Christmas,
Decem

Jeevan,

For your

book collection

Love, Richard

My Mother
Golda Meir

My Mother
Golda Meir

A SON'S EVOCATION OF LIFE WITH GOLDA MEIR

BY Menahem Meir

ARBOR HOUSE New York

To my mother and my father
in loving remembrance

To my wife Aya

To my sister Sarah

Acknowledgments

For their invaluable and generous help in recalling images and events described, I wish to express my thanks to Moshe Allon, Mordecai Gazit, Simcha Dinitz, Itzhak Eylam, Isser Harel, Frances Minor, Zvi Netser, Samuel Rothberg, Zeev Sherf and Yaakov Shimoni.

I am also indebted to Toby Mostysser for her professional and sensitive skills in helping to organize the material in this book. A special heart-felt appreciation to my dear friends Miriam F. Werner, Harry Simmons and Gideon Ziv.

To my sister Sarah and brother-in-law Zecharia, my sons Amnon, Daniel and Gideon, and to my wife Aya in particular, I owe my unbounded gratitude for their patience and steadfast encouragement during the process of writing this book. Their support was most important.

Author's Note

IN THE PAGES that follow I have set down some recollections of life in my family which, because of my mother, was not an ordinary one. I have done so in the hope that these fragments will be of interest, even of use, to those who, in years to come, may want to know something more about her.

—M.M.

CHAPTER 1

THE ROOM IN which I sit is my mother's living room. She has been dead for five years. Sarah, my sister, lives in it now with her husband Zecharia. But it is still very much Golda's room; the other half of the modest semidetached house on a suburban street in greater Tel Aviv in which, she on the right hand and my wife Aya, I, and our three boys on the left, made our home during those years when mother was successively Israel's minister of labor, foreign minister and finally prime minister, and in which she went on living after she retired. Part of that time she also stayed, of course, in official residences in Jerusalem, some more attractive than others, but this little house was where she felt she really belonged.

Sarah and Zecharia have made no attempt to preserve as a shrine what is now their half of the house; they haven't changed it nor turned it into something of their own except perhaps for the rows of Zecharia's ceramic pots and bowls arranged, a little tentatively, on the stairs that lead from the living room to what was my mother's study and totally unadorned bedroom.

Wherever my eye falls I see, in contrast to the plainness of mother's furniture and the blandness of the carpets and curtains, what I suppose you might call the exotic trophies of the high offices she held, though even these, like the now-empty sentry box outside the front door, are singularly inconspicuous. Perched on the sideboard, barely noticeable because no one has polished it, is the large and splendid silver Dove of Peace presented to my mother by Pope Paul VI, the giant porcelain bowl given to her by the city of Philadelphia, an antique sterling samovar she received in Moscow, and the jeweled box she brought back from the King of Cambodia. On the wall opposite me pose flights of dancers painted by Raphael Soyer (whose portrait of Golda hangs in the Washington National Gallery) and Kokoschka's oil of her—both are attractively and admiringly inscribed; on the copper Persian tray that served her as a coffee table still sits the silver cigarette case Sadat gave her ("from a new grandfather to a grandmother"), while on the simple shelves are the books written by some of mother's famous friends—and the small row written about, and by her.

Everything is low-key, making no statement other than hinting at the kind of life mother led and the sort of people she encountered; but unless one knows whose room it had been, there is no way of telling that only recently, or so it feels to me, it was a room to which heads of state and ambassadors, TV personalities and celebrated authors drank coffee with my mother and hung on her every word.

It was her room and yet, sitting here, it is about my father, Morris Meyerson, who never lived here, that I am impelled to write first.

For many years, Sarah and I were the children of a woman whose austere bun, deep voice, orthopedic shoes and capacious handbags were recognized, literally, around the world, a woman like a movie star who was known everywhere by her first name

—and of a man about whom few knew or cared at all. Then, in the last years of Golda's life came a spate of books and dramas about my parents. Ostensibly they were about Golda Meir but, without exception, my father was featured too, though never flatteringly and never accurately. In this room, he is absent but in those books, plays and TV spectaculars he was there, a poor second to mother, at best weak and dependent, at worst feckless and indecisive, anyhow always unsuccessful.

For me, and for my sister, he was a great deal more. He was tender, kind and warm, a model of what a man and a father could be, a gentle knowledgeable mentor who indicated for us that, somewhere beyond the confines of my mother's consuming patriotic and political concerns, there lay another world. This was the world he opened up, eagerly and affectionately, for Sarah and me. Art, music, literature, psychology, sociology, an appreciation of all these is a part of my father's heretofore unacknowledged legacy to us, and part of the gift that he made to Golda so many years ago in another world and at another time.

Although neither Sarah nor I are the subjects of these recollections, it is perhaps necessary for me to explain, or maybe the word is even reveal, one cardinal fact about ourselves and our parents: nothing about the real causes (for there must have been more than one) of their separation is known to either of us. We were almost completely taken unawares by their parting.

Today, in this epoch of intense, maybe exaggerated emphasis on the importance of "communicating" or what passes for it, of a growing disavowal of the so-called generation gap and of the high priority given to candor for its own sake, no matter how hurtful, my parents' refusal to turn us into participants in the domestic tragedy that befell them may appear to people younger than myself not only ill-advised but even eccentric. "Tell All" is the current imperative; "Truth Liberates," "By all means inform the patient that the cancer is indeed terminal,"

9

such are the guidelines of the 80s. But my parents, though so different from each other, shared a deep belief in the blessing of reticence, in the personal working-out of personal problems, in the easing of life for its inadvertent victims.

At least that is how I, as a middle-aged adult, interpret their taciturnity, their strict observance of the amenities, and their capacity for retaining the obvious and deep liking they had for each other. Maybe, their separation notwithstanding, love remains the valid word for it after all.

This is not to say that there was complete silence on the topic, or that we remained unscathed by the trauma of separation or that our own antennas didn't function. All that I want to say is that neither of my parents abdicated the strong parental role, all subsequent legends to the contrary notwithstanding, including my mother's own mea culpa on this score and persisting sense of guilt.

The formal reason proffered to us by mother in those days was that her career had driven them apart and that Morris needed a woman who would be at home with him more, not pulled in a thousand directions, not trying to juggle Zionist fulfillment, social justice, the progress of trade unionism and peace in the Middle East all at once, and we accepted this as the truth because in large measure, it must have been that. In the event, no such perfect woman ever emerged for my father as far as I know, though I once had dinner with him and with a lady to whom he seemed particularly attentive, and I wondered afterwards about a special bond between them; but my father didn't divorce my mother and he didn't marry again.

Nor did she. And though there were broad hints in the books and films about other men—and when we grew older there were rumors of romances—to the best of my knowledge, mother never entered a permanent and full relationship with anyone else.

To a considerable extent, both my parents' marriage and their parting were inevitable. They had much in common, and much that divided them. Both were players in the drama of the immigration of the masses of persecuted Jews from Eastern Europe to the U.S. in the early 1900s. Both came from economically marginal families; both came from homes in which, albeit to differing degrees, traditional Judaism was observed; and both enthusiastically and successfully absorbed the new Western culture to which history had introduced them.

They met under circumstances that typified the kind of questing, earnest young intellectuals they were. My mother had run away from Milwaukee to her elder sister Sheyna's Denver apartment when her parents refused to let her go on with high school. At this point, she was still in her teens, rebellious and prepared to support herself by working in a local dry cleaning establishment. My father, who was living with and supporting a consumptive sister in Denver, was earning a meagre living as a sign painter.

Despite these lowly occupations, they spent their evenings, as did thousands of such uprooted young Jewish intellectuals, drinking tea with lemon, and arguing loudly, in a mixture of bad English, good Yiddish and indifferent Russian about European politics, Communism *vs* Socialism, the proper direction for American democracy and how the return of the Jews to Palestine (mind you, all this years before the Balfour Declaration) could turn that Promised Land into a paradise for Jewish workers.

My mother, in her memoirs, has described her meeting with Morris.

"One of the less articulate young men who came to Sheyna's often was a gentle, soft-spoken friend of theirs, Morris Meyerson . . . I think I first noticed him because although he was almost entirely self-educated, he was so well versed in the kind of things that neither I nor most of our friends knew anything at all about.

He loved poetry, art and music and knew and understood a great deal about them, and he was prepared to talk at length on the merits of a given sonnet or sonata to someone as interested (and as ignorant) as I was."

Viewed from the distance of more than half a century, it is interesting to me that these intense men and women are so recognizable. Many of the issues they debated with such vehemence are being as vehemently debated today not only in smoke-filled and overcrowded and overheated rooms in Colorado but on campuses all the way from San Francisco to Jerusalem; the one major alteration being that today Morris, Golda and Sheyna would all be attending university themselves.

They were part of the same milieu and fell in love. What I believe drew my parents to each other and what they were unable to resist was finding in the other so many complementary qualities. Mother was drawn to father's admirable (and enviable) erudition and sensitivity while he, I am sure, was overwhelmed by her vivacity, her dynamism and her charm.

In truth, however, the attributes that attracted them to one another turned out to be precisely those that resulted in the failure of their marriage. Golda, one of the most naturally gregarious people I have ever known, was at her best when surrounded by others, and got most satisfaction out of life when she could shape the reality around her by persuading people to support her own deeply held views. What I mean is this: my mother flourished in, and was utterly fascinated by, the perpetually turbulent political climate of the Zionist movement, something in which my father had much less interest.

Morris, however, excelled in the private virtues, in one-to-one relationships, in doing unto others what you would have done unto you. In principle and by temperament he was an internationalist, a pacifist, an anarchist. Moreover, it strikes me now that in his attitude towards his clearly remarkable young wife, and his two small children, he was a forerunner of that much-praised contemporary creation, the genuinely liberated man. Not a house husband, though my memories are vivid of his washing dishes, helping my mother to tidy up, making furniture (in the early days of their married life in Jerusalem he made most of their furniture because they were too poor to buy any), a mender par excellence of anything that needed mending, an understanding and permissive partner who extended to my mother the fullest possible measure of freedom. If you must, go! Travel, lecture, fund raise, work for Zionism, Socialism and the Jewish people. If there were conditions, they were the kind she could readily accept, but I doubt that there ever were any.

My mother, though, needed more than freedom, more than self-expression or self-fulfillment. Those too, of course, but more than this, she was driven to become a moving force, a full-time participant, in the Zionist mission. While mother, from the start, saw in Zionism the enduring solution to Jewish minority status and persecution and was becoming active in the American Zionist movement, my father envisioned a world in which religion and state would at last cease to separate people. In a letter dated August 1915, written when he was still in Denver and mother was back with her parents in Milwaukee, he made clear his opinion that a Jewish state could do little to solve the problems of the Jews.

"I don't know," he wrote to Golda, "whether to be glad or sorry that you seem to be so enthusiastic a nationalist. I am altogether passive in the matter, though I give you full credit for your activity, as I do to all others engaged in doing something toward helping a distressed nation. . . . The idea of Palestine or any other territory for the Jews is, to me, ridiculous. Racial persecution does not exist because some nations have no territories but because nations exist at all."

To be sure, he was eventually to feel otherwise. The Holo-

13

caust turned him into a convinced Zionist, and he was able to witness for himself the way in which the newborn and beleaguered State of Israel welcomed to its shores hundreds of thousands of Jews from Europe and the Arabic-speaking countries of the Middle East and North Africa.

The differences in their personalities rose to the fore when they immigrated to Palestine in 1921. After a nightmarish journey from New York and a trying, not to say draining, first few months in Tel Aviv—both of which Golda has described vividly in *My Life*—they became pioneers in a young kibbutz in the Jezreel Valley (the Emek, in Hebrew). In a long and detailed letter to his mother, he describes the beauty of Merhavia and its surroundings and the life on the kibbutz that he seemed to enjoy it. He writes about the flora in detail, about the beautiful sky in the early twilight and the dawn, about Nazareth and Mount Gilboa. But above all he extols the joy of ploughing with two horses the vast tract of virgin land. He also writes about the wonderful physical feeling of fatigue after a day's work in the open fields.

It was only after he caught malaria, an illness which lays low the strongest of men, that he began to sufffer badly from the unremitting summer heat and the damp-to-the-bones winter cold. It was then that he found the unalleviated physical labor tedious and injurious to his health.

Although neither she nor my father ever told us this, Golda writes in *My Life* that their relationship underwent its first major crisis at Kibbutz Merhavia. I imagine though that it had been subjected to stress even before they departed for Palestine. For a while, en route there, they had stopped off in New York. New York for my father was one thing; theater, music, bookstores, all expensive and mostly beyond his reach but at least they were there and could be aspired to. For my mother, New York was mainly the focus of Zionist activity in the States, the site of constant meetings with Labor Zionist colleagues, a place for a taking from and giving to people with whom she was becoming increasingly identified—and above all, it was the place from which she was going to leave for Palestine.

After arriving in Tel Aviv, in the first months before their acceptance in the Kibbutz Merhavia, my father wrote to his mother in America enthusiastically about the charm of Tel Aviv as a new city despite the problems of adjusting to very primitive conditions, in a small rather shabby apartment shared with Sheyna and her children, with sand and flies everywhere. He wrote of his thrill of being in an all-Jewish city and his good fortune in obtaining work as a bookkeeper for a British firm. Mother too was earning a modest amount, giving English lessons to a few students. While the two worked bringing in enough to cover basic expenses, Sheyna remained at home taking care of the house and looking after the children.

Nonetheless, after Merhavia, they entered into what today passes for a "commuting" marriage. There was a short and exceedingly difficult period (including really horrendous poverty) in Jerusalem, and then, when I was four, mother moved with me and Sarah to Tel Aviv, where she went to work for the Women's Labor Council. My father stayed on in Jerusalem, working as a bookkeeper for *Solel Boneh*, the building company run by the Histadrut (General Federation of Labor) until he moved to Haifa. In effect, they had already parted, but there were months when Father was at home with us and my mother travelled abroad as a fund raiser for the Histadrut and a novice Labor Party delegate to international Socialist conventions.

Even when they were essentially living apart and father joined us only on weekends, my parents went on making a home for us. Friday evenings and Saturday afternoons, either the house filled with guests or we went to friends. And in between we enjoyed being quietly together, father absorbed in his book or paper, mother bent over work she had taken home from the office, Sarah and I reading or doing homework. Saturday mornings, father made breakfast and took Sarah and me for walks or, when it rained, helped me arrange the stamps in my collection or construct towers and bridges from the erector set he had bought me.

About many things that matter, my parents were of one mind. They made it clear both by precept and example that they expected us to be truthful, clean and tidy: baths before bed, bed at fixed times always preceded by a story, hands washed before meals, clothes put away, beds made in the morning. Mixed with this fundamentalism was their shared, if somewhat exalted, image of what responsible Socialist children in that new society they were building should be like. They endlessly extolled the value of work for the joy of doing a job well, not merely for wages, and impressed upon us their high ideals of public service.

Most importantly, at any rate for me, they were united in their support and encouragement of my growing interest in music. Father, who had brought with him to Palestine his old gramophone and a precious collection of classical and romantic records, took me (aged six) to my very first concert, played his favorite pieces for me over and over again, and listened, year in year out, to my cello practice from the first feeble squeals to competently produced pieces. Both my mother and father put out the month's salary that my cello (and later Sarah's violin) cost, and scrimped for our biweekly music lessons; though I must say it was mother alone who accompanied me—whenever she could—to and from those lessons, carrying the heavy instrument until I could carry it myself.

With full agreement between them in so many areas, who can blame us for accepting at face value the explanation that economic necessity, jobs that took them to different cities, was what kept them apart. Separations of that sort were commonplace in those days: like so many other Russian Jewish husbands, my grandfather, Golda's father, had preceded her mother to the U.S. by several years, saving up for the family's steerage fare, and Sheyna had come to Palestine long before her husband arrived there.

So when the "official" and irrevocable break came in 1940 (when I was fifteen), I took it badly, and blamed mother. I neglected doing homework and didn't concentrate in class. I withdrew from friends, choosing only a select few for comfort and companionship, and consoled myself with my cello. What was even more serious, in my mother's eyes, was that I quit the Labor Zionist youth movement that I had joined as a matter of course and much worse dropped out of high school. But as children generally do, after a while I managed to adjust.

My father remained a central and loving figure all my life. From this point on, Sarah and I had two homes; one with Golda, whose life was to bring us—and later our families—into ever-increasing and exciting contact with the people and forces most responsible for the building up of the State of Israel; the other, tranquil, inner-directed, with Morris in his one-room rented flat where life seemed to continue as before.

There we established patterns that lasted for years: we ate choice brunches, the ingredients of which he shopped for with great care; we riffled through the overseas editions of the *Times* of London and the Manchester *Guardian* that were his greatest luxury; we battled with and generally solved the sophisticated crossword puzzles (the harder the better) he was addicted to and on behalf of which he sent us scurrying to his battered eleventh edition of the *Encyclopedia Britannica,* and we read *Macbeth* and *Ulysses* together while he patiently and happily explained their subtleties. And, of course, I played for him.

* * *

17

The bookstore my father ran in Jerusalem in 1930 with money that Sheyna's husband, Shamai, raised in the States, might have made this country a happier place for Morris than I think it was. For a moment, I see him there: the shop is on Jaffa Road, one of the city's main thoroughfares. It's late afternoon, Jerusalem's most becoming light. Inside people, who must have been there for hours, are browsing. Father, smoking his pipe, also has his head in a book. He doesn't like disturbing the customers or "pushing" them, as he puts it, to buy. Besides, it's more interesting to read than to sell. When Sarah and I come in, father looks up delighted. He takes a book, a present for us, from the store's single shelf of children's books, gives each of us a hand, and we're off for the ice cream parlor down the street. During which time the boy who works in the store helps himself once again to cash from the till—an unsuspected perfidy that goes undiscovered until the bookstore has to be sold at a considerable loss. Sheyna, for all that she loved my father, never quite forgot his losing so much of her husband's hard-earned money.

A postcard from Golda, Zurich, 1937.

Dear Morris,

From the first minute that I reached Zurich till now—meeting after meeting. Not one minute of rest. It seems that [the Zionist] Congress will last at least two weeks. I am counting the days till I'll be home. Deliberations are difficult. I hope it will be for the best.

Your Goldie

From Golda, aboard the S. S. *Sphinx*, 1938.

Dearest Children,

. . . I feel as though I've been away from you for a whole year

. . . Please, please write about everything . . . and help Father. He's very tired. Take good care of him . . .

From Morris, February, 1940.

Dear Menahem,

. . . When people sometimes stop writing to their nearest and dearest, look for one of two reasons (and nothing ever happens without a reason): either because they are all too happy and carefree or because they are too troubled and miserable. I'll leave it to you to guess which it must have been in my case . . ."

From Morris, Abadan, Iran, 1943.

. . . I'm glad you enlisted. It's good for one's body and soul. Drills and discipline will make you into a "tough guy" . . . Now that I've got a son in uniform and a daughter in a kibbutz I feel you have all grown up . . .

From Morris, Abadan, Iran, 1945

My dear Menahem,

. . . it would indeed be difficult for me to analyze and lay before you on paper all the threads that had woven themselves into that frame of mind that results in prolonged silence. Nor, do I think, would it be easy for you to grasp and follow; and, if you followed and grasped, it would only fill your young life with a sadness I'd rather spare you. Suffice it to say that it has its origin in the same deep, dark well as other aspects of my troubled existence, and is only one other facet of a life utterly unhinged and frustrated, which has been my lot now for oh so many ages . . . when your letter came, I was enwrapped in a tangle of dreams, planning and elaborating ways and means of how to arrange my life so as to help you. I believe with all my heart in your musicianship and am confident that the 'means' will be found when the time comes. My remaining [here for

19

Solel Boneh] for another season or two could be a partial solution.
And don't think pitifully what a "sacrifice" that would be. For what
has Tel Aviv to offer except my bare, cheerless room on Maaze St.
and the meetings with you? . . .

New York, May 1951. On the night flight going back to Israel,
mother looks drawn and her breathing becomes shallow. After
a while we call the stewardess and, alarmed, ask for oxygen.
Channa, my first wife (we had only recently married), and I
whisper to each other about Morris' fatal heart attack of the
previous afternoon. At Lod airport, where the entire family
waits for us, mother is tight-lipped and pensive. Even afterward,
she talks little about father's death, as little as she does about
other personal experiences. Channa's mother tells me that my
father died while visiting her in Golda's Tel Aviv apartment,
where she was staying while mother was abroad. About his
death, my mother wrote years later in her memoirs:

> . . . It was not a bereavement that I either could or wanted to talk
> about with other people, even my own family. Nor am I prepared
> to write about it now, except to say that although we had been
> apart for so long, standing at his graveside, I realized once again
> what a heavy price I had paid—and made Morris pay—for what-
> ever I had experienced and achieved in the years of our separa-
> tion.

As for myself, I have frequently pondered that price. Might
Morris' life have been substantially better in the States? Had the
renascent Hebrew culture been too great an obstacle for a man
so lacking in self-confidence about his fluency in a language that,
in fact, he handled well? Would he have returned to the States
were it not for Sarah and me? (To these questions, of course,
there can be no answer.)

CHAPTER 2

AND MY MOTHER? Where and when do I first see her —through that inaccurate, unreliable and yet always meaningful inner lens that is the mind's eye? In Jerusalem, I suppose; in that city of war and peace that was to be a major station in her life, and yes, a terminal also—for that is where, in the end, she was to die. But the memory is of a young and attractive woman, though not a contented one; a woman, like the century, still in her twenties, who sits with me, handing me something to eat on the stoop that leads to the dilapidated one-story house in which, having left Merhavia, we now live. Together in the choking summer heat, my mother and I sit, silently, idly, staring at the large dry, thorny field in front of us. Rocks, burnt water-starved bushes—and dust. I remember a horse-drawn carriage passing on the dirt road and, a few feet away, an Arab boy grazing a herd of goats. But I have no idea today why that one memory endures.

My father, lucky to have work at all at a time of such great economic stress, was paid his less-than-living wage in vouchers that decreased in value as they passed from my mother to the waiting hands of a landlady, a milkman, a grocer. Like other women in this run-down neighborhood, outside the walls of the Old City, my mother took care of Sarah and me and kept house, in conditions that—by any standards—were those of poverty. Like a villager, she drew our water from a bucket sent down to a rainwater cistern and boiled it before we drank it; she cooked in an out-of-doors tin shack that was our kitchen; and she lit our rooms with a smelly kerosene lamp that all too often exploded. Until Sarah was born, Golda and Morris rented out one of the two rooms and, when that became impractical, Golda took in the weekly washing (which she did on an iron washboard) from the nursery school I went to so that school fees wouldn't have to be paid. Every now and then, Shamai came from Tel Aviv with gifts of fruit and cheese that he and Sheyna had prepared, having guessed (since my parents were too proud to tell) how and on what we were living.

Cared for, loved and secure, I had no sense of the growing tension in my mother's life, of the friction that was eating at her marriage or of the anxiety that gnawed at her because she was unable to buy enough meat and milk to ensure us a nourishing diet. Or enough fuel to keep at bay the bitter Jerusalem cold in winter. Nor, until many years later, did I have an inkling of the tremendous frustration she felt, so totally isolated from the national and political activities that were her life's blood. Having come to Palestine to join others in building a nation, she was now, in fact, virtually alone; barely managing to keep her family together; and about as far from self-expression as a young, talented and energetic woman could be.

Little wonder then that when she met a friend who offered a job in Tel Aviv as secretary to the Histadrut's Women's Labor Council, she found the challenge irresistible*. Within a few

*Overcoming initial trepidations—Is it fair to uproot the children? Am I the right person for the job?

months, she had us there, herself, Sarah (aged two and a half), and me (aged four), housed in an airy two-room flat with a large balcony overlooking the sea. We were still without gas and electricity, but our new surroundings in this still new city represented a change for the better, and mother's new position was truly the start of a new life for her—and us.

For a small boy, Tel Aviv was little more than the glaring sun that bleached the world white on summer days, the clear, warm sea water I swam in and the deep sand that led up to the doorstep on our as-yet-unpaved street, filling our shoes and, for much of the year, scorching our toes. But gradually, unavoidably, the impact of Tel Aviv began to make its way into my consciousness as it had into mother's from the very first.

What did Tel Aviv mean to my mother then—this out-of-the-way, virtually trafficless, almost telephoneless town with its tacky stores, narrow streets, and red-roofed pastel-painted houses that peeled almost as soon as they were built?

Well, for a start, Tel Aviv was the world of the Histadrut, the Labor Movement. This was not only the place where mother worked, but the organization whose ideals—the building of a Socialist-Zionist nation in which Jews could live, for the first time in thousands of years, in freedom, dignity and equality—she totally, utterly and permanently shared. Every morning, she set out to this world, face shining, hair pulled back, ironed skirt and starched blouse; a woman going to do battle for social justice in a low red building not far away from us (what *was* far away then?) in which everyone from janitor up first-named everyone else. There, in what was perhaps the most genuinely egalitarian setting in the world the women all dressed as my mother did; the men all wore khaki shorts or slacks and short-sleeved open-collared shirts; and salaries were all determined not by education, job or rank, but by the number of one's dependents and the years of seniority; typists could and did earn more than

23

"executives." Mother's salary, for years, remained less than that of the woman with seven children who cleaned and served mid-morning tea.

The Women's Labor Council concerned itself, in the 30s, largely with the setting-up of training farms for Jewish girls who, like their male counterparts, had come to Palestine to work the land but who knew nothing of agriculture or, for that matter, of any other trade. Although my mother tended to regard women's organizations with a certain reservation, she was enthusiastic about this project because it made it possible for young women both to develop themselves in only recently opened up ways and to participate fully, as pioneers, in the work underway in Jewish agricultural settlements throughout the country.

Even then, she saw in her modest, very limited job that through the Labor Movement she could contribute to the larger good and take her place in the larger scheme of things. I imagine it is hard for anyone living outside of Israel (and perhaps also for Israelis growing up here today) to envisage the all-encompassing role of the Histadrut in the pre-state days. When no government looked out for Jewish interests—the British Mandatory government had its own concerns that lay in the opposite direction—the Histadrut functioned as a *de facto* government. Far more than the standard labor movement fighting to better the working conditions of its members (though it did that too), the Histadrut created a structure, the detailed ways and means by which that workers' paradise, so ecstatically talked about by the young idealists in Denver, could really be established in Palestine.

Its accomplishments ranged from the kibbutz, a model of cooperative living, all the way to cooperatively managed enterprises of almost every sort, projects that performed the double duty of doing the things that needed to be done in the homeland and of providing the Jews there with a livelihood. There were

Histadrut-created and -run factories, the Histadrut building-and-contracting company (in which Father worked), Histadrut-managed low-cost eating places that served homestyle food, a Histadrut sick fund that provided medical insurance and built hospitals and clinics, a worker's bank and loan association, and Histadrut-affiliated schools that Sarah and I attended. The Histadrut had a daily newspaper, *Davar,* and a repertory theater, the *Ohel,* to see to it that the spirit of the new Jewish worker was as well nourished as the body. While the Mandatory government had its seat in Jerusalem, Tel Aviv was the competing core from which all Histadrut activities radiated.

And beyond this Tel Aviv of mother's, enclosing it, was another even more wondrous one: it was the first, and in those days the only Jewish city in the world. Unlike Haifa and Jerusalem, senior towns with long histories and mixed Arab-Jewish populations, Tel Aviv had been created only twenty years before, in 1909, mainly by Russian and Polish Jewish immigrants. It was the only city anywhere with a Jewish mayor, an all-Jewish City Council, Jewish policemen, and an all-Jewish proletariat—a city where we felt we belonged, where we felt at home. It was, in fact, where the Jews were rehearsing for statehood, where new immigrants disembarked, and where the children in the street spoke only Hebrew. Autonomous, exhilarating, unlovely, it was destined to become the site of the declaration of Israel's independence, the nation's cultural capital—and the backdrop of an abiding traffic problem!

With all this, there was also the world of our home, a home which despite everything, was warm and well run. Neither my mother's hectic political activities nor the sparseness of its furnishings (her bed was in the "living room" and doubled as a couch), made it any the less so. After school, there wasn't long to wait before she came home. If we wanted, we walked the block or two to Sheyna and Shamai's and the cousins, Chaim, Jonah and Judith with whom we were being brought up almost like brother and sister. And in the evenings mother gave us supper, listened to us recount the day's doings, and got us into bed. Then, as millions of working women have always done, she started her second job. She washed, mended, scrubbed and cooked. Thursday nights were special, as they were all over Tel Aviv; the small apartment filled with the aroma of Shabbat cooking—freshly baked challah, chicken soup, gefilte fish, all the traditional Jewish foods, which mother prepared for us, for father and for the many guests who inevitably dropped in.

Like mothers the world over, she worried about our health. Are you dressed warmly enough? Did you have a good lunch? Was that a sneeze I heard? We answered automatically, as children do, until one day near-disaster struck. Sarah developed a debilitating, misdiagnosed kidney disease which changed the way we lived; introduced me, for one, to anxiety, empathy and fear. Also it forced my mother again to face terrible choices, something she would have to do over and over again.

For three tense years, doctors, pills, injections were Sarah's standard, bravely accepted fare, while my mother daily and painstakingly preparing a misprescribed carbohydrate diet, developed new lines in her face and a heavier, less lively gait. I too, underweight and supposedly afflicted by a heart murmur, became yet another source of anxiety and my mother, exhausted, mobilized fresh resources in the unavailing struggle to fatten me up.

It is only now that I am a husband, a father and old enough to be a grandfather, now that I am married to a woman who works (Aya is a child psychiatrist) that I can start to appreciate the tremendous burden my mother bore so stoically during what were, for her, crucial years. In *My Life,* she admits unhappily to the pangs of conscience that assailed her about working so intensely at a time when Sarah was so ill:

. . . On the days when she had to stay in bed, leaving her with someone else wasn't simple, and when she was up and around, she had to be watched all the time. Sheyna and my mother were of great assistance, but I always felt I had to explain and apologize to them for going to work in the morning and not coming back till the afternoon.

And she was even more conflicted about going out again, to Labor Party meetings, in the evenings once or twice a week.

Worse yet was travelling abroad, something she was already beginning to do in connection with her work. A letter which she wrote to Sheyna in 1929 on the way to a meeting of the Socialist International in Brussels, expresses the pull of opposing calls:

. . . I ask only one thing, that I be understood and believed. My social activities are not an accidental thing; they are an absolute necessity for me. . . . Before I left, the doctor assured me that Sarele's health permits of my going, and I have made adequate arrangements for Menahem. And yet you can understand how hard it is for me to leave. But in our present situation I could not refuse to do what was asked of me. Believe me, I know I will not bring the Messiah, but I think that we must miss no opportunity to explain what we want and what we are to influential people.

One thing is clear. I have only two alternatives; one to cut off my connections with all outside interests as I once did at Morris' insistence, or to go to another kibbutz. I have no further strength for my present life. My sole problem is what is better for the children. Perhaps you will not believe me but I tell you if I were sure that the first way were wholesome for the children I would not hesitate a bit, but I am doubtful. . . .

But when mother was with us, she was really there; attentive, kind, considerate, witty and a healer of wounds. I never felt that I was second to her other interests, or that I was being neglected

27

for the sake of her ego or personal advancement. Whenever she left the house, she explained—according to our age and ability to understand—exactly where she was going, and why.

I remember an evening when I must have been six and mother had left for a Labor Party meeting after telling us she'd be home early. Sarah and I just couldn't fall asleep. We talked and giggled, went through our repertoire of songs, and then when mother still hadn't gotten back, we dressed and marched off to fetch her from party headquarters. Climbing the stairs, we found ourselves at the back of a tightly packed smoke-filled meeting hall, and there was mother. She was standing up in front, counting raised hands, so we too raised our hands, hoping to be noticed and wanting to participate. Mother smiled and beckoned, and when the meeting ended, she introduced us—as she would do increasingly in later years—to all her colleagues. On the way home, she put into simple words what the meeting had been about and what those raised hands meant. Actually, I think, it was our first lesson in the political life of a democracy.

Still when she travelled, twice to England and once to the United States, we felt forlorn, watching her fold her clothes neatly into those large, inelegant suitcases that were part of my childhood landscape, and seeing her off, blowing kisses and calling out last-minute instructions and promises until the boat or train that took her away disappeared entirely. True, there were always the letters (however slowly they arrived) which father read to us and helped us to answer, taking down our dictated replies and encouraging us to draw pictures. And once, in a burst of high technology, she even sent a recording to which we listened, untiringly, on father's hand-operated but beloved gramophone.

Yet meetings and travels aside, during those first years in Tel Aviv, Golda seemed little different from the working mothers of many of our schoolmates, and her chairing meetings and count-

ing votes seemed to us to be the normal course of events. I
suppose our lives would have gone on indefinitely in this way,
interrupted only by occasional partings and the inevitable hurt
of separations, if Sarah's illness hadn't taken a turn for the
worse, propelling us all into a new order of adventure.

1932. Mother, Sarah and I are off to America. Mother had
already been there this year, fund raising for the Histadrut,
when father's urgent cable ("Sarah ill. Suggest you return.")
called her home. What was to be done? Sarah was weakening.
Puffy, in pain, often blank-eyed, she looked deathly ill. One
pediatrician, I recall, cruelly assured Golda that some children
with this condition live to be twelve or thirteen! He counselled
patience and continuing Sarah's till-now ineffective proteinless
regimen. Everyone around advised against going abroad; the
long journey itself might kill her, it was said. But mother, never
one to accept verdicts of doom or to allow herself, her family or
her country to be trapped between alternative death sentences,
determined to take the immediate risk as against what seemed
like a sure, slow dying, and opted with father for the off-chance
of a cure at New York City's Beth Israel Hospital.

To finance the unhappy venture, mother signed up for a two-
year stint with the Pioneer Women, the recently formed sister
organization in the United States of the Women's Labor Council. And, of course, I was to be taken along. So one August
morning, the usual pattern of our separations was reversed.
Father stood alone on the platform of the old Tel Aviv railroad
station, while Sarah and I chuffed and chugged off with mother
on our way to Port Said, where we embarked on our voyage. For
me, it was one glorious voyage though, let it be clear, my notions
of luxury do not accord either with past fact or with present
adult recall. The fact was we were all jammed into one small
tourist class cabin, but I was entranced: the magnificent crew in

its splended whites, the wonderland of the playroom with trains, bicycles and games such as I had never seen before; the decks like uncharted continents spread out for us to explore; the dining room with its sparkling tables and chairs. Everything so beautiful. And mother all to ourselves. She had no meetings, no speeches to make, no business to transact, no place to go. We sat on the deck, talked, read and sang together, and mother played shuffleboard with me for hours.

Yet looking back, those days of enforced leisure must have been terrible for her, travelling in that agonizing attempt to save a small daughter's life. Firmly rooted in Palestine by now and happy, she was reluctant to leave for two years, and less than enthusiastic about the new job. Also there was very little money, and, worst of all, no guarantee that Sarah would get well.

Characteristically, though, no tension showed in her face or behavior. She fussed over Sarah but without visible depression or panic. Was it reticence? Protectiveness? Faith that things would work out? Would it have been better if she had shared or even shown her anxieties? Who knows. Again, only the questions have survived the years.

In New York, we were swept into the Goodmans' huge embrace. Fanny and Jacob Goodman, the people in whose spacious Flatbush apartment we stayed during the whole of our first year in the United States, were two of Golda's friends-cum-comrades-cum-contemporaries who, like others of their special, invaluable ilk, were to play a continuous role in our lives. Not many are still alive but I want to pay tribute to those who are. They were wonderful people, unbreakable links in a chain that reached across Europe and the States to our flat in Tel Aviv and would reach, with time, to Jerusalem and the prime minister's residence. Known collectively as *haverim* (friends in Hebrew) they were much more than that. They were adopted family, sharers in the Socialist-Zionist vision, men and women whose convictions and temperament turned them into a large extended family that could always be called upon, always counted on to help, to rally, to keep a secret and to counsel. Mother had many such *haverim* and till this very day I am still in touch with some of their children.

Two things of considerable family significance occurred during that stay in America. Sarah was cured within six weeks, emerging from Beth Israel a healthy child who, to top everything, had learned the English alphabet and even some phrases and songs. And mother at last received the opportunity to demonstrate the impressive abilities that were to win for her an elected position on her return to Palestine, and were to bring her into those leadership roles which she exercised for the rest of her life.

Characteristically, mother, whose organizational flair was later to be on international display, managed to do everything at once; to start a new job, to start us off in a new life, to see to it that we didn't kick over the traces of the former life to which we were due to return within two years; in short, to get everything, herself included, organized. And bear in mind that one of us was a convalescent child who had been sick for years. It was a formidable assignment for a lady on her own—and I think it says as much about her as did the fact that she had—again when times were less than rosy—up and taken herself off to Palestine because that was where she felt she had to be. Now she had to be in the States and she coped as determinedly with all of the problems of relocation.

One example of the kind of effort she made was that, during the entire first week of school, mother sat next to Sarah and me in a first-grade classroom translating into Hebrew every word the teacher said. Later on, once we had improved our faulty English, she felt it was her duty to see to it that we shouldn't forget Hebrew, so she spoke to us only in Hebrew and hired a friend to give us private lessons. And I remember the vigor (where did it come from?) with which she tramped over New York with us: the American Museum of Natural History, the Hayden Planetarium, the Empire State Building, the zoo—all educational, good for us and a "must."

Some weekends, we met relatives: Morris' sister and her husband in Philadelphia, and Aunt Zipke, Golda's younger sister whose American name was Clara. A warm, emphatic, bustling auburn-haired lady with opinions that tended, particularly later in life, to be diametrically opposed, on some crucial issues, to those of her world-famous sister. Her own problem-filled and valiantly lived life would make a book of its own; so would her close quarrelsome relationship with my mother and her deep affection for and lasting trust in my father. But although she belongs also in these recollections, at the time of which I now write she was mostly just one more person, albeit an important one, in that extended family, that so cushioned those two years for us—and made them possible for Golda. Three decades later, Zipke would become a part of our lives, as Sheyna had been all along, but in the meantime, she was mother's "American sister," different from the rest of us but kin.

What did Golda do? We used to ask this question though the answer made less sense to us then than it would today when fund raising is so integral to community organization, especially to Jewish communities. She made speeches; she helped organize the outings, raffles, bazaars and other functions that brought in the dimes and quarters which funded the women's training farms and helped settle new immigrants in Palestine. And she went to meetings. She worked like a demon, travelling drafty trains and buses for hours to and from Cleveland, Chicago, Winnipeg and other stops of the vast American hinterland, staying one night with this comrade's family, one night with that one; away from us for unbroken stretches, sometimes for as long

Mother's high school graduation photo. She is second from left in the first row.

ISABELLE HILL
Secretary

CARL HARPKE
Treasurer

JOHN KEELEY
President

Officers
Of the

JUNIOR
CLASS

GOLDIE MABOWETZ
Vice President

The program for mother's junior class at Milwaukee's North Division High School.

Mother's parents with her younger sister, Clara, in Milwaukee.

My parents were newlyweds in this photo, taken in 1921, before they left for Israel. Mother is seated at far left; my father is standing behind her. Regina Hamburger Medzini, standing third from left, a close friend of mother's since grade school, and Yossel Kopelov, standing fourth from left, made the trip with them.

My parents (standing) pose with Sheyna's family. Sheyna is seated, center, next to her son Chaim and daughter Judith. Sheyna's husband, Shamai Korngold, is seated next to her.

A photo of me taken at around age one and a half.

My sister and I pose with our father.

A portrait of my mother and father in 1919, taken shortly after their marriage.

This is the passport picture of Sarah, me and mother for our trip to the United States in 1932.

Mother working at Kibbutz Merhavia.

A photo of my mother and father (left) and their close friend Yossel Kopelov taken in 1920, just before they left Milwaukee for Palestine.

Mother and father sharing a tender moment in Milwaukee, 1920.

In 1934 mother, Sarah (right) and I returning to Israel from the United States aboard the S.S. Esperia.

My sister and I pose together in 1936.

This photo of Golda's parents, Bluma and Moshe
Yitzhak Mabovitch, was taken in Herzlia, Israel in 1940.

In 1969, while on a state visit to the U.S., enroute to the West Coast mother returned
to the school in Milwaukee where she studied as a child.

My children, Daniel, Gideon and Amnon pose with mother in 1966 at the official residence of the foreign minister.

as a month at a time, and once for two months. Each time she left, she sat us down to explain that "Not all American Jews understand us." And that "It is my job to tell them why we need a Jewish homeland in Palestine and how we live there." Someone, she said, had to describe a kibbutz, and talk about how swamps were drained and immigrants welcomed and taught to grow oranges and take care of cows and chickens. It was her job, she said each time, to tell some of the Jews of America to come and help and to tell others to give money "so we can help ourselves." And as we listened to our mother, like the millions who listened to her in later years, we were wholly persuaded that we too must do our "job" and let her go. Nonetheless, I dreaded her absences, and during those seemingly endless weeks gave our hosts a hard time, especially Malka Sheinkman, with whom we stayed our second year in Manhattan.

But what stayed, the residue, was my beginning to realize, really for the first time, that my mother was *not* like other mommies, not even like other working mommies. My first insight I think might have been at a summer camp run by the labor movement where Sarah and I spent part of our vacations. We had some trace of a special status with the counselors there: already we were becoming "Goldie's children"—a designation that filled us with a confusing mixture of pride and annoyance as the years progressed. And I remember too a Passover we spent with mother in Detroit at the home of the parents of Lea Biskin, her close friend who also worked with the Pioneer Women. All week, people dropped in for tea and *Pessachdicher* cakes and to hear what mother had to say. "Goldie, do you really think that women can work as hard as men on farms?" "Goldie, what do you think, should the children learn Hebrew or Yiddish?" "Goldie, tell me, how many immigrants can Palestine absorb a year?" People leaned forward, urgently asking, pushed close to hear her replies, and analyzed her words among themselves. Not Delphic, not an oracle, already she was a woman whose opinions people wanted to hear. A strong woman, a very clever woman, they said to each other. A mother to be proud of, they said to us, and so we were.

Then finally, home at the end of the second summer; sailing with us was a group of Golda's Labor Party associates and some youngsters whom she had personally encouraged to come to Palestine. In the evenings Sarah and I sat on deck or in the public rooms, submerged in the talking, but coming to life to join in the Yiddish and Hebrew songs, and watching mother, always at the center, the focus of people's attention. I can see them now, those young people listening wide-eyed to what she, a living example of self-realization and commitment, had to say about the country to which we were travelling through the night. They listened as one listens to a leader, to a colleague, to a parent, to someone of optimism, courage and authority. Mother was indeed proving herself.

Haifa at last, Mount Carmel, the white houses rising as if out of the sea, and father, on the dock, full of admiration and exclamation: "How wonderful you look Sarahleh! And you, you've grown, Menahem. What fine English you speak!" We kissed and hugged and then set off for Tel Aviv, the city that was ours and familiar but that would never be quite the same again.

CHAPTER 3

MY MOTHER WAS now firmly launched on a career which, however modestly it started, was to culminate within four decades in her assumption of the highest executive office in the land—and the blaze of power and fame. No sooner had we returned home from the States than she was invited to join the Histadrut's Steering Committee, where, from now on, she would have a voice in what is known today as the decision-making process. In short, she had formally entered public life.

Her first assignment was to organize a minute twin-duty tourist department for the Histadrut; a unit to welcome foreign dignitaries to the country and show them around it (sometimes Sarah and I trailed along) and, at the same time, subtly underline the Histadrut's own accomplishments. Within the same year, having carried out this assignment with success, she was elected to the Histadrut Secretariat. This step up placed her in what was, had a Jewish government already existed, the august equivalent of a cabinet post and thus, in fact, a position of considerable clout. By 1936, she was put in charge of the Histadrut's "Mutual Aid" functions, i.e., its social welfare program. This included acting as the chairman (later on she laughed at the word "chairperson" and thought it ludicrous) of the medical insurance scheme, supervising the working conditions of Jewish laborers in the army camps that the British were then busily constructing all over Palestine, and, above all, trying to help solve what was becoming a massive unemployment problem.

An awesome assemblage of tasks for anyone; no wonder my mother's health, though not yet actually poor, began to show signs of wear and tear. There were even twenty-four-hour stretches—rare to be sure, but they did happen—when she was flat on her back with an excruciating migraine headache, prone, pale and exhausted on the couch, cold compress on her head, impatiently waiting to recharge her batteries. How much of this was due to her being a workaholic, to her compulsive undertaking of what amounted to two full-time jobs at once? Personally I think, a lot. No one can work the way my mother did all her life, keep frustration and fatigue so well hidden and at bay most of the time, and not pay a steep physical penalty. "What I really need," she used to say wryly, "is a wife." Saying this inevitably provoked comments such as "She's the only real man in the cabinet" etc., but in reality, Golda wasn't at all or in any way lacking that elusive quality loosely termed femininity.

On the contrary, throughout her life she was quite self-assured both about herself as a woman and in her professional capacities, not ever feeling, I think, the need to obliterate the one in favor of the other. And she had her share of vanities. She wasn't chic, but she was well groomed: although she never used makeup, her nails, in later years, were always manicured and lightly varnished; her clothes conservative but carefully chosen (this white dress for the reception in Kenya, this beige lace for dinner at Nixon's), a critical eye out to what would be appropriate—to her age, her station (whatever it happened to be) and her mission. She enjoyed the line of a well-cut suit, the feel of good fabrics, the bright addition of a piece of jewelry and she was fascinated by the many glamorous women she encountered. Most recently, the family was touched and amused to see how drawn she was, for instance, to Anne Bancroft who portrayed her in the play *Golda* (of which more later). And I am sure that, regardless of how she would have reacted to the final product, my mother would have been absolutely delighted to know that Ingrid Bergman was "Golda" in the TV series that (again, for reasons that must wait) I never saw for myself.

She worked well with all people, and with men always as an equal, neither inferior nor asking for concessions. Unlike many of the early pioneer women who forced themselves to perform the most difficult physical labors in an attempt to prove equality, my mother took it totally for granted. Fighting specifically for women's rights was something that seemed to her unnecessarily limiting. Here, within the Jewish community of Palestine, most of these rights already existed, and when they were absent, it was her bounden duty as a human being and a socialist to see that the wrong was rectified.

She said this herself, loudly, clearly and often because, of course, people wanted to know how she felt about being such a prominent woman. It was a point interviewers always emphasized, understandably enough, but irritatingly. In her autobiography, she had the last word on the subject.

> I am not a great admirer of the kind of feminism that gives rise to bra burning, hatred of men or a campaign against motherhood, but I have had great regard for those energetic hardworking women within the ranks of the labor movement who succeeded in equipping dozens of city-bred girls with the sort of theoretical knowledge and sound practical training that made it possible for them to do their share (and often more) of the work

37

that was going on in settlements throughout Palestine. That kind of constructive feminism does women credit and matters much more than who sweeps the house or who sets the table. . . .

And she also wrote:

. . . . being a woman has never hindered me at all. It has never caused me unease or made me think that men are better off than women . . . nor have men ever given me preferential treatment.

She didn't relish being compared to Ceylon's Madame Bandaranaike or to India's Mrs. Ghandi of whom she disapproved in any case (I have a suspicion that, political chasms notwithstanding, my mother would have admired Mrs. Thatcher's able and unself-conscious comportment as prime minister).

But it was as a hard-pressed woman having found room within herself to be a *mater familias* also to her parents, let alone to her children, that I thought about my mother recently, as I stood for a moment one evening at the site of the charming pocket park, a little garden and fountain, that the city of Tel Aviv (though Golda asked to have nothing named for her) is creating in her memory, just outside our house. Standing there I thought how this commemorative patch of flowers, grass and shade trees would have pleased her parents, and decided then and there that my grandparents must have their place in these reminiscences because though neither individually nor collectively do they explain my mother's uniqueness, she is, after all, what they produced.

They came to Palestine in 1926. They sold their house, their truck and their grocery store in Milwaukee and came to join two of their daughters. I don't know whether it was Golda or Sheyna who lured them here, but their home became the place we spent many many weekends and holidays, a high-ceilinged house that grandpa built with his own hands in a new town, just north of Tel Aviv, on a hill from which, like our own Tel Aviv apartment, one could see the Mediterranean.

My grandfather was an amazingly handy man ("Those are golden hands," my mother said pointedly), a fine carpenter, a cabinet-maker really, who taught me to saw planks with a handsaw, how to hammer nails with some fair precision, how to put together doorframes and window frames. My grandmother was also practical, her natural tendency being to make herself useful, so in Israel she decided that her kitchen would not only provide meals for us, but also hot lunches that she sold at scrupulously fair, and, need I say, exceedingly low prices, to the workmen who were constructing houses throughout the area.

Holidays never being as blissful as memory cosmetically records, I nonetheless think back with a recaptured throb of pleasure to the solemn preparations we made periodically for going to grandpa's. The great awkward bundles of clothes and bedding (who had a washing machine then?), the long, roundabout route from Tel Aviv to Herzliah (there were no speedways either), then the first sweet glimpse of the house on the hill and the first sight of the cousins waiting. The sharpest memory is of the annual Passover Seder that has remained my favorite holiday. Grandpa—gray-haired, tall, dignified—presiding so importantly; my mother, Sheyna and grandma bustling, serving, clearing, admonishing; and all of us singing the Pessach songs that encapsulate so much history and bind Jewish generation to Jewish generation.

Golda had been a rebellious outspoken runaway adolescent, but in Herzliah, for years, I saw her as a remarkably dutiful daughter, forbearing with her peppery critical mother ("Goldie, *why* so many cigarettes? Have a piece of chocolate instead," or "He's taking up the *cello*? Why the cello? There haven't been *Klesmers*—Yiddish for musicians—in this family ever before!"),

39

and respectful and attentive with her father. Grandpa had been a mildly successful immigrant in Milwaukee, active in the Jewish community, liked by his cronies and customers but not anyone of status. In Herzliah, however, he turned, to everyone's surprise—not least his own—first into a landowner (three acres of orange groves) and then into a pillar of the community with whom other pillars took counsel. My mother, I believe, was as proud of him as he of her and proudest perhaps that in her parents' home, the Jewish self-defense underground, the *Haganah,* had installed a secret arms cache. It was in a specially built double wall on the balcony and I don't think even my grandmother knew about it! At last Golda's political and national fervor was echoed by grandpa, and she came to value greatly what she saw to be his persistence, principles and leadership, while in her mother she learned to enjoy the sociability and practical common sense that she herself had inherited.

As for my grandparents, they came to see in my mother a woman whose earlier judgments turned out to be right, a daughter who could be depended on, so it was to my mother, for example, that they went for financial advice—strange as that seems to me since Golda took no interest whatsoever in amassing capital or property, aside from the one purchase of the house we lived in. Still I remember mother and Shamai sitting up evenings with grandpa, helping him figure out where he could get a loan to finance the upkeep of the groves until they paid for themselves. If her talents as a fiscal counsel were belatedly disclosed, her ability to arbitrate was long known to us, and no one in the family was surprised by her role in a bitter dispute that once broke out between the members of a nearby kibbutz and my grandfather. The kibbutzniks worked their fields on Saturdays. Grandpa, something of a skeptic as far as religion was concerned ("Is there really a God? I'm not sure anymore," I heard him say in the months before his death), was nonetheless observant. Like other religious Jews, he regarded adherence to Jewish law not as a strictly private affair concerning only himself and his Creator, but as something binding the Jewish people, as the glue maybe holding together the House of Israel.

So when the kibbutzniks ploughed and dug on the Sabbath in full and brazen view of worshippers in the small Herzliah synagogue, grandpa was outraged. The issue was explosive; the arguments shrill; there was even a possibility of a fistfight. The situation was tense, and might well become threatening. "You talk to them Goldie!" said grandpa. *"You're* friends with the leaders of the kibbutz. You can talk to them better. You're good at that."

She was—and she did. My parents were nonbelievers themselves, belonged to the same generation as the wicked kibbutz Sabbath-breakers, and, generally speaking, shared their orientation. When grandpa came to visit us in Tel Aviv, averting his gaze, he ate off plates on which, in contradiction to Jewish dietary laws, both dairy and meat meals had been served; but when grandma came, she ate on her own plates with her own cutlery so she could have her meals with us but on separate "kosher" dishes. But religious observance or its absence were not ever issues, everyone did what made them comfortable. Thus it was reasonable that despite their differences, grandpa felt he could count on Golda's common sense and negotiating skills to create order out of the chaos being wrought by hot tempers and opposing ideologies. Sure enough, a compromise was reached: the kibbutzniks would go on working on Saturdays, but not outdoors where the visibility of their labor offended. They could be Godless if they so chose, but only where no one except God Himself can see you, mother said cleverly, and the kibbutzniks agreed. Grandpa's admiring hug was a very far cry from the early chastisements of Milwaukee.

Mother's relationship with Sheyna was changed during these

years. Throughout my entire childhood, Sheyna (nine years Golda's senior) was the grownup, much-looked-up-to older sister for whose approval Golda so yearned and whose criticisms so stung her. Small, thin, fine featured, sparing of words but adamant of opinion, Sheyna, in a way, was the conscience of the Mabovitch family. Or, anyhow saw herself as that. My mother had spent many hours of her own childhood in Pinsk, in the decade before the Russian Revolution, listening from her perch on a kitchen shelf to Sheyna and her friends plot a better world. For her, Sheyna was the family's first Socialist and first Zionist, and the fact that she had come to Palestine with Golda—at the drop of a hat as it were—and thus provided such enormous moral support and physical help during those discouraging early days was in itself a source of vast gratitude and even deference. Without Sheyna's presence and pluck, mother undoubtedly would have had an infinitely harder time juggling the opposing demands of public and private life. Sheyna may have been a bit sharp-tongued and a bit self-righteous and old-fashioned about motherhood, but it was with her that we stayed when there was no one else.

I think back on those weeks at Sheyna's with great fondness: being there was like being in some benign army; up at six, morning swims with Shamai, a hearty breakfast (Sheyna was a dietician) and off on time for school, in the afternoons the odd excursions to an "educational" film (Sheyna permitted no other), homework and exactly half an hour's worth of "The Children's Hour" on the radio. Sometimes Sheyna was a trifle more attentive than was comfortable, such as when she inquired daily as to our health and physical fitness or probed, "Menahem, have you done *all* your homework? . . . Have you practiced your cello?" etc. Matters that my parents left to my discretion. Yet, for all of us, Sheyna was a tower of strength (though "tower" is hardly the word) and an aunt one could always come to for support and advice.

It was after our return from the United States that adjustments began to be made in what might be labelled our relative status. Sheyna now fully accepted mother's dedication to her work—perhaps because Golda's talents were becoming apparent also to the public. In the meantime, she herself had gone with her four-year-old to the States to study nutrition (Shamai was already there), leaving her grown daughter and a teenage son behind in mother's charge, and now she was organizing a chain of modern Histadrut-subsidized kitchens, all of which meant that she was better able to understand mother's need for a world beyond the home, and also the conflicts and pressures this kind of need entailed. As mother's career progressed, Sheyna yielded more and more of her authority and increasingly demonstrated her admiration for the sister who had so unreservedly admired and relied on her. In years to come, she began to collect photographs of mother and press clippings about her, and to our embarrassment, kept these on open display in her room.

In 1950 Uncle Shamai died. Sheyna, once so indomitable and indefatigable, withdrew from control of her own life; she stopped shopping and cooking for herself, and waited for us to help take care of her as she used to take care of us. On Saturdays it was now mother who went to Sheyna's home carrying bags of food that she prepared in Sheyna's kitchen; terrain that, only shortly before, she had barely been allowed to enter. And toward the end of Sheyna's gradually dimming life, it was mother who personally financed and directed the publication of a rather terse autobiography (a hundred unadorned pages) that Sheyna had penned at some point so that she might be able to see the printed book while she was still lucid enough to take pleasure from it. But it came out too late, something for which mother bitterly blamed herself.

*   *   *

Zionism took (and still takes) many forms. I liked, in particular, mother's story of one of her more off-beat encounters. Returning in the mid-30s from a Histadrut mission to the United States, she brought back to us the following account:

> I boarded the plane from Los Angeles to San Francisco, where there was to be yet another meeting. To tell the truth, I was excited and a little nervous. This was the first time I'd ever been in such a contraption though I imagine there'll be others, and it's certainly quick. I was watching the passengers come aboard when I noticed a short, bright-eyed man with a violin tucked under his arm. He sat down right next to me and straight away he introduced himself, "How do you do," he said. "My name is Bronislaw Huberman. You are Mrs. Golda Meyerson, aren't you?" I can't say that I didn't feel flattered to be recognized by this great musician and I was very sorry that I wouldn't have time to hear him perform. But what he told me during that plane ride was more exciting than any concert. He's planning to establish a symphony orchestra right here in Palestine, where all the Jewish musicians who are being forced out of Germany and the other countries in which they're not wanted will be able to come and play. It took me a few minutes to absorb what he was saying because who would ever have thought such a thing possible. But soon enough it hit me: how wonderful it will be, having our own Jewish orchestra. Of course, I promised to do everything in my power to help, and I certainly will!

The Palestine Symphony Orchestra came into being officially at the end of 1936, with a gala concert held in a spacious Tel Aviv fairground pavillion. Marshalling all his impressive energy, his great prestige and his impressive international connections,

*Mother and I posing with my wife, Aya, and my mother-in-law,
Cila Pinkerfeld on our wedding day, June 25, 1956.*

My children, from left, Daniel, Gideon and Amnon.

A photo of the extended family: from right, next to Golda is Zechariah (my brother-in-law), myself, Aya, Jonah (Sheyna's son), Sheyna (mother's sister), Chaim (Sheyna's son), my sister Sarah, and Sarah and Bella, Jonah's and Chaim's wives, respectively.

A budding young cellist.

Relaxing in our backyard. I am holding Amnon, while my wife provides a comfortable seat for our son, Daniel.

Amnon, Shaul, Golda, Gideon and Daniel at a Philharmonic Orchestra function for the Israel Conservatory of Music.

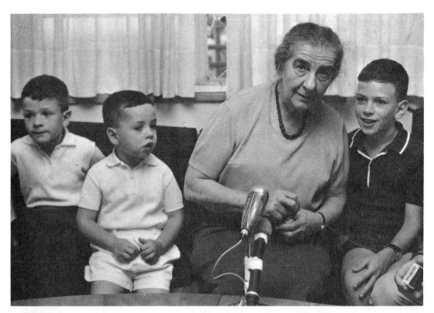

*In Ben-Gurion Airport, a press conference with the grandchildren on mother's
return from a trip to the U.N.*

*Mother and I pose with French musician Serge Baudo (left), after a special youth
concert given by the Israel Philharmonic Orchestra in Tel Aviv. Mr. Baudo
conducted the orchestra and I was cello soloist.*

Mother receiving one of many honorary doctorates.

At Kibbutz Revivim in 1972, from left: Shaul, Golda, Sarah, Naomi and Zechariah.

Huberman financed the venture and chose and brought the musicians together, enlisting no less than Arturo Toscanini, himself a refugee from fascist Italy, to conduct at the inaugural performances. The meeting on mother's very first plane ride resulted, not surprisingly, in Histadrut-sponsorship of a series of workers' concerts (they are still given) which the family attended with almost religious devotion, Sarah and I obediently taking afternoon naps so as not to be tired during the performance, and mother sometimes hosting the musicians on behalf of the Histadrut at after-concert parties where we rubbed elbows with the great.

Today, the Palestine Symphony's offspring, the Israel Philharmonic Orchestra, is an institution with a worldwide reputation, but I can still effortlessly retrieve the incredible excitement of those first concerts at which so many of the best musicians in the world gathered. The Jews of Palestine were starved for culture; many of them were highly educated, cultivated German and Austrian Jews who, flocking to Palestine during the early years of Hitler's rise, had brought with them their taste for the sundry amenities of middle-class European life. Elegant shops suddenly appeared on Tel Aviv's main streets; sidewalk cafes served whipped cream with everything—on tables covered with cloths for the first time in the *Yishuv*'s history; and the sounds of Bach, Beethoven and Brahms, though certainly not unknown before, became more familiar to the ears of Tel Avivians. The German-speaking Jews, arriving in the thousands, transformed the very face of Palestine, and raised for all time our standards of music, journalism, architecture and industry, among others.

What made the opening of the symphony so memorable, apart from Toscanini's appearance, was the background against which it took place: the Arab riots that had begun in April 1936 with the murder of nine Jews in Jaffa and which, as a result of British laxness not to say collusion, continued on and off for a terrible and bloody three years—in the first of which alone there were 2,000 attacks on Jews and Jewish property, and 80 fatalities! Trees, so lovingly planted one by one, and precious crops raised with such difficulty in isolated settlements were wantonly burned to the ground, Jewish houses were destroyed, and any Jew travelling the interurban roads literally risked being stoned or shot at. Tel Aviv, with its concentration of Jews and its tightly organized self-defense system was relatively safe, but everywhere else, everywhere outside the city, fear accompanied us most of the time and so did grief. Almost daily, the newspapers and the radio told of yet another victim. The actual words still ring in my ears: "The high commissioner regrets to announce . . ." So the fact that Toscanini and other gifted artists had knowingly and willingly entered this atmosphere to be with us, filled our hearts to overflowing.

Mother continued to be drawn to music and to musicians even through the hectic days of her five-year office as prime minister and with pride and emotion was to assume the honorary presidency of the noted Rubinstein piano competition, on the grounds that, "Although I don't know much about music, I love and have a special affinity for three musicians—for Casals, for Rubinstein and for my son!"

The "disturbances," as the British euphemistically termed the years of Arab riots and general strike (designed, unsuccessfully, to paralyze the country) didn't, of course, stop my mother or any-one else from using the roads to Jerusalem or to outlying settlements even immediately following Arab raids—though we used to say "goodbye" to her in the mornings with hearts in mouth, and Sarah and I waited at home in the afternoons far more frightened for her than she had ever been for herself.

The intolerable situation did result in efforts, of very different kinds, to solve what in those days, curiously enough, was also known as the Palestine problem—though then the Palestinians were us, the Jews! One such attempt was that of the British Peel Commission, headed by the eponymous, which conscientiously and under heavy guard toured the length and breadth of the country, and within a year delivered itself of a cautious set of recommendations. What the commission proposed was that Palestine be partitioned, divided into two states; one, an Arab state to occupy most of Palestine's 45,000 to 50,000 square miles; the other, a Jewish state to be squashed into a paltry 1,000 square miles, with a tiny Jewish enclave in Jerusalem that would connect to the coastal canton by a slender and perilous corridor. The Arabs rejected the partition outright, as biased in their favor as it was; the Zionist leadership convened somberly in Geneva to discuss it, and finally, urged by David Ben Gurion, then head of the Jewish Agency, accepted the severe truncation on the grounds that at least it would provide some haven for the Jewish refugees fleeing Europe whom no one except the *Yishuv* wanted. Mother, along with close friends from the party (Berl Katznelson was one) joining a minority, firmly opposed what she was sure was an unviable division—though when World War II broke out, bringing with it the extermination of the trapped Jews of Europe, she was to look back on that militant stand as lacking real foresight, taking comfort only in the fact that it was not her opposition but total Arab rejection that had caused the plan's demise.

Today, I reread letters we wrote to and from Geneva then and I marvel at how hard she worked to take us into her world and somehow to keep in touch with ours while what mattered most to her was placed in such dreadful jeopardy.

From Menahem, Tel Aviv, June 13, 1937

Darling Mamma,
    We were so happy to receive your letter. The books you sent are

wonderful. I was especially happy when I saw the second one on how to paint with oils. The book on Rembrandt is less important to me, but interesting, and the shirts are also nice. Yesterday, on Saturday, father, Sarah and I went to Sheyna's and we took a cab to see the new house they're building . . . If you really want to know what I would like from Switzerland, I want only two things, one an easel and good painting supplies, and the other an electrical meccano set, so I can build a radio, telegraph, etc . . .

From Menahem, Tel Aviv, July 12, 1937

Shalom Mamma,
. . . Today I read the speeches of delegates to the Congress in the newspaper and it seems to me that the debate is very stormy. . . . You probably voted for partition against your will, but don't worry, it will all be alright . . .

From Menahem, Tel Aviv, July 29, 1937

Shalom Mamma,
Today I got back from the camp at Moshav Ben Shemen. It was wonderful. We worked in the agricultural school, and swam in the pool. All the kids from the Youth Movement went to camp mainly to work and to get used to working on the land, to physical work that is, in the fields, gardens, and with the cattle. . . . Ima, be well. Even in Switzerland you can take care of your throat and teeth. We have plenty to do. I'm reading Treasure Island *by Robert Louis Stevenson and the English isn't difficult at all.*
Mother, in times like these there are Arabs who are friendly towards the Jews. For instance, when we were at camp, we went to tour the area and met with an Arab sheikh whose father had had ties with Weizmann and even helped us get the Balfour Declaration, and whose grandfather was on good relations with the first Jewish watchmen during Turkish times and worked with them hand-in-hand. It's

*hard to believe that there are Arabs like these today. When we got
to his home, he gave us water because we were very thirsty. The next
day the young sheikh came to the camp and we gave him bread and
cocoa. He divided the piece of bread between the head counsellor and
himself, a sign of brotherhood among the Arabs. . . .*

Postcard from Golda, Zurich, July 30, 1937

My Dearest Ones,

*We have been having meetings for two days already and discussing
the issues of the Congress. I found five letters from you here. It was
wonderful. I was so glad that Menahem went to camp and hope that
all went well. Write me and tell me what you are doing during the
holidays. I was very happy with your grades at school and in your
music studies. I also think that you, Menahem, should study painting, but we must find a good teacher. Ask someone who knows.
Sarah, what did you do when Menahem was away? Morris, I'll
write you soon. Be well.*

From Sarah, Tel Aviv, August 12, 1937

Hello Mamma,

*How are you. We're fine. We'll see each other in about two more
weeks . . . Tomorrow Menahem and I will go to Herzliah to spend
Saturday with grandma and grandpa . . . There was an article in
the newspaper about you, saying that you spoke up very strongly
against partitioning the country. Good for you. Menahem says that
Dr. Weizmann doesn't have any sense because he favors partition
. . .*

Postcard from Golda, Zurich, August 18, 1937

My Dear Children,

I got your letters. Your opinions on partition are very interesting to me. No one in the party voted for partition. When I get home I'll explain to you what our decision was . . .

*   *   *

The other effort, this one on the part of the Jews alone, was more fortuitous. The looting, burning, well-poisoning and killing by wildly incited Arab mobs were accompanied, as I've mentioned, by a general strike with which the Arabs hoped to force the British to end Jewish immigration, in effect to annul Britain's commitment to a Jewish National Home as expressed in the Balfour Declaration. One day, obeying orders issued by the Arab High Committee (it was headed by the Mufti of Jerusalem, who had instigated the riots with the open support of the Axis powers), all the Arab busdrivers abandoned their buses; all the Arab farmers withheld their produce from market, and all the Arab longshoremen stopped working, thereby closing the Jaffa Port. Everything ground to the proverbial halt; the "Palestinian problem" now incorporated the threat of economic strangulation. The only possible response, if Jews wanted, as we did, to survive, was for us to step into the vacuum. So Jewish drivers armor-plated and drove the idle Arab buses; kibbutzim brought their fruits and vegetables to towns and cities; and it was decided to construct a new harbor, a wooden jetty actually, in Tel Aviv. I don't think anyone alive in that city on the day the "harbor" opened for business has forgotten it. It was, in every sense of the words, a national holiday, proof positive that we could indeed do everything ourselves. By the thousands, Tel Avivians crowded together at the waterfront, singing and dancing while the longshoremen (to a man Jews from Salonika who refused pay for the day's work) unloaded one sack after another of cement from the Yugoslav ship that was the first to anchor there, with every one dashing into the water to take a turn at helping out. Within a few weeks, an iron jetty replaced the wooden one and an enclosed bay formed for tugboats and barges to unload their goods.

But what's a Jewish port without Jewish ships? So the first Jewish maritime enterprise, *Nachshon* (named for the first Israelite to leap into the sea, at Moses' command, during the Exodus from Egypt), was launched. And in 1937 and '38, mother was sent back to the States to resume a pattern of coast-to-coast travelling; this time to sell *Nachshon* shares at dozens of parlor meetings and public gatherings. Once again, people all over the States were listening raptly to her simple, clear statements about the need for their help. "We *must* train our people for work on the sea," she told them, "just as we have trained them, all these years, for work on the soil. This is one more step toward the independence of a nation."

It is chilling to note that while no one could have known or foreseen the wave of immigrants that would arrive during and after the Holocaust, in the voluminous correspondence that my mother conducted in the 30s with shipping companies in England and elsewhere, she was already discussing, alongside purely commercial matters, the transporting to Palestine of Jewish immigrants and refugee children from Europe.

As for me, like any ten-year-old boy, I had my own reasons for being enthralled by the new harbor and *Nachshon*. Not only had my trip to the United States several years before equipped me with brave fantasies of becoming a sea captain myself, but from the balcony of our flat I could watch the tugboats bring in the lighters piled with cargo and, if I used binoculars, I could make out the flags and the names of the anchored ships. That they were docked in Tel Aviv was, for me, like the formal recognition of one country by another, and it gave me a sense of living in a country that was part of a wide world.

From Menahem, Tel Aviv, February 1, 1937

Dear Mamma,

   Today is the first of February. Remember that you promised to return at the end of the month. So there are thirty days left. But I'm hoping that you'll finish sooner and return at once aboard a Nachshon *ship with the Jewish flag waving on its mast . . . The concert we went to was very successful and we'll listen to it again on the radio. . . .*

From Menahem, Tel Aviv, February 21, 1938

Shalom Mother,

   On Thursday the first tourists are going to arrive at Tel Aviv Port. We will be going there ourselves soon with the whole school. Today we had an arithmetic test. The teacher gave us only one question, very difficult and complicated. No one could work it out. All the brightest pupils tried and tried, wrinkled their foreheads, and couldn't. Only me and a friend managed to solve the problem . . . Your return is already overdue, but never mind. Come back in a month . . . If you manage to purchase the two ships, that will surely encourage people to buy more shares and the company will grow and expand its routes to everywhere in the world where there are Jews . . . Mommy, if you want to bring a nice present, I suggest a children's encyclopedia, like the Book of Knowledge . . .

From Menahem, Tel Aviv, January 8, 1938

Hello my dearest Mamma,

   On January 15, I'll be playing at a concert dedicated to Jewish composers at the music school . . . Everything is fine at school. This week they changed the work groups. I've just finished working in the kitchen, and now I'll be doing handicrafts. We're binding books for the school library and they come out exactly as if a real bookbinder had bound them. It's very interesting work for boys and girls, unlike embroidery, which is work for girls and boys can't get used to it. The teacher says I'm doing very well with the bookbinding . . . Now we are studying Isaiah; *you can't imagine how beautiful it is . . .*

If the issue of immigration hadn't rapidly turned into a matter of survival for the Jews of Europe, the high romance, the thrill of the new port and of *Nachshon* might have lingered longer. But though the Final Solution came nearer to realization, and Arab violence was making Arab aspirations unequivocally clear, the British, reacting to blackmail, began to give in. Never mind the tightening noose, the gates of Palestine were closing to the Jews. Immigration quotas were critically reduced and visas becoming impossible to obtain. In Europe, the Jews were being doomed, and we sat in our homeland, helpless.

Then there was a glimmer of hope. Franklin Delano Roosevelt sponsored an international conference on refugees at Evian-les-Bains, France, at which the "representative" countries on whose conscience the plight of the Jews seemed to weigh somewhat might discuss a "just solution of the refugee problem." Since there was no Jewish state, however, the United States and Britain cynically determined that there was no way of having an official Jewish representation and decided that immigration to Palestine wouldn't even be discussed at Evian.

Mother attended the conference, along with Dov Hos, head of the Histadrut's political department, "in the ludicrous capacity of the 'Jewish observer from Palestine,' " as she put it in her autobiography. This was her first painful encounter with the world's polished diplomats and negotiators, and she describes better than I can the despair and rage that flooded her as the conference degenerated into an exercise in rhetoric:

53

> Sitting there in the magnificent hall, listening to the delegates of thirty-two countries rise, each in turn, to explain how much they would have liked to take in substantial numbers of refugees and how unfortunate it was that they were not able to do so, was a terrible experience. I don't think that anyone who didn't live through it can understand what I felt at Evian—a mixture of sorrow, rage, frustration and horror. I wanted to get up and scream at them all. "Don't you know that these numbers are human beings, people who may spend the rest of their lives in concentration camps, or wandering around the world like lepers, if you don't let them in?

Mother would frequently quote Dr. Chaim Weizmann's pithy pronouncement: "The world is divided between those countries that expel the Jews and those that won't let them in."

Having thus momentarily stilled their consciences and disposed, so they hoped, of the tiresome problem of the Jews, the delegates went home, leaving the British to complete the betrayal. In May 1939, the Chamberlain government, in the wake of the failure of the Peel plan and in response to Arab threats to join the Axis, issued its infamous White Paper. Masterminded by the man who had just signed Czechoslovakia over to Hitler at Munich, this document virtually decreed the end to Jewish immigration—a grand total of 75,000 would be allowed to enter Zion during the next five years, and then none at all, ever, without Arab consent. This, at a moment of history when it was known by all concerned that the lives of hundreds of thousands of Jews (no one dreamt then of millions or of worse than concentration camps) who had no place else to go depended on this one single refuge. Nor did any protests, demonstrations or hunger strikes in Palestine itself make any difference. The British, blinded (one can only believe) by their fear of a fancied Arab uprising, were deaf to any appeal. Their minds were made up;

the White Paper was not going to be revoked. The only thing to do was for the Jews of Palestine to take matters into their own hands—as far as possible. At a London conference preceding the promulgation of the White Paper, David Ben Gurion had already declared to a shocked British audience that if legal immigration were stopped, *illegal* immigration would become the order of the day. The *Yishuv* would not remain inactive, whatever the price of action. In August of 1939, one month before the outbreak of World War II, Golda was called away urgently to the Zionist Congress then taking place in Geneva, where Ben Gurion now announced his intentions to the leaders of World Zionism, many of whom feared the results of an activist Jewish policy. But Ben Gurion, placing Jewish lives above international politics or Jewish popularity, resoundingly affirmed the *Yishuv*'s absolute commitment to bringing Jewish refugees to Palestine and continuing its settlement and defense. "The Jews should act as though we were the state in Palestine, and should so act until there will be a legal Jewish state," he declared, a declaration with which my mother was in wholehearted agreement.

As a rule, when mother went abroad, Sarah and I tried to dissuade her: Why is such-and-such a mission necessary? Why must you, of all people, be the one to go? Why now? And she would sit with us and patiently explain until she gained our "consent." This time we asked nothing. No questions. We knew for ourselves that if she was needed in Geneva, that was where she had to be.

From Golda, Geneva, August 21, 1939

Dear Children,

Today I received your second letter and I am delighted that you found good friends on your holiday. There's no greater joy in the world than close friends and good company. I hope that you have received my letters and cards . . . A Rabbi from America spoke yesterday against "illegal" immigration and Berl Katznelson replied in a wonderful and great speech. The entire Congress felt that, at this terrible hour, it is good that there is someone who can present our case so well. There is a heavy feeling of the danger of war. I pray that this won't happen. It's impossible to contemplate the killing that will take place throughout the world . . . I miss you both very very much. We'll see each other soon, I promise. If war breaks out, don't worry. I'll come home at once. . . .

From Menahem, Tel Aviv, undated

Shalom Mamma,
    . . . I am sure that times will be good one day for our people, and not only for our people, but for everyone. I don't love our people more than others who are human, not scum like the Nazis, with Hitler and Mussolini at their head. One of these days we'll all live happily. There'll be a socialist democratic government and everyone will live in brotherhood and there won't be any more wars . . . I'm glad you went to the dentist.

From Menahem, Tel Aviv, (undated) 1939

Mamma!
    Really the time to return to your homeland has come. I know how much you miss us and how hard you're trying to come home. I also miss you. Mamma, we were so happy when we got the telegram saying you're coming back, but surprised when we received the second one. Never mind if it takes another week or two, because I know that you're not abroad for your own sake . . .

From Golda, Geneva (undated) 1939

Darlings,

. . . Today I leave for Marseilles. All the Yishuv *delegates will go home from there. Don't worry. We'll certainly all be home in a few days. If we don't get passage on an ordinary liner, the Jewish Agency will charter an American ship for us. Regards to everyone in the family. Many kisses. See you soon. . . .*

CHAPTER 4

FOR REASONS EMBEDDED, I imagine, in their wrath-and-glory filled history, Israelis are much given to ceremonies. As Golda's son it was only natural that I myself and, of course, my family, should have been the recipients of hundreds of invitations to all kind and manner of ceremony. For years and years, in fact for as long as I can remember, dedications and commemorations, graduations and installations literally punctuated my mother's calendar; and Aya and I were included sometimes as interested and enthusiastic participants sometimes feeling duty bound to keep mother company. It is therefore by way of being a bitter irony that the one ceremony I missed was the signing of Israel's Proclamation of Statehood —something I would dearly have liked to witness both for its intrinsic importance and because it was one of those moments in history for which no record, reportage or even first-person account can ever substitute for actual participation.

Like everyone else who was not one of the lucky 200 people who, by secret invitation, jammed into the little Tel Aviv Art Museum on Rothschild Boulevard on the afternoon of May 14,

1948, I am more or less familiar with the details: the simple hall so hastily swept and scrubbed and decorated with a few flowers here and there; the large photograph of Theodore Herzl that hung between two improvised Star-of-David banners; the representatives of all the *Yishuv*'s political parties in their bought-for-abroad dark suits; and David Ben Gurion, totally out-of-character in a buttoned-up shirt and tie, briskly reading the less-than-one-hundred words that brought to a formal end two thousand years of homelessness and the humiliating deadly helplessness of the Jewish people.

But not only was I not there; I wasn't even in the country. Instead, I was thousands of miles away, incongruously getting ready for the Manhattan School of Music, cursing the distance between myself and the tremendous events taking place at home. I remember watching the modest, earth-shaking procedures in a little Trans-lux newsreel theater somewhere in New York, sitting alone in the dark, staring up at people whom I had known since childhood, now suddenly transmuted, elevated might be the better word, into the founding fathers of a new-born state, members of a provisional government. I remember thinking that I'd caught a glimpse of my mother signing the Proclamation—and I can retrieve, to this day, the astonishing but well-suppressed urge I had to get up, right then and there, in that three-quarters-empty movie house and announce at the top of my voice that what we were looking at, there on the screen, was the beginning of something absolutely new, something of great significance; not just a newsreel. There, in black and white, nurtured by ancient roots, and grown in long-neglected and blood-stained soil, a Jewish state was bursting into being. And my own mother was part of that wonderful happening. I would have given a lot to have been with her that hot spring day in Tel Aviv.

She talked quite frequently about the ceremony, about the

extreme almost unbearable strain that had preceded and was to follow it, and how, although it wasn't much more than Ben Gurion's understated reading and an odd bit of music and was, anyhow, the prelude to the mass Arab invasion and the darkest days of the War of Independence, it was quite simply the single most wonderful moment of her life.

> When my turn came to sign, my hands shook and the tears just rolled down my cheeks. I could barely see the document in front of me. . . . Whatever happened now, whatever price any of us would have to pay for it, we had done it. We had brought the Jewish State into existence—and I, Golda Meyerson, had lived to see the day.

She had returned from Evian prepared to embark on any course of activity that might conceivably aid the Jews of Europe. By comparison, the lot of the Jews of Palestine was an easy one, easy, in fact, even by comparison to that of many other peoples caught in the crossfire and the destruction of the war. Of course, everything was rationed—sugar, oil, eggs, textiles, shoes, all the basics; at night there were blackouts in Tel Aviv and we sat in darkened rooms sweltering behind closed shutters and drawn curtains in the suffocating summer heat. And, naturally, for a long time, there was the undercurrent of terrible fear: Would Rommel make it across Egypt? Where would the Italian bombs hit? They had struck at Tel Aviv twice, causing many fatalities. A school friend of mine had been killed. Would they do it again? And, above all, would the Axis invade? And what if there were indeed invasion and conquest? But those tended to be night fears; in the daytime, at least until 1943, life went on in basically familiar patterns with only a highly increased British presence serving as a visible reminder of carnage beyond Palestine's borders.

But the surface serenity was shattered by collective anguish as the dimensions of the Holocaust became clearer, like the still indistinct shapes of a monster at long last emerging from the concealing fog. We had no idea then of the numbers involved, but the *fact* of the extermination camps, their ghastly purpose and the reality of the liquidation, faced us, as the British, adamant, continued to block, thwart and undermine each attempt on our part to save our brethren.

The forces at our disposal were puny; a handful of unseaworthy ships and their unreliable mercenary crews hired mostly at blackmail prices to transport the fleeing Jews to Palestine. But those who *ran* the secret exodus were, like my mother, deeply committed to, and profoundly involved in, the organization of these escape routes, and what they accomplished—even if not statistically spectacular—is forever to their credit. Psychologically, the demands made upon them were complex: my mother serves as a good example, I think. Like so many Israelis, she had tended to idealize the British, not, of course, as empire-builders or the holders of the Palestine mandate, but as a great nation, like her own and like the United States she so admired and I would even say loved, genuinely democratic, genuinely sensitive to the value of each individual human life and genuinely striving (if not always managing) to be on the side of the angels. It was doubly difficult therefore for her to accept the "insane" (her word) and cruel British pursuit of those wretched little hellships with their cargo of anguished beings who had lost everything but their own lives. She saw the British, at one and the same time, as saints and as devils and was never able to explain adequately to herself, or to others, their brutality and indifference where Palestine was concerned.

At war's end she stood before the Zionist Congress in Basel and voiced the overwhelming feeling of frustration she had experienced in the years when one-third of the world's Jews were being annihilated and she, strong, healthy, intelligent, had been unable to help rescue more than a very, very few.

> Why are we *now* pressing our demand for a Jewish State? When did it become clear that we must have total control over our lives and immigration, that these must be in the hands of Jews, not as a distant aim, but as a desperate, immediate need? Let me tell you when we understood this necessity: when we, the six hundred thousand Jews of Palestine, despite everything we had created in the country and endured during the long years of war, were powerless to rescue millions of Jews from certain death. All that stood between our readiness to rescue the Jews of Europe and the certainty that death awaited them at Hitler's hands, the one and only thing that blocked their way from death to life, was a political regulation laid down by strangers— the White Paper. The British Government placed itself between us and the millions of Jews lost in Europe, practically within our sight, and we could be of no help. The White Paper was like an iron wall erected between us and Hitler's victims. It was then, when our helplessness was so tragically revealed, that the argument among us as to the goals of Zionism came to an end. Zionism, redemption, and rescue became a single concept . . . and we knew that there was only one way of fulfilling Zionism now—and that was by creating a Jewish State.

For Golda, as for all Jews, the Holocaust was a watershed, dividing modern history into before and after. Not that, though it is often so claimed, the birth of the Jewish state resulted directly from the slaughter. There were Zionists long before that —and my mother was one of them—but the Holocaust did effect crucial and permanent changes in attitude. For one, it made the Jewish state imperative. If before, a Jewish homeland was envisioned as a place in which Jews might live in freedom and dignity, after the Holocaust a Jewish state was regarded as a *sine qua non* if Jews, as a nation, were to survive. If, before the Holocaust, many Zionist leaders were content to dream of a Jewish state to come into being in some distant, indeterminate future, after the Holocaust the timing for the state became *now*.

It was all long ago, almost another world, but one scene from those days somehow has not lost its colors or faded. It was 1942. We lived then in a new apartment, the first we ever owned, in a workers cooperative erected by Solel Boneh that faced the sea. One evening my mother came home tired and, what was more unusual, visibly upset. She washed her face, put on a housecoat, sat back in her chair and closed her eyes for a minute. Then she said, "It's bad enough that the rest of the world doesn't and won't help us, but our own people, some of them, just don't understand what is at stake."

What was at stake, she said, was making contact with the Jewish underground in Poland. Only a few months ago, the first reports of death camps and gas chambers had reached us and we were still incredulous. But my mother was among those who knew instinctively and at once that these reports were based on truth. Now, a Histadrut emissary had come back from Turkey where he had contacted a group of rather unsavory characters, some perhaps even Nazis, who moved freely about Europe and were willing, she told us, to do the liaison job—to the tune of £75,000, which was then maybe a single king's ransom but not much money for possibly saving hundreds of human lives. The Histadrut and the Jewish Agency decided to go along with the venture; each offered £25,000 from its own budget, agreeing under the circumstances to overlook the question of what proportion would go to the Polish-Jewish freedom fighters themselves, and what to these unorthodox, available go-betweens. The rest was to be raised from private contributions and mother had been asked to help raise these funds.

> You know, there are people even here in this country who are better businessmen than Jews. Today I met one of the wealthiest men in Palestine. I went to Tiberias where he's on holiday. When he heard my proposal, I could see him counting the bills in his head. "How do you know the money will ever reach the Jews?" he asked. "As a matter of fact," I answered, "I know that most of it won't. But if even ten pennies out of every ten pounds gets to them, that'll be more than they have now." But he was too concerned about his money and he turned me away empty-handed. He didn't understand.

She shook her head as though to shake away the pain and the shock and then we talked about something else. But I never forgot how drawn her face was—or how agonizing the revelation that even in Palestine not everyone believed that the worst had happened.

A more dramatic, if equally unsuccessful, attempt to establish contact with Jewish underground movements in Europe in which mother was also involved concerned the sending of Palestinian Jews, parachutists, behind enemy lines in the Balkans and Northern Italy. It is a story many know, but some do not. It mattered a great deal to Golda so I'll tell it for the benefit of those for whom it is new.

It was a scheme that the Jewish Agency had been urging on the British for years as a way of simultaneously aiding the war effort by helping Allied prisoners of war, particularly captured airmen, to escape, of making contact with the partisans, and of sabotaging Axis targets—all this while furthering our own increasingly frenzied efforts to aid Jewish resistance and escape wherever possible. For years the British had vetoed every suggestion, terrified that we would ask for too much in return, perhaps make reciprocal demands for immigration and for the Jews to be allowed to play a more prominent role in the war against Hitler. But by the summer of 1943, motivated by their growing need for reliable and skilled saboteurs and liaison officers, especially in the Balkans, they grudgingly agreed to a watered-down version of the original proposal.

A few months later thirty-two parachutists, young Palestinian Jews, came to the Histadrut offices to say goodbye. My mother had had no hand in selecting them or in working out the details of their beyond-belief hazardous missions, but as a member of the Histadrut Secretariat she had been one of those who decided in favor of the plan; and she felt responsible for every action they undertook and for each individual who was putting a life on the line. As they walked into her office, as she shook hands and offered encouragement and praise, she had no illusions at all about the dangers they were taking upon themselves, their chances of survival, or even the degree of success with which they would meet—and indeed, seven of the thirty-two never returned. Some of those volunteers were acquaintances; some she had never seen before. One of them, Enzo Sereni, was a long-time friend whom mother had first met at Givat Brenner, the *kibbutz* he helped to found in the 1920s when he came to Palestine from his native Italy. I remember him very well; he was strikingly different from Golda's other Labor Party colleagues. At forty, his age when he parachuted into Italy, something of the rarified atmosphere of the well-to-do, assimilated, highly cultured family in which he was raised—his father had been personal physician to the King of Italy—still clung to him. He had retained the air of a sophisticated Italian intellectual, of a man who could afford the luxury of a philosophical turn of mind, of pacifist convictions, and of religious feelings curiously but smoothly combined with his practicing socialism. He was older than the other parachutists, a man with a family and a rich and active life behind him. He had played and was still playing a leading role in the *Haganah,* and he had served as an overland conductor of Iraqi Jews escaping into Palestine. But also he had served as the editor and publisher of an effective Italian anti-fascist newspaper. In short he was truly a man of parts, often at our house, a wonderful talker. The day of his leave-taking, mother confessed that she had tried to persuade him not to go. "He isn't young enough. He won't withstand Fascist imprisonment if he is captured and, anyhow, we need him here." But even as she argued, she knew that her words were useless, and she parted from him with a heavy heart. Unfortunately her misgivings were justified. Enzo was caught almost at once, imprisoned by the S.S., transported with other Jews to Dachau, and killed there by the Nazis.

Another parachutist my mother talked about later and often, always with pain, was a young woman, Hannah Senesh, who had come to Palestine from Hungary in 1939 to live, as my mother herself had once wanted to live, a pioneering life on a *kibbutz.* Like Enzo, she too was a writer; the diary and short lyrical poems she left behind recording her love for the land and her sense of a special personal destiny made her a national symbol of heroic youth cut off and sacrificed for the common good. For Golda, Hannah Senesh's death—in Hungary, where captured, imprisoned and tortured, she was finally shot—focused two specific and, I think, characteristic emotions.

One was that sense of responsibility I've just mentioned; it verged on and overlapped with a sense of guilt that she felt and would continue to feel through the '73 Yom Kippur War and afterwards for each casualty, a feeling that, when she was prime minister, would cause her to toss and turn through sleepless nights, thinking and rethinking each defensive or offensive mili-

tary action on the agenda. I remember that after World War II
Golda met with Hannah Senesh's mother, one of the first postwar immigrants, and I think it may be revealing to record
Golda's off-the-cuff description of that meeting. Speaking in the
fall of 1946 at a Labor Party convention that had been called to
discuss ways of responding to the still-in-force hateful British
White Paper, she described two encounters, one with the parents of an unnamed boy who died in a *Haganah* action, the other
with Mrs. Senesh:

> Yesterday the parents of a young man who didn't return, a
> mother and a father who cannot accept the fact that this is their
> fate and that their son will not be back, begged me to give them
> one word of hope, even though in the depth of their hearts they
> knew that this hope no longer exists. I want to tell you that if
> there can be feelings of guilt that we took this boy from his
> parents, I felt those feelings yesterday. And I felt them also when
> I met with Hannah Senesh's mother. Hannah Senesh too was not
> sent on her mission by a foreign power; Hannah Senesh too
> didn't undertake a course of action that she had chosen on her
> own; she and her friends did what they did because *we* sent them,
> because they knew that their going was *our* desire . . . They
> obeyed our call, they went, and they did not return. . . .

She often spoke of the *Diaspora* as a place where Jews lived and
died at the beck-and-call of others, where they lost their lives in
other people's pogroms and in other people's armies. Forced
conscription of Jewish youth had been a standard terror in Czarist Russia (my mother's own grandfather was subjected to it),
and she was convinced that only in a Jewish homeland would
Jews be able to control their destiny. But with choice comes
responsibility, and this was to weigh on her more heavily with
each passing year—and each passing war.

The second feeling that focused on Hannah Senesh's death, as well as the death of the other girl parachutist, Haviva Reik, also a kibbutz member captured and put to death behind Nazi lines, was a strong and abiding sense of identification, as a woman, and, what's more, a woman of spirit and vigor. It occurs to me as I write that had mother been less than middle-aged in those days, less of a winded chain-smoker, less of a harried up-and-coming party leader, she might have herself answered the call that urged on those young women. As it was—and I shall come to this—she was not to lack for opportunities to demonstrate her own courage.

The saga of the parachutists was only one aspect of a larger, multifaceted *Yishuv* endeavor to take part in the battle to the death against Hitler. Virtually the entire Jewish population of Palestine was mobilized one way or another, and our own family, in fact, typified the kind and range of this involvement.

Take Sarah first: like other adolescents, students and young working people, she was then a member of one of the *Yishuv*'s many youth movements. These tended to be not totally unlike scouts in the United States and Britain; they were, however, politically oriented, each group run under the auspices of a political party, and their activities involved real work, farming, guarding, etc., not just camping and knot-tying, though they did those too. For their adult sponsors and mentors, they represented the future, the way in which Zion would be rebuilt; each movement stressing a preferred alternative to the other. In 1943, the leaders of Sarah's group sent out a call to its youngsters, appealing to them to enlist for what might be termed the two-pronged service that has always typified Israel's defense approach. On the one hand the kids would be prepared for *kibbutz* life (i.e., nation-building as that particular political movement saw it); on the other hand they would receive military training that would ready them for enlistment in the *Palmach*, the *Haganah*'s striking force. The Palmach was created in 1941 when the danger of a German invasion of Palestine convinced the *Haganah* high command that the *Yishuv* was in need of a fully mobilized and properly trained force able to provide some measure of defense both against an Axis attack and against the inevitable Arab harassment and rioting that would follow, in that grim case, upon a British withdrawal. The *Palmachnikim,* men and women alike, were schooled in guerilla tactics and intelligence activities, and Sarah was soon taught to operate a wireless, a feat she was very proud of and one, I must say, that I admired and even envied.

After a gruelling breaking-in period in a northern *kibbutz* she was sent off to Revivim. Revivim then was not only one of three isolated Jewish outposts in the Negev; it was actually the southernmost Jewish settlement in the country, plunked down together with its two "siblings" in the middle of acre upon acre of scorching sand and very little else. Here this knot of teenagers that included my young sister was expected to irrigate and work the soil and, when and if the time came, to defend it against Egyptian army attack. Not an easy assignment for seasoned troops and when you think of it, an astonishing undertaking for boys and girls fresh out of high school.

For many years now, Israeli guides have proudly shown off the miracles of irrigation to one batch after another of wide-eyed tourists who can feel their skin drying as they walk from air-conditioned buses to greenhouses that burst with Negev-grown tomatoes and cucumbers or through burgeoning fields of wheat and cotton. But in 1945, when Sarah joined up, the promise of Revivim and the other Negev *kibbutzim* far exceeded the reality. Above all, they were the advance guard, the heralds of a vast desert reclamation program (the British had firmly dismissed 85 percent of the Negev as being "entirely uncultivatable") masterminded by David Ben Gurion and defying the White Paper restrictions on the areas on which Jews were permitted to settle or the amount of land they could purchase. The program had two main goals: to make room for the hundreds of thousands of would-be Jewish immigrants the British were still hunting and blockading but who, one day, somehow or other would enter the country; and to set the as yet uncertain borders of a still non-existent state. If today the Negev is both fertile and secure—and it is both—this is so only thanks to the vision and guts of youngsters willing to live in the primitive and dangerous conditions that Sarah and her friends lived in during those first years. . . .

I remember going to Revivim with mother in 1946. Without letting Sarah know beforehand (no telephones in *kibbutzim* in those days), we drove down in a Jewish Agency car, bumping along the potholed single road that meandered southward through Beersheba, still a ramshackle dusty little Arab town with minarets rising picture-postcard-style above higgledy-piggledy shops and small stone houses into the sky. By the time we turned southeast from Beersheba we had long passed areas of sizeable Jewish settlement, and the road, bordered solely by wide expanses of sand and scrub, seemed bleakly to be going nowhere. Finally we turned right at a sign announcing that we were all of five kilometers from Revivim, where there was no road at all, and we drove in the ruts of earlier cars, both of us choking with the thick and blinding dust that lifted in the wake of our tires.

By the mid-50s Revivim would boast fruit saplings, a factory for the production of silo elevators, real houses, and not only all the other taken-for-granted components of normal life but also the very latest of agricultural equipment and kitchen and laundry facilities for a population of about eighty members. But that day all there was to see were a fortress-like structure with the obligatory watchtower, a chunky water tower, one common room that served as a dining room, tents in which the *kibbutz* members slept and little patches of vegetables that were, in effect, important participants in Revivim's farming experiments. Everything else was yellow sand that periodically rose and resettled in furiously destructive mini-sandstorms.

"How in the world will Sarah ever manage here?" mother asked me, and herself, on our parched way home. Amazingly enough, Sarah had looked fine, and mother knew, better than most, how much it mattered to her to be directly involved in what was happening in the country, and part of the dramatic "redemption," as it was then a bit bombastically but quite accurately known, of the Negev; Israel's future, Ben Gurion said. But the Revivim tea had tasted as though it were steeped in brine; the sand and disorder in the tents had not escaped mother's sharp eye; and the sun had beaten down on us almost unbearably—not that summer glare was new to us. How could she help but think of the frail little girl who had almost died of a kidney disease. I could see that she was torn between deep concern for Sarah and equally deep pride in her; a pride that later she would express in public speeches dotted with references to "my daughter in the *kibbutz,*" but that she never, to my knowledge, openly confessed to Sarah herself.

How much she thought—during that first visit while Sarah's friends excitedly told her about their work and interrogated her about the Jewish Agency's plans for developing the Negev—of her own days in Merhavia and whether she felt twinges of envy or regret I don't know. This belonged in the realm of the introspection that was so foreign to her. But I remember a story she told me about a friend from Milwaukee, an ardent Zionist who had burst into bitter recrimination when *her* daughter took her at her word and emigrated to Palestine. I had a feeling then that mother may well have had in mind this example of how not to behave when she kept her worries from Sarah and even tempered whatever she said to me on the subject. Besides which,

71

there was Golda's code, shaped by the society in which she lived and worked: one didn't complain or praise too much, or permit oneself weaknesses of any avoidable kind. Stoicism and socialism were, so to speak, the two banks between which the river of life inexorably flowed as it moved in the direction of that independent Jewish state that she—and almost everyone else I knew —so yearned for and the bringing-into-being of which so totally absorbed them.

For my part I joined the Jewish Settlement Police, in order to do so quitting the Palestine Philharmonic Orchestra that had accepted me only the year before in 1943 as its youngest member. Unbecomingly garbed in a British uniform (a raised, flat-top Turkish Kolpak hat, khakis, puttees and lace-up boots), and trained to use a military rifle, I was assigned to guard German and Italian POWs; others in the unit guarded British arsenals, radar stations, warehouses and strategic plants, such as the oil refinery in Haifa.

The major advantage of the *Palmach,* which was a semilegal organization ("semi" meaning that when the British wanted, or needed to, they worked with it quite openly; when not, not), was its independence. Answering only to the *Haganah,* that is, to the Zionist leadership, it was prepared, both in terms of motivation and of method, to protect strictly Jewish interests, the Jewish lives and property of which the British were so contemptuous. In contrast the Jewish Settlement Police were more limited. As our title indicates, we were trained only in police work, and the arms issued to us were restricted—no machine guns, not even hand grenades. However, serving under direct British supervision and sanction we did have one advantage: legal arms with which we could defend isolated Jewish settlements and which, since most of us were anyhow naturally more loyal to the *Haganah* than to the British, we could sometimes put at the *Haganah*'s disposal, in addition to giving its activities support and cover whenever possible.

The paths that Sarah and I had chosen to follow during the demanding years of the struggle (*Ma'avak* in Hebrew), as it was to be known, represented the two poles of the majority *Yishuv* approach to its wartime dilemma: here we were caught between two enemies—a greater enemy, the Nazis, and a lesser one, the British. The question was how to cooperate with the British in fighting a common enemy (even where they didn't necessarily want or accept such cooperation)—and how and how much to oppose them on our own behalf. Ben Gurion had defined, in ringing terms, the position that actually guided us: "We shall fight the war as if there were no White Paper and we shall fight the White Paper as if there were no war." Obviously we would in no way interfere with the British war effort, as the Arabs consistently threatened to do and, to a large extent, as in Iraq, actually did, but the preservation of Jewish life within these self-imposed limits was a very complicated matter—which is why more than one approach was adopted.

The British attitude went like this: use them (the Jews) when you badly need them but don't let them get an edge. At times, when the Nazis seemed to be gaining ground in the Middle East, Balkans, etc., the British entered into brief alliances with the *Palmach,* seizing on it as the only reliable pro-Allied source of fighting power anywhere in the region; and then the authorities would turn a blind eye to the so-called illegal existence and weapons of the *Haganah.* But no sooner did the immediate peril subside than their round-ups and arrests of *Haganah* members, the brutal searches and confiscations of precious *Haganah* arms, were renewed—and often with a vengeance.

Similarly, with regard to our attempts to serve in the British Army: when World War II broke out, thousands of Jewish youths volunteered. What happened? First, the British insisted that Jews could only enlist on a parity basis with the Arabs; then, when Arab enlistment proceeded at a snaillike pace and the British so urgently needed manpower, the principle of parity was quickly abandoned and a policy of letting Jews enlist but keeping them out of combat units (using them as drivers and in the ordnance, service and medical corps and generally treating them as "natives") replaced it. It was only toward the very end of the war that the creation of an all-Jewish brigade was finally permitted, by which time, though the brigade fought with distinction on the Italian front in 1945, it was robbed of any real impact in terms of the arch-enemy.

So we sat out the war, mother, Sarah and myself, each doing what we could in our own way, each feeling that it wasn't enough. Mother had a number of tasks that she fulfilled with her usual diligence, among these negotiating pay and work conditions of Palestinian civilians in British wartime industries and serving on the local War Economic Advisory Council, but these were activities that seemed trivial in the face of what she knew really needed doing.

In the meantime the kind of ordinary things that happen to people anywhere, and always, also happened to us. Sheyna became ill and was operated on. Mother developed a new health problem, gallstones, and I took hasty midnight walks to fetch our family doctor, Else Ascher, an elderly woman with a strong German accent, who brought with her the relief of a morphine injection.

And Sarah and I were growing up. In joining Revivim she was cutting a path out for herself different from the one my mother had taken and, in that way, was assuming an independent identity. And I suppose that there was something of this too in my decision to become a professional musician. But as Golda became more and more of a VIP if not yet a celebrity, for me becoming myself wasn't always easy. I remember sitting on the stage, first in the conservatory and then in the Philharmonic, with mother and (before their separation) also my father in the audience, my fingers moving on the cello's fingerboard, and my right hand drawing the bow across the strings; but something being not quite as it should be. It was the sense of withholding energy, of denying the audience some of myself. Was it because I was afraid to compete with my too successful mother or unwilling to outshine my father, who had never received much recognition for his talents? Even now the diagnosis escapes me, though that constraint, in one version or another, has persisted for years. I felt something of the same way meeting girls and wondered instantly if they liked me for myself or because I was Golda Meir's son, and I remember feeling far freer, more sociable, with people who didn't know my background at all. Whenever I could, I kept it to myself.

And of course we waited, all of us, for the war's end. Several years later, at that same Zionist Congress in Basel at which she spoke so movingly of immigration, my mother described the utter frustration of sitting out those dreadful years:

> I won't dwell at length on what we went through in Palestine during the war. With all our hearts we wanted to participate in the war, in that fight that concerned us first and foremost because it was against us that it was initially declared. As long as the war was only against the Jews, we stood alone, without allies; but once it embraced the entire world and we asked to join and fight, a long and unfortunate chapter began. In the end, our young people breached the wall and won for themselves the right to go to the front as Jews, as a Jewish unit, going to battle under a banner of their own. Imagine what and how we suffered before at last permission was granted for a few dozen men and women to be

dropped as parachutists into Nazi-occupied countries, there to try to contact Jews, to bring them tidings of Palestine, to encourage them and help them to rebel against their conquerors. Consider for yourselves what we in Palestine felt when we were denied the right to provide what little help we might have given to Jews trapped in the charnelhouses of Europe!

The only thing that somewhat alleviated this feeling of powerlessness and the immense tension of the waiting was hope: the single hope that when the war ended the British, no longer vulnerable to Arab threats, would return to their senses and finally make good their promise to foster creation of a national homeland for the Jews in Palestine. Come victory, we expected free immigration, unrestricted settlement, and a due measure of independence. It seemed the least, the bare minimum that the civilized world could do for the tormented and bereaved survivors of Hitler's Final Solution. As mother said it in Basel: "We truly hoped that a better world would emerge and that the rights of the Jewish people would be recognized."

CHAPTER 5

I T WAS REASONABLE that when Labor scored an overwhelming victory in Britain at the end of World War II there should be grounds in the *Yishuv* for optimism. For my mother, the facts seemingly spoke for themselves.

> For years the British Laborites have bitterly condemned the Government's restrictions on Jewish immigration and upheld the Zionist cause, charging that we were betrayed. I know these people, I like them and I trust them. Things will be different now. *They* will not let us down, I promise you.

True, "they" were British and non-Jews, but they were also, like Golda herself, Socialists and Zionists and, as she said, for years had been enthusiastic about our experiments in socialism, our *kibbutzim* and the various institutions of the Histadrut. Mother had fond memories of many of these men and women, the members of Parliament she had conducted around Palestine during her early days with the Histadrut, those she had met on various tours of England, and also of Lord Attlee, the new prime minister. She had even been to his home, and I remember her coming back with the glowing report that this was a man who helped wash the after-dinner dishes just like Ben Gurion did.

Moreover, there was a new world mood. Or so we thought. Few who had seen the camps, the crematoria, the skin-and-bone survivors could remain unmoved; the western media now printed horrific eyewitness and first-person reports, and the U.S., which had emerged into global leadership, seemed in particular to be conducting a kind of conscience-stricken soul-searching that everyone expected to result in a new, enlightened British policy.

Afterward, when it became clear that we'd been wrong, my mother was to say wryly, "The Labor Party is wonderful, in opposition." I suppose it was the intensity of our hopes that predisposed us to believe. We were, you might say, a stricken population; hardly a family had not lost relatives in Europe. Mother, who got off relatively "unscathed," had close relatives, aunts and uncles, who had been wiped out. In the 30s a second or third cousin of hers, an enthusiastic and pretty girl, had actually been to Palestine (on one of the agricultural training farms mother had raised funds for) and then had gone back to Pinsk for a visit in '38, never to be seen again. Mother never forgave herself for letting her go.

Like others, we waited for the better news that didn't come and prepared ourselves to welcome long-lost relatives, who also never came.

It is tempting to conjecture that, had the new British Labor government conducted itself more kindly and with better sense, Ben Gurion might not have stood up in the Tel Aviv Museum on that May afternoon in 1948 to proclaim the establishment of a Jewish state in the Land of Israel, and that independence might thus have been postponed to a more convenient date, or even have taken a different form. In any event, that very summer after

the war the new British Foreign Secretary Ernest Bevin trucu-
lently declared that the British government would effect no
changes whatsoever in the White Paper on Palestine. Since the
legal immigration certificates allowed in the White Paper were
just about used up, this meant a critical worsening of a very bad
situation. In an act that, in the light of the *Yishuv*'s mood, could
only be interpreted as provocative, the British government
refused a plea by no less a personage than the U.S. President
Harry Truman to make a one-time gesture of mercy and permit
the immediate entry of 100,000 displaced persons from Germany and Austria. Instead it placed a paltry and insulting 1,500
certificates a month at the disposal of the Jewish Agency. Whatever direction events might have taken had the British acceded
to Truman's request, their flat refusal to do so marked the
beginning of the *Ma'avak*. From then on, every restrictive and
repressive British measure only strengthened our determination
to achieve freedom.

Let me say here that though my mother took an active part in
the final approval of most major Haganah actions—whether it
was bringing in "illegal" immigrants, freeing those the British
caught, imprisoned and threatened to deport, increasing its supply of weapons, maintaining an "illegal" radio station, defend-
ing settlements on territory that the White Paper put out-of-
bounds for Jews, or anything else—she was never carried away
by the David-and-Goliath romanticism of pitting ourselves
against the British Empire. Countless evenings that fateful summer, we would sit on the balcony discussing, of all things, the
morality of stepped-up opposition. I don't remember hearing a
word about honor, heroism or glory; there was no gloating over
successful Haganah escapades, no expectation of "grand" victo-
ries. The atmosphere was of grim, resigned determination. The
British were forcing us to choose between *their* interests, whatever those might be (there seemed to be more anti-Semitism

79

and sheer obstinacy involved in their stand than *realpolitik* as such), and *our* flesh-and-blood. There was no way we could or would deny or refuse the survivors of the camps; no way we would permit other peoples' Keep Out signs to deprive them of coming home. And, by the way, there were also the urgent needs of the would-be immigrants fleeing Moslem countries; ever since the outbreak of World War II, Jews in many Arabic-speaking lands were living in fear; older Iraqi Jews to this day tell, with unabated horror, of the pogroms that followed the 1941 pro-Axis coup in that country. So we knew we could come down on one side only, make one choice only. And we did just that.

This is not the place for a history of the *Ma'avak* nor am I the proper author of such, but in terms of my mother's involvement, there are certain events I feel I should mention.

The first, I suppose, once the struggle got under way, was her appearance before the Anglo-American Commission of Enquiry —it was the *eighteenth* ineffectual fact-finding body to have been dispatched to Palestine since the inception of the British Mandate—following Attlee's rejection of Truman's proposal. "One more committee," mother sighed as she prepared the testimony that, as a representative of the Histadrut, she would be called on to make. "Maybe this one will be better than the others. After all, they're Americans and not so hand-in-hand with the Arabs."

Today, looking over her testimony, as I guess one would call it, before the commission, what I want to emphasize is how little what she had to say was touched by the standard rhetoric of resistance, war, opposition, rage, anger or violence . . . by the vocabulary, in short, of most contemporary liberation movements. She spoke then, as always, very simply, to-the-point, without any attempt to impress, anxious only to inform and to communicate. The same way essentially in which she spoke to us, the operative word being "clearly." Her explanation to the commission of why the Jews returned to Palestine in the first place is a case in point:

> The men and women responsible for the activities of the labor movement in Palestine came here some forty years ago to lay the foundation of what we like to call a labor commonwealth. They came mainly from eastern Europe, from countries where Jews endured persecution or, at best, existed on sufferance. It was the generation described by the Hebrew poet Bialik in a famous poem written after a wave of pogroms in czarist Russia. He expressed his anguish over Jewish helplessness in life and death:
> I grieve for you my children; my heart is sad for you.
> Your dead have died in vain and neither I nor you
> Know why you died or wherefore, nor for whom,
> Even as was your life, so senseless was your doom.
> This generation decided that the senseless living and senseless dying of Jews must end. It was they who understood the essence of Zionism—its protest against such a debased existence. . . .

And as to how we built the country:

> The pioneer generation had yet another purpose in coming here: their second aim being the creation of a new society built on the basis of equality, justice and mutual cooperation. When they arrived here they were faced with tough realities; their mission to conquer not their fellowmen but a harsh natural environment, marshes, deserts, the malaria-bearing mosquito . . .
> The accomplishments of the labor movement in the villages and towns, in industry and in agriculture were due mainly to two factors. First, these young Jews who wanted to live a life of dignity felt that they had no alternative; they had come here to make a success of it. Another factor was their unlimited faith in man. Throughout these years, in spite of all the obstacles put in our

81

way, never once did the members of the labor movement, or the young generation it trained, give up the hope that humanity, all progressive people, would realize the justice of our cause.

She went on to clarify to the venerable commission how she felt about the United States and British labor movements:

> From the very beginning of the labor movement in Palestine we were in close contact with the international labor movement, with the British Labor Party and Trades Union Congress and with the labor federations in the United States. We believed in these organizations, in their programs and policies, and were certain that they, above all, in deep moral sympathy with our purpose, would help us.
>
> Probably one of the greatest factors in helping us to overcome our initial difficulties was the fact that from the first, from 1917, we received constant encouragement from the British labor movement and, later, from the U.S. labor movement. Perhaps this is why the blow that we have sustained lately has been felt so very keenly by us . . .
>
> Must we conclude that even those whom we totally believed in —those in whose hands it lies to bring about a happier and juster world—also do not understand our cause and what we are doing?

But even in this profound disillusionment, there was no rancor. Golda ended that speech on a note of optimism, restating, once again, our constructive aims:

> We are certain that, given an opportunity of bringing large masses of Jews into this country, of opening the gates of Palestine to all Jews who wish to come here, we can go on building upon the foundations laid by the labor movement and create a free

Jewish society built on the basis of cooperation, equality, and mutual aid. . . .

All of this notwithstanding, during the months that the committee deliberated, the conflict with the British escalated. Not only did the Royal Navy, Army and RAF continue tenaciously to pursue the refugees on land and sea, but the British government put forth additional constraining measures. "Illegals" who were caught were carted off to detention camps and threatened with deportation while, pedantically, their number was subtracted from the measly 1,500 monthly quota. When the Haganah refused to halt immigration, organized a break from Atlit, and, to bring the point home, widened the scope of its activities to include attacks on British installations related to immigration—troop-carrying trains, naval and aviation fueling stations, and weapons—the British upped the ante with a retaliatory set of "emergency regulations." In effect these introduced martial law; each Palestinian Jew became a criminal until proved otherwise, and each British soldier, officer and policeman was allowed to search, harass and arrest on the slightest whim or suspicion.

One of the most galling things that the British did during this period was to extend their interference with our "illegal" immigration overseas by pressuring those who were willing to help us—either openly, which was rare, or covertly, which happened now and again. One outstanding example was the matter of the two Haganah ships, the *Fede* and the *Eliahu Golomb,* which were caught at the port of La Spezia on the Italian Riviera just before they were due to leave for Palestine.

Under British pressure the Italians detained the ships—and a war of nerves began. The more than 1,000 refugees aboard, already at wit's end, refused to leave the ship; they called a hunger strike, announcing that if anyone tried to force them to disembark in Italy they would sink the vessels and kill themselves. My mother, convinced that the refugees were desperate enough to go through with their threat, suggested that fifteen leading figures in the *Yishuv* undertake a hunger strike in the DPs' stead and do so in Jerusalem.

Sarah and I went to see my mother on the third day of that fast. It was being held in the Jewish Agency headquarters in the center of Jerusalem, the place in which it would surely attract maximum press attention. There were cots for the fasters. Visitors were everywhere: well-wishers and supporters from the Histadrut, the National Council, and just plain friends and relatives milling about, while outside the Agency compound a large, silent, sympathetic crowd expressed its feelings by maintaining a vigil with the fasters. Golda had just been released from the hospital after a bout of illness and had virtually twisted her doctor's arm to get him to sign the required medical certificate allowing her to participate in the hunger strike. She accomplished this in her typically logical and effective fashion. All right, she told her disapproving physician, I'll fast alone *at home* if I'm not allowed to fast with everyone else in public. By the time we got there she was in good spirits and no more the worse for wear than any of the others. Sarah and I had come to be with her at the Passover Seder that was to be held with the strikers that very evening.

"Seder," of course, is the traditional annual ceremony commemorating the Exodus from Egypt, and is partly focussed on a many-course ritual meal. Not sharing in this meal makes it impossible, by definition, to hold a Seder. So the rabbis consulted each other and finally informed the strike leaders that not to eat a Seder meal would actually constitute a desecration of the holiday!

What to do? After a short deliberation the group decided to hold a *symbolic* Seder. The story of the Flight from Egypt would be read, as it is read in almost every Jewish household every-where every year; the strikers would half-sit half-recline around the Seder table, as they do every year; and, as for the meal itself, each person would observe the injunction by eating a miniscule piece of *matza* "the size of an olive." Needless to say, it was one of the most moving Seders we ever celebrated. About a day and a half later the ships were released, and at least one battle had been won in an ongoing and rapidly intensifying conflict.

What followed was the stubborn British refusal to abide by the recommendations issued that May by the Anglo-American Com-mittee. *No,* Bevin replied to the committee's suggestion that restrictions on land sale to Jews be lifted, and *no* to the sugges-tion (a repetition of Truman's) that 100,000 displaced persons be allowed immediate entry into Palestine. Again, the excuse given was that if so many Jews were admitted it would take an entire British division to put down Arab opposition.

That reasoning, of course, had a counter-logic that was begin-ning to make itself felt in the *Yishuv*. If the Arabs could cause enough trouble to sway, if not shape, British policy, then the Jews would at long last have to cause more trouble of their own, distasteful as this might be. To drive home the point the Haga-nah carried out a major military action of a new sort. On the night of June 16, 1946, in one simultaneous operation it blew up all of the frontier bridges in Palestine, cutting all of the land links between Palestine and the neighboring countries.

Predictably, events snowballed. Less than two weeks later, on Saturday, June 29, on a day forever after called the "Black Sab-bath," the British set out to show the Jews just who was boss, and who distinctly was not. One hundred thousand British sol-diers and fifteen hundred policemen raided dozens of Jewish settlements in search of the "illegal" arms so slowly and assidu-ously collected for self-defense, literally tearing apart floors, walls and ceilings. They dragged thousands of settlers off to detention camps in Atlit, Rafa and Latrun and imposed curfews on all the major cities with large Jewish populations. And, most dramatic of all, they swooped down on all the major national Jewish institutions, including the Jewish Agency, the National Council and the Histadrut and jailed hundreds of people—including many children. I was one of these, picked up at home like many other teenagers and hauled off to the local high school, where a British officer was suddenly installed. My name was checked against a "wanted" list. When I was cleared of any visible connection with the Haganah I was curtly dismissed—with a satisfying sense of having joined the battle, and a growing anxiety about what lay ahead.

Oddly enough, mother went untouched. To this day none of us is sure why; maybe simply because the British didn't want to tangle with a woman in her position, though they had no compunctions in general about rounding up women; maybe because with all the other Jewish leaders either in prison or hiding (Ben Gurion happened to be in Paris), they needed someone to negotiate with; maybe (so she herself once remarked) because they thought she still held U.S. citizenship. In any case, I think she felt a kind of indignation about being left out of things, though she was happy enough when *I* came back safely late that evening.

For mother and for the rest of the *Yishuv* the Black Sabbath marked the point of no return, finally revealing beyond any possibility of rationalization the depth and illogic of British hostility on the one hand and creating, on the other, a total willingness on the part of the *Yishuv* to undergo whatever had to be undergone and do whatever had to be done to gain independence. To use Golda's own description:

> The twenty-ninth of June, when the British government arrested the leaders of the *Yishuv,* was a turning point in Palestine.

In this action the government overreached itself . . . On the twenty-ninth of June it set out to break the spirit and backbone of the *Yishuv* with one concentrated blow attempting to smash whatever independence the Jews had acquired in Palestine. In taking the Agency building it proposed to manifest to all that the Jews were deluding themselves into believing that they were independent and could elect leaders of their choice.

It was not long before the government realized its ignominious defeat . . . Above all, these blows strengthened our determination to demand that full measure of political independence which can be attained only through the establishment of a Jewish state.

This cool, concise summary made several years after the fact has a firmness of tone that contrasts with the hesitations and self-doubts that my mother actually experienced from this point on. On account of the mass arrests she was now acting head of the Political Department of the Jewish Agency, replacing Moshe Sharett, locked up at Latrun, and thus essentially chief executive. "It's terrible to be responsible for other people's lives," she told me around this time. In her new position she had moved from the advisory and consultative role she formerly held to become the person whose yea or nay was to determine whether this or that action was to be taken or not.

That September she chaired a party meeting convened to discuss the ways and means of further fighting the White Paper. Others more familiar with military operations (though she, alas, was to learn more at first hand soon enough) talked about specifics. But mother's introductory remarks set the tone:

I was *not* brought up in an illegal movement. Nor was I brought up on anti-government activity. I confess that the organization of a protest rally when the White Paper was published struck me as being difficult, and when I saw youngsters march against the British army and police force that had been called up, it terrified me. I didn't believe that I would ever get used to seeing such things or that the time would come when I would be required to ask my friends to take even more difficult and more dangerous paths . . .

Not everyone endured such qualms of conscience, had such patience or maintained such moral standards; and my mother was to pay for her moderate stand. It was during the *Ma'avak* that I first saw burly young men from the Haganah walking unobtrusively (or anyhow trying to do so) a short distance behind her, or standing around in front of the house attempting to look like passers-by. Bodyguards (of whom my cousin Jonah was sometimes one) to protect her not from the British but from the hotheads in the Jewish population, namely, the young men and women in the dissident military organizations: the *Irgun Zvai Leumi* (National Military Organization), headed from 1943 to 1948 by Menachem Begin, and the Stern Group, as the *Lochemi Herut Israel* (Israel Freedom Fighters) were known.

The *Irgun* had split from the Haganah (during the 1936–39 Arab riots) over the Haganah's policy of restraint, *havlagah* in Hebrew, and later, the even more militant Stern Group had in turn split off from it. Neither against the Arabs in the 30s nor the British in the 40s was the Haganah willing to engage in counter-terror; it maintained a tight rein on its members and restricted its actions to self-defense on the one hand, and to the achievement of specific goals such as immigration on the other. Unnecessary bloodshed, reprisals, retaliation were to be avoided at all cost. The *Irgun* and Stern Group, however, were guided by other values and driven by other motives: anger, revenge and punishment were their prescription for ending Arab and British provocation. Between the Haganah and the dissidents there was a fundamental, unbreachable difference of opinion, approach, judgment and understanding.

As acting head of the Political Department, Golda was immediately responsible for all the *Yishuv*'s military actions. She decided policy matters. Haganah commanders consulted with her on all operations having political ramifications—and almost everything did in that time of troubles. At the same time she was also the *Yishuv*'s representative in political negotiations with the mandatory government; and it was to her, among others, that the British government turned for help in hunting down *Irgun* terrorists. Her reply to this request was a loud and clear negative: "We will not become a nation of informers, nor make informers of 600,000 Jews, with each one watching a neighbor or friend and reporting on what appears to be wrong with the person under suspicion." But out of her office flowed endless condemnations of *Irgun* tactics; and she fully supported and encouraged Haganah efforts (including the temporary preventative abducting of possible perpetrators) to forestall *Irgun* actions that would unquestionably result in the injury or death of innocent people. To these restraining actions the dissident organizations responded with their customary violence, and though mother was never harmed, she was frequently threatened.

Her opposition to terrorism was based, I think, on her sound political instincts. The actions of the *Irgun* and Sternists drew adverse and bitter publicity not only in England but throughout Western Europe and the U.S., and exposed the entire Jewish community of Palestine to repeated British arms searches, constant curfews, mass arrests and even deportations. And finally, in refusing to abide by the authority of the Jewish Agency, they seriously undermined the foundation of national discipline on which the Zionist leadership had been building for thirty years and which was, in the eyes of most people, basic to a successful statehood.

Even deeper than these pragmatic considerations, ran Golda's ingrained moral convictions; these, I am sure, were really at the

89

heart of her objections to the *Irgun* and the Stern Group. "They degrade the moral stature of every Jew!" she said to us and to others on more than one occasion. She never had any animosity to Arabs as Arabs or to British soldiers as British soldiers. But terrorists who struck at the innocent as well as the guilty, unwilling or unable to make the distinction in the first place, filled her with revulsion. I don't think I can overstate the strength of her feelings. Hers was a world view that recoiled from violence. Even at home, when Sarah and I were children, the one taboo consistently and rigorously enforced was against any physical fighting. Not that my mother believed in turning the other cheek or that she was a pacifist. Far from it. But the image created by her opponents in Israel and mostly abroad of a tough shoot-to-kill lady was totally false. Self-defense, in her eyes, was one of the cardinal tenets of Zionism, and she admired greatly the initiative, resourcefulness, courage and dedication of the Israel Defense Forces. It was murder, kidnapping and mindless collective punishment that she so abhorred.

When I left for the United States at the end of 1946 Palestine was virtually a police state and the British army an army of occupation. During the next year things got worse. As the Haganah stepped up its "illegal" immigration and the tide of refugees swelled into a flood, the British deported the DPs to camps in Cyprus in which the living conditions were even more primitive than they were, at that point, in the postwar camps of Germany and Italy. One time my mother went to Cyprus to see for herself and to negotiate the early departure of orphans (of whom there were many) to Palestine. Despite the cruelty of the deportations and the refugees' discomfort, there was no reduction in their numbers. Nor, despite often irrational counter-measures, was there any letup in Jewish settlement of land areas such as the Negev (formally forbidden by the White Paper) in the support of the *Yishuv* for its elected leadership, or, to give them their due, in the reprisals of the *Irgun* and Stern Group. By 1947 it was quite clear to the British that as long as they stayed in Palestine the country would be an armed camp and they the permanent warders of a small, poorly armed but powerfully motivated foe engaged in a life-and-death struggle against them. In February Bevin finally tired; he wiped his hands of the whole matter and referred the Palestine problem to the United Nations.

The outcome is familiar. The United Nations created a Special Committee on Palestine (known as UNSCOP), composed this time not merely of British and U. S. investigators but of eleven representatives of the world community who, not yet demoralized or corrupted by Arab oil, were likely to make an impartial evaluation.

My mother testified before this committee as she had before the others. A few months later a report was drawn up that led the way to the decisive November 29 partition of Palestine into a Jewish state, an Arab state and an international zone comprising Jerusalem and its environs. For neither Arabs nor Jews was this an ideal arrangement: the land allotted to Jews—any allocation was too much in Arab eyes—was one eighth the the area envisioned in the Balfour Declaration and so fragmented that Jews and Arabs would both be required to pass through each other's territory in order to get from one of their own enclaves to another. Moreover for mother and the rest of the *Yishuv* a Jewish state without Jerusalem was like a body without a soul. Still, my mother had come a long way, and seen a great deal since she had so fiercely opposed the Peel Partition scheme a decade earlier and now, like almost everybody else in the *Yishuv*, she was happy to have anything at all to call our own.

But the Arabs were already rattling their sabres. They turned down a state of their own, since the price for it was a Jewish state, and made a determined effort to take Jerusalem by force, gaining increasing control over the main road between it and Tel Aviv and hoping in this fashion to starve out Jerusalem's Jewish residents and lay siege to the city they coveted.

The U.N. vote came in at midnight on November 29, 1947. Jews poured into the streets of Haifa, Tel Aviv and Jerusalem, bursting into joyous song and wheeling in circles of ecstatic dance that swept up everyone, even the British police, so long symbols of the hated Mandate authority. Mother was in Jerusalem at the Jewish Agency building. In the compound below an excited crowd was calling out for a speech. So it was from the balcony of her office that mother addressed not so much the celebrating crowd below as the Arabs:

> You have fought your battle against us at the United Nations . . . Now the United Nations—the majority of countries in the world—have had their say. The partition plan is a compromise; not what you wanted, not what we wanted. But let us live together in friendship and peace.

I think that she hoped (but I'm not sure that she believed) that those words would have an effect. It was, of course, not to be so.

The very next day Arabs ambushed a bus travelling from the coastal town of Natanya to Jerusalem, killing five passengers and wounding seven. Within a week an outburst of arson and rioting resulted in further deaths and injuries, and not long after that Arab irregulars from neighboring countries began to attack the settlements. These were all portents, the beginnings of a war that was to result in independence—but also in the death of a shocking percentage of the citizens of the about-to-be-born Jewish state.

CHAPTER 6

LTHOUGH SHE IS not generally thought of in this way, the fact is that for much of her career my mother was an emissary for the Histadrut, for the Jewish Agency, for the Provisional Government (after statehood was proclaimed) and of course for the State of Israel itself. Better known as an important cabinet member, as prime minister, as one of the three women heads of state in whose office policy was made and from whose office orders issued, she actually spent many years—all her adult political life, one might even say—serving the labor movement and for many years collaborating closely with David Ben Gurion.

I want here to talk about my mother's relationship with Ben Gurion. Of all of the people with whom she worked toward the creation and development of the state, no doubt Ben Gurion was the only person she ever considered indispensable.

She first met him, or rather first heard him talk, when he came to Milwaukee during World War I to recruit for the Jewish Brigade for Palestine and to urge young men and women to come to rebuild the land; she was still an adolescent he barely noticed. She met him again at Kibbutz Degania (where she had been sent from Merhavia to attend a Labor Party meeting). As she became more active in the Histadrut and the Labor Party, there was more and more opportunity for their working together.

Over the years they developed a relationship of mutual trust and respect. Unlike the other people she worked with, Ben Gurion was never a crony, a comrade, of Golda's. He didn't come to the house; she didn't make social calls on the Ben Gurions; Sarah and I barely saw him outside of public forums. But she considered him a man of almost unprecedented vision and foresight, Israel's greatest leader and most astute and courageous statesman.

Not that the reverence was ever blind, or her behavior ever servile. When the need arose she disagreed with him and even stood against him publicly—as in her original opposition to the 1937 Peel partition that he supported. (I wonder if here, though, she didn't gain confidence from the fact that Berl Katznelson, the philosopher of the labor movement and one of the few people whose opinion Ben Gurion himself really respected, saw the plan as a British ploy to get the *Yishuv* to agree to a land area that wouldn't have been given to us anyway.) But in most matters she simply saw things the way Ben Gurion did, both of them being, I suspect, the same kind of idealistic pragmatists, willing to take leaps that seemed reckless to some, into a future that they thought possible and worth reaching out for. So, when it came to defying the British about the White Paper in 1939, by undertaking the *Ma'avak* in '45 and by insisting on statehood in '48, my mother saw eye to eye with B.G., as he was known to all those who preferred *not* to call him "the Old Man," which was his other sobriquet, though mother always referred to him by his full family name.

Within the framework of Labor-Zionist philosophy both Ben

Gurion and mother advocated an activist stand regarding the conflict with the British mandatory policy—as distinguished from the more moderate approach usually expressed by Dr. Weizmann and Sharett. Also in the early years of independence, in the face of terrorist incursions by the *fedayeen* infiltrators, mother usually supported Ben Gurion's retaliation policy.

While mother clearly admired Ben Gurion, something of the long-standing respect in which he also held her can be gathered from a letter he wrote in 1957 to Dr. Israel Goldstein, then the president of the American Jewish Congress, when mother received the Stephen Wise Award for outstanding service to the Jewish people:

> . . . The Jewish people is rich in great men, perhaps more than any other people. But it doesn't fall short of great women; we are perhaps the only nation that remembers not only its founding fathers but also its mothers. Sarah, Rachel and Leah are not, in any way, inferior to Abraham, Isaac and Jacob. And just as we were fortunate to have a great woman (Deborah) leading our people in the days of the Judges, so again, in our own time, we have a great woman in our midst, a noble, talented and wise woman who has accomplished a great deal and who stands in the forefront speaking for an independent people, in the person of Golda, as we all call her, affectionately and respectfully . . .
>
> Her service, performed with the accompanying grace of a Jewish woman, has brought honor and glory to our nation. You couldn't have found a more worthy recipient for this award than Golda Meir; she is the most precious gift that American Jewry has given to Israel!

Such superlatives were rare for Ben Gurion, and even rarer was such a revelation of personal feeling, so when I think now of their mutual esteem and the intimate working relationship maintained for so long, the break between them in the early 60s appears to me to be no less than tragic, perhaps the first of the two great tragedies in my mother's life, the other being the Yom Kippur War. It happened over what is known as the Lavon Affair.

The Lavon Affair began in 1955 with a serious Israeli security blunder that resulted in the arrest of Israeli intelligence agents in Egypt, and the establishment of a committee to determine who was responsible—Pinchas Lavon, the controversial minister of defense Ben Gurion had appointed, or a certain "Senior Officer." Each charged the other with having given the disastrous order, and in the flurry of claims and counter-claims the committee was unable to apportion guilt. Lavon, however, was forced to resign, with his reputation tarnished. But this was only the beginning. Initially top secret, as mother felt it had to be, the episode lay smouldering until 1960, when the volcano exploded. Lavon claimed that false evidence had been given at the original inquiry and demanded that Ben Gurion publicly clear his name, which B.G. refused to do, declaring that he had never made any accusations in the first place so there was nothing to withdraw. Instead, he agreed to the formation of a ministerial committee (it was nicknamed the committee of seven) to re-evaluate the earlier inquiry. This commission also concluded that there had been insufficient evidence to point a finger either at Lavon or at the Senior Officer. Here, in my mother's opinion, the matter should have ended.

Here, however, was in fact where the sparks really began to fly. Instead of accepting the commission's verdict, Ben Gurion continued to insist on an earlier demand for a full judicial hearing to look into the matter in depth. All over again. In all fairness, he was probably motivated by his profound concern for the morale of the army, an army that he had helped to build out of the pre-state's conflicting paramilitary groups, and whose irreproachability and freedom from factionalism were, he believed, more essential to Israel's security. But even so, he seemed to my mother to have lost all sense of proportion as he embarked on a vicious and vindictive attack on Lavon, Levi Eshkol, on the committee of seven and, by implication, on the rest of the government—including Golda!

Actually my mother had never regarded Lavon as being the right man for the critical defense portfolio. She knew he was clever, ingenious even, and in another position might have made a significant contribution. But he wasn't, she felt, the man for that ministry; he was impulsive, quarrelsome, and when Ben Gurion had picked Lavon to replace himself for that job (Sharett was then prime minister), Golda joined with such colleagues as Zalman Aranne and Shaul Avigur to try to dissuade him. But once Lavon had been both cleared and punished—after all, he had been forced to resign as defense minister and later virtually compelled to resign as secretary of the Histadrut—she couldn't see why the matter shouldn't die a natural death instead of being endlessly pursued.

The affair unfolded like a Greek tragedy, in which the death throes come slowly and even the peripheral characters (of which mother was, in a way, one) get caught up in the consequences of the bunglings of the great. For several years, in forum after forum, in cabinet meetings and party meetings, in Knesset sessions and newspaper headlines, Ben Gurion vented his spleen and demanded that what he called justice be done for the good of Israel. The committee of seven, he said again and again, was stupid, immoral, and had acted under improper jurisdiction, withholding evidence and obstructing justice.

All of these charges mother took to heart, and the bad feelings they engendered resulted not only in Ben Gurion's resignation as prime minister but in the bitter personal break between my mother and himself, a rift that lasted almost to the end of his life. What happened? After all, there had been disagreements before as to what policies should be undertaken and how these should be implemented. For the most part mother deferred to Ben Gurion's judgment as being more penetrating than her own. "Even when he's wrong in theory," she used to say, "he's usually right in practice."

So what was different about the Lavon affair? Now, years afterward, when almost everyone concerned is dead and no young reporter likely even to identify Lavon, it's possible to speculate that as a cabinet minister (my mother had served for seven years as minister of labor and was then foreign minister) she felt herself responsible for the government's actions, and she had both more at stake and more self-assurance in pressing her views. But even this, though an element, doesn't account for the sharpness or the depth of the quarrel. Some people accused mother of being one of a "troika" together with Aranne and Pinchas Sapir, who was then minister of trade and industry, that was trying to force B.G. out of office by making his life a misery. But this is nonsense; in at least one cabinet meeting that I know about mother responded to Ben Gurion's threat to resign by leaving the room and drafting her own letter of resignation. Later on, friends persuaded her to withdraw it, but at the time she felt that if Ben Gurion left, the entire government should go with him to give the voters a chance to choose leaders in whom they could feel fully confident.

When I try to analyze what it was in this imbroglio that pained mother enough to undermine years of such dependence, regard and friendship, I see her on a hospital bed, a strong woman whose sturdy body had knuckled under the punishing schedule of her work—and the trials of the spirit. The occasion was the aftermath of a Labor Party meeting at which Ben Gurion mercilessly attacked the committee and its supporters, directing especially venomous charges at Levi Eshkol. By then Eshkol had replaced B.G., at his own request, as prime minister, but had enraged him by refusing to set up the judicial hearings about which B.G. was so obsessive. At the end of the diatribe my mother rose to her feet and in a brief but heartfelt speech came to Eshkol's defense, but she couldn't conclude what she had to say because she collapsed. On the following day Ben Gurion came to the hospital to see how mother was.

Levi Eshkol was one of my mother's closest friends, for decades laughing and arguing with her in that throaty voice of his, in a Hebrew richly interspersed with juicy Yiddish idioms and anecdotes. He was one of the Labor Party members mother had met way back in the 20s and typical, she said, of the practical idealists of his generation. Contrary to a reputation for not being able to make up his mind, ill-earned during the Six-Day War, Eshkol was a great doer: the man who had supervised the founding of nearly 400 Jewish settlements, who had organized an extensive search for water with which to irrigate them; and who had done far more than he was ever given credit for to build and maintain Israel's armed strength. When mother was minister of labor Eshkol was minister of finance; and in those days of not enough money for anything, they were often at odds over the housing budget. "The immigrants need houses," mother would proclaim. "You can't milk a house," he used to say. "What we need is milking cows!" And at one point the dispute became so sharp that mother almost resigned before Eshkol found the housing money. But these differences were never personal. And when Ben Gurion turned on Eshkol, for decades his "absolutely loyal follower," as mother phrased it, she was, literally, sickened by the one-track ruthlessness of it all.

When I reached Beilinson hospital that night, following the party meeting, the doctors would let me do no more than look at her. She had had a minor stroke. It did no significant damage, but in the meantime she was in no condition to speak. (In the course of a thorough examination, an enlarged lymph gland was noticed and the first diagnosis of lymphoma was made.) But on the following days she had a good deal to say about the affair. The words "confidence," "trust," "mutuality" came up over and over again—indeed, whenever she talked about Ben Gurion henceforth.

"How can he attack the loyalty, integrity and intelligence of people who have worked with him for decades?" she asked, shaking her head. And not only Eshkol. Aranne, Sapir, Mordechai Namir, Shaul Avigur and she herself were all, she noted, subjected to his vituperation.

Each one of the men that Ben Gurion attacked was more than just a lifetime colleague, he was her comrade in arms, a friend, one of those who visited at our home and would often stay over for a bite. Ben Gurion had been much venerated, sometimes almost held in awe, a father figure, but these men were peers, members of mother's own generation; and if she respected Ben Gurion as a leader, with these people she felt almost kin.

Today, public memory and political fashion being what they are, I don't suppose the average young person in Israel knows more about them than that a given street or city square has been given this name or that—but I can visualize each one of them. Zalman Aranne, tall, fine-featured, with the sharp mind and lively curiosity that befitted Israel's minister of education and culture. A man who married late in life, he used to come to our house for warmth, for conversation and books, to which he freely helped himself from our open shelves. Whenever he came over there was a lively debate and his voice used to rise to a high pitch, though by the end of the evening when I accompanied him to the door he usually calmed down enough to assure me, "Don't worry, the books are as safe with me as if they were in the Bank of England."

Shaul Avigur, who had set up the Haganah's justly noted intelligence service and, when World War II ended, headed the

Mossad, directing the intricate still-illegal immigration from Europe, was, mother said, a "born conspirator." He was also a quiet, resolute man, and in his later years ailing, who never said more than was absolutely necessary, never adorned a noun with a nonessential or revealing adjective and was the personification of honesty and authority.

Then there was Mordechai Namir, who had once studied the violin and who first worked with mother when she was minister to Moscow and he the legation's counselor. When she became minister of labor Namir took over the ambassadorship from her; when she was appointed foreign minister he took over the Labor Ministry, then became secretary of the Histadrut and mayor of Tel Aviv, a post for which mother had been suggested but was indignantly turned down by the religious parties. Namir lived about a block away from us, in the same complex of cooperative houses, and, then a widower, he used to drop in on Friday evenings and Saturday mornings to talk shop and, like Aranne, to have some company.

Pinchas Sapir was among the dynamos of that generation. When he died mother was convinced that he had actually worked himself to death. He was a huge, bearlike, balding, bespectacled man; gauche, good-hearted, sentimental, prone to strong expressions of both pleasure and grief, and a master manipulator of money and men, a builder more than a thinker. In the 60s he was Israel's minister of trade and industry and moved mountains to bring factories and plants to—and thereby make viable—the development towns that mother as minister of labor had helped to establish in the 50s. She regarded Sapir as the king of improvisors, a man of formidable drive and imagination whose instincts were uncannily reliable. A bit younger than Golda, he used to come to the house frequently to air and try out his ideas. She always listened very carefully, probed and explored every angle with him, and when she felt that he was on to something supported him to the hilt, no more deterred than he was by the barrage of criticism that his remarkable improvisations sometimes evoked. They continued to work hand-in-hand when she was prime minister and he her minister of finance. I remember when the news of his death reached her in the summer of 1978 and she was quite ill herself. Aya and I were with her in Caesaria, where she was resting up in a seaside house lent by a loving friend. As a result of treatment for her lymphoma she was immobilized at the hips and now confined to a wheelchair. When the news came over the radio she kept very still, turned white, closed her eyes and looked as though she wanted to cry or faint but couldn't do either.

It was at Beilinson Hospital that mother spoke to me of these men, whose dedication, loyalty and integrity were beyond doubt. Ben Gurion's attack, she felt, was a betrayal, a wiping-out of decades of devotion. "He talks as though all those years never existed," she said. And it was not only a personal betrayal. Friendship and politics were inextricably interwoven in this intricate web. In casting aspersions on her friends and herself, Ben Gurion was dividing the party at a time when party unity, and not only army morale, so mother believed, was vital to the nation's well-being.

The Labor Party has been split in too many ways and too often to discuss here, and I doubt that its fissures are of much interest today. But the issue of unity was a burning one in the 60s for a number of reasons, one being that everyone in the labor movement, including Ben Gurion, was seriously worried about Menachem Begin and his militaristic chauvinism. Mother was sure that a Labor Party split would, someday, enable Begin to construct a coalition with other right-wing groups (as, in fact, happened) and thus, as she saw it, to subvert the egalitarian and socialistic underpinnings of the democracy that they had all created. As it was, the Labor Party's younger generation, men

102

like Moshe Dayan, Shimon Peres, Yitzhak Navon, Chaim Herzog and Senta Yosephtal were not only drawn into Ben Gurion's camp but at times seemed the tacticians and instigators of many of the battles he led. And, when Ben Gurion actually went and formed a new political party, Rafi (Israel Workers' List) he did so together with Peres and Dayan.

Apart from ideology, my mother felt, the labor movement was built on trust and personalities. Ben Gurion was now tearing at this fabric.

This sense of Ben Gurion's betrayal of herself, her friends and their party gnawed at her like an ulcer for years. The architect of the State of Israel, the one leader who had always before disclosed, for the benefit of the rest of them, what was the essence of almost any important issue, seemed to have become a shorn Samson once he himself was opposed and ready, for the sake of a petty vendetta, to tear down the temple, not of the Philistines this time, but of the Israelites. So when Ben Gurion invited Golda to his 80th birthday party at the Negev Kibbutz Sde Boker, where he had gone into "exile," but pointedly excluded Eshkol, she felt it would have been hypocritical for her to attend, though I'm sure her conspicuous absence wounded them both. A sort of rapprochement was made in 1971 when mother did go down to Sde Boker for Ben Gurion's 85th birthday, and he, earlier that year, came to Revivim for the party that Sarah's kibbutz held for mother in celebration of the 50th anniversary of her *aliyah* to Israel. By now, both were tired of the affair, and when Ben Gurion showed up mother was very touched. Until he actually made his appearance no one had been sure that he would come, since by now he was quite frail. Nonetheless, he got up in the kibbutz's dining hall, praised mother, and read out, I recall, in an unsteady voice but one full of emotion, the letter that fifteen years earlier he had written to Israel Goldstein commending Golda's wisdom, talents and achievements.

So the relationship came full circle, though it was too late for the scars to heal.

During the short, crucial, determining years in which the State of Israel was created, the period stretching from just before the U.N. Resolution through the Proclamation of Independence to the end of the War of Independence, mother was still, as Ben Gurion's cherished envoy, carrying out the missions that he assigned, however difficult or hazardous or both. In fact, her activities during these months can be grouped around three such pivotal missions. The first, least productive but most exotic, was climaxed by her two secret meetings with King Abdullah of Transjordan (King Hussein's grandfather), one in November 1947, the other in May 1948. Frequently written about, these were meetings of peace, or, more accurately, meetings intended to forestall Transjordan's participation in the all-out war that the Arabs were vociferously threatening should we dare assume the rights and status of an independent nation.

The first meeting took place at Naharayim, on the east bank of the Jordan River. From all accounts, King Abdullah felt friendly towards the Jews of Palestine, had little liking for the fascist Mufti of Jerusalem Hag Amin El-Husseini, and was in open rivalry with other Arab leaders. In exchange for being allowed to annex the Arab areas of the soon-to-be-announced partition, he would have gladly kept himself and his crack British-officered, British-trained Arab Legion off the battle line. Abdullah assured mother, as she often told us later, that as a Bedouin and a king he was an honorable man, and especially—he would never break a promise to a woman. In any case mother came away from that meeting somewhat skeptical. As she told me soon afterwards, and before Abdullah reneged on his promise, we were dealing neither with an independent ruler nor a democratically elected one. He was far from being his own man.

Would he manage to withstand the pressure of other Arab states or the threat of assassination that has hung like the proverbial sword over the head of every single Arab leader who has had any dealings whatsoever with us? That was what worried mother. Furthermore, Ezra Danin, the Israeli Arabist who accompanied her, along with Eliahu Sasson, warned that the Bedouin monarch's truths tended to vary greatly with time and place.

By their second meeting, circumstances had changed. Though war had not been declared, and the neighboring Arab countries were still waiting for the British to depart before making their massive and concerted attack, Arab troops in the guise of volunteers were already operating throughout the country; the precious Jerusalem-Tel Aviv road was in jeopardy; Jerusalem itself under ruthless seige; the only road to the Negev blocked; and, worst of all, as they withdrew, step by step, the British methodically handed control over to the Arabs. Besides which, Abdullah had already committed himself to the Arab League.

Nonetheless, he agreed to a second meeting in spite of the perils involved. Heavily committed to the war against us, Abdullah insisted that this time the rendezvous be held in Amman, at the home of a trusted friend. Also, he indicated that he could take no responsibility for anything that might happen to his Jewish visitors en route to their rendezvous with him. For us the stakes were high, and even the slimmest possibility that Abdullah could be induced to change his mind was worth the risk. Mother and Danin, dressed up as Arabs, made their way through the night in a series of cars, Danin wearing traditional Arab headgear and speaking fluent Arabic, and my mother swathed in the heavy veil and voluminous dark robes of an Arab woman huddled silently in the back seat, praying, no doubt, that she wouldn't be directly addressed at any of the ten checkpoints they eventually passed.

To be frank, I don't know what kept mother going on that nighttime journey through hostile territory. Her sense of the mission's importance? Her confidence in Danin, whose expertise had been called on so often and whose self-assurance was catching? Or, maybe, just another manifestation of her overall disregard of the kind of things that throw most people. Anyhow, I am reminded here of a story told by Ze'ev Sherf (an Israeli public figure and former cabinet minister, who was a very close friend of Golda's) of a ride he took with mother between Tel Aviv and Jerusalem at a time when no Jew in his senses made the slow transit along the narrow winding stretch except for official purposes, and only in an armored convoy under Haganah protection. Even then one was a sitting duck for the Arab snipers who perched comfortably on the bordering, protecting tree-filled hills. On this particular trip the convoy was attacked and a mutual friend in the next car shot dead. As the bullets whizzed past them, mother hid her face in her hands. "What were you doing, Golda?" Ze'ev asked her afterward. "Covering my eyes," she answered. "I'm not really afraid to die, you know; everyone dies. But how will I live if I'm blinded? How will I work? What will I do without eyesight?" So, here too, as she drove with Danin . . . "Golda, are you afraid?" he asked on their way to Amman. "No," she answered, "I'm not a hero, but I can do what is necessary."

At the meeting, so marked by misunderstanding and cross-purposes, so disappointing in the end, Abdullah made what he may have regarded as a magnanimous offer. If we would only postpone our proclamation of statehood and halt immigration for several years, he would be delighted to take over the whole of Palestine and merge it with Jordan, treating the Jews well and giving them due representation in the Jordanian parliament. If the situation weren't so grave, the proposal might have been regarded as ludicrous, even pathetic. Mother and Danin, master-

ing bravado they couldn't have felt, tried to impress Abdullah
with the strength that they knew, even better than he, our armed
forces didn't possess.

The meeting ended with zero gain. Years later I heard Danin
complain that once the conversation ended, mother was in such
a hurry to report back to Ben Gurion that she didn't let him eat
more than a few mouthfuls of the sumptuous Middle Eastern
feast their host had prepared for them. But, more seriously,
when mother asked Abdullah about his earlier pledge, his answer justified the doubts that followed their first meeting. "Then
I was alone. Now I am one of five," he said, the others being
Egypt, Syria, Lebanon and Iraq. On the way back mother and
Danin saw Arab troops, tanks and Howitzers massing along the
border.

With the failure in Jordan, the ongoing fighting and the certainty of immediate attack by five Arab armies there was some
question about whether statehood would actually be proclaimed. To mother's and others' relief, Ben Gurion went ahead
as planned, though Yigal Yadin, the Haganah chief of operations (later to become Israel's second chief of staff of the Israeli
army) and Yisrael Galili, its de facto commander in chief (who
was to become my mother's esteemed friend and colleague),
both informed him that in their estimation we had no better than
a fifty-fifty chance of winning any major engagement. There
were other pressures as well. Up to the very day of the Proclamation, the Americans were pushing an alternative plan, trustee-
ship to replace the Mandate, instead of the statehood they had
voted for earlier. And the British high commissioner—he had
once helped my mother to get the orphans out of the Cyprus
detention camps, a man she regarded as a kindly if ineffectual
person—also came up with a new proposition to put off the
expected hostilities: like Abdullah he suggested that independence be postponed for a more "propitious" time. Today, years

after we won that war, and other wars intended to wipe us off the map, the idea of postponement after all the *Yishuv* had been through seems inconceivable, but in those days there were leaders, including mother's friends Remez and Yoseph Sprintzake, quite willing to entertain it.

Writing about that abortive Abdullah meeting makes me wonder, as I have often done before, why Golda, of all people? Why did B.G. send her—a woman? Why did she agree to go? Formally, as head of the Jewish Agency Political Department (Sharett, released from Latrum, was sent to the U.N. in New York) she was the natural envoy. But was it really natural for a woman to be an emissary to an Arab leader, even one as westernized and cultured as Abdullah? On the one hand, perhaps, for the second meeting at least when the trip had to be made in disguise, her gender was an advantage, permitting her to travel incognito and sparing her, as a good Arab wife, the unwanted questions of legionnaires at the checkpoints. In his autobiography Moshe Dayan reported that Abdullah once told him that because Golda was a woman he was actually forced to join the Arab nations in their war against us, since otherwise he would have been placed in the impossible position of accepting a woman's ultimatum. A poor excuse, of course, on Abdullah's part, because this meeting had been planned in advance with his consent, and naturally he could have dictated his conditions. Myself, I am certain that mother was sent on this mission because of who and what she was: because of her bravery, composure, skill and, above all, her readiness to undertake whatever task had to be done, no matter how tiring or how dangerous.

All of which serves to introduce the matter of clandestine trysts. The trip to Amman, I believe, was the first of many in a long line of such meetings. In the years to come, when mother was foreign minister, there were many secret meetings. In Paris she met with the Shah of Iran to discuss the vital matter of oil purchases at a time when Iran was virtually our sole supplier; meetings with Mulla Barazani and his son, the fiery leaders of the Kurdish liberation struggle against the Iraqis, a cause for which Golda had much sympathy, seeing as it was not unlike our own fight for freedom, and which, moreover, the Shah, in perpetual conflict with his northern neighbor, had asked us to support as part of the oil deal; and meetings too with other Arab leaders in unexpected places and at unexpected times.

Secret meetings have long been part (and how not?) of Israel's diplomacy. In this history-burdened and forever restless region in which inter-Arab rivalries are part of the way of life, and Arab leaders openly negotiating with Israel have good reason to fear assassination—Sadat being only the most recent example, while Abdullah himself was killed in 1951 (and who knows if his dealings with Golda weren't motivating factors)—those who want to speak with us tend to do so on the sly. There has been a marked difference between their violent public condemnations and their private expressions of goodwill. "The Arabs will have to resolve their own squabbles before they're ready to live in peace with us," was one of my mother's most frequent observations; and it was the source of a good deal of frustration, I think, that nobody outside of Israel, not even our "best friends," seemed to realize how rocky the diplomatic terrain here was.

On a more personal level, the clandestine engagements involved something of a to-do. There were code names (I can reveal that Abdullah was known as "the friend"), misleading information to the press, large bouquets of flowers that arrived at the house without cards or signatures, and other gifts as well. From one head of state came a magnificent strand of perfectly matched pearls, an oddly warm and personal gift from a man who wouldn't dare even to consider open diplomatic ties or open talks. And I remember, too, seeing mother off: midnight rides in private cars to the airport, the last stretch to a government plane along some uncharted runway, only the associates directly involved present to say goodbye.

Why was I privy to these secrets? Mother was by no means a garrulous lady. She didn't drop names of people or places, or half-told stories or other hints of things she wanted kept quiet. The same discretion that governed her personal life was the law of her public career, as I'm sure any member of her tightly muzzled cabinet or contemporary newspaper reporter in hot pursuit of sensitive information can verify. So where did I fit into the picture? And why? Two reasons: one is that these clandestine rendezvous all involved a measure of risk; if anything happened to Golda she wanted someone in the family to know; and secondly, like all leaders my mother endured a certain isolation, and the family, always so important to her, was the only place where the loneliness of leadership, in spite of a multitude of friends and comrades, could be mitigated at all. Male leaders confide in wives. Mother confided in Sarah and me. So, Sarah and I learned early on to keep our counsel. So, by the way, do our own children, for whom government business was, from their earliest days, ordinary breakfast table conversation. We listened to what we were told, asked no questions, carried no tales.

One tale that I am free to tell here—not such an important one anymore but it does suggest something of the flavor of those hush-hush meetings. The date: 1958; the occasion: a visit to Switzerland to meet with the Turkish foreign minister, Fatin Bustu Zorlu. The meeting was scheduled to take place at a time when Egypt and Syria joined forces to form the short-lived United Arab Republic. Both Israel and Turkey had reason to fear what looked as though it might become a strong alliance; Israel for obvious reasons, Turkey because of the border skirmishes it was then having with Syria. The talks, of course, were to be absolutely secret. Although we had consular and trade relations with Turkey it was considered wiser to keep the meeting out of the press and public eye—and so mother's trip was disguised as a much-needed convalescence.

I was invited along to serve, among other things, as a decoy. Who, after all, would question the filial propriety of accompanying a convalescing mother—mother, in fact, had only recently been treated for a blood clot in her lungs and had just left the hospital—on a short vacation? It was only natural for somebody to be with her to perform the small, essential but wearying chores of packing and unpacking, and opening her mail—which meant keeping the letters at a proper distance from my face and tearing the envelopes open only after I held them up to the light to make sure they contained no explosives. And only natural too that a woman resting up in the luxurious Burgenstock hotel overlooking the lake of Lucerne set among the most beautiful mountains in the world might also want to do some easy sightseeing, and that her son would take her, as I did, on a day's trip to Interlaken and an evening in Lucerne, where we listened to the pianists Clara Haskil and Geza Anda accompanied by the festival orchestra. In the intermission we were introduced to Artur Rubinstein, who was in the audience, and a friendship between Golda and the maestro was struck. On learning that I was a cellist, Rubinstein, in a magnanimous and gallant gesture, suggested: "Let's play sonatas together." Unfortunately, I didn't have my cello with me on this trip.

I was also invited, let me confess, because convalescence was really in order, and mother's doctor insisted that she travel not only in the company of one of his assistants but also with someone from the family. To be frank, my presence was required mainly because of mother's character: like others of her generation, she refused to have any truck with illness. The dialogue was always the same: "How do you feel?" "Fine," a monosyllable that ended any chance of finding out more. If she was unusually tired, pale or drawn, if she coughed suspiciously or was short of breath I was to see to it that the doctor was told and that she didn't overexert herself—not easy considering her natural pace and scorn for medical precautions.

In any case the ruse, as others, was effective; the Israeli ambassador with his wife and children visited mother at the hotel, fully accepting her explanation of a needed rest. It was left to Reuven Shiloach, then head of the foreign ministry's Middle Eastern desk, to arrange the top secret meeting at the home of a leader of the Lucerne Jewish community, a villa vacated for the day.

CHAPTER 7

THE SECOND MISSION, a more successful one, was to the United States, and its purpose, as of many previous and subsequent visits, was fund raising. As early as 1946 Ben Gurion, with typical intuition, foreseeing the ensuing war with the Arabs, had gone to the U.S. himself to raise money for arms and manufacturing equipment for the Haganah's infant, and secret, weapons industry (*Ta'as* in Hebrew). Now with the resolution and the Arab declaration that they would "throw" us into the sea, there was literally a life-or-death need for a massive immediate arms build-up. The Haganah's inventory was pathetic: around 10,000 rifles, under 2,000 machine guns and 200 other guns, and a total of around 550 two- and three-inch mortars, only nine light aircraft, eight with single engines, not one cannon or tank, no fighter planes or warships and a critical lack of military vehicles. At the same time soldiers had to be outfitted, bed-and-blanketed, and given medical care; immigrants still pouring in needed, somehow or other, to be housed and absorbed and the economy maintained at working level both to sustain the fighting and so that, when it was over, there would be a normal life to resume. This was no small order, and various representatives had already been sent to the States only to return with generous but still inadequate contributions.

Now, about a month and a half after the U.N. adoption of the partition plan, and with the country well into an undeclared war, Ben Gurion prepared to go to America himself. Mother agreed that the need for money was urgent, but felt he shouldn't leave the country just when his vision and leadership were most needed. Maybe she could collect the funds just as well, she suggested. God knows my mother wasn't inclined to bragging or to overconfidence, but she did have a realistic sense of her skills and of what she could accomplish. To begin with, she knew that she was less needed in Israel at this exceedingly crucial juncture than was Ben Gurion. But beyond that, she knew what her talents were; she had raised funds before and done it well. Both literally and figuratively she shared a common language with American Jewry; she was able to communicate the *Yishuv*'s needs simply and clearly, and had the even rarer ability to move people, to address herself to their deepest feelings and instincts. Apparently others in the Jewish Agency executive shared her evaluation of herself; when she insisted on a vote, she was elected to do the job.

We met at Idlewild (today Kennedy) airport on a freezing winter Friday afternoon. Because time was so short and the road to Jerusalem (where most of her belongings were) under the constant attack of Arab snipers, she had arrived from Tel Aviv with only an overnight bag. We drove directly to the Sulgrave Hotel, and there for the first time she met with many of the American Jewish leaders who were to become close personal friends of hers—and of the State of Israel. Raisers of invaluable funds for development, reconstruction and defense, and lobbyists with Congress and presidents, they were the men (and women) who did most to lay the foundations for, and maintain, the tight U.S.-Israel ties during mother's lifetime and help create the cooperative, involved orientation of American Jews.

Before I write about this meeting and the subsequent campaign, I'd like to say something more about these men. They were a different breed from the Jews mother had worked with previously. Not socialists, not back-to-the-soil, live-on-the-land Zionists, not immigrants nor even—in many cases—the children of immigrants, and not primarily of Russian- but also of German-Jewish descent, they were well-established, in some cases fabulously wealthy, hard-working, hard-headed American-Jewish industrialists. Some ten to fifteen years younger than Golda, their dedication to the Jewish state derived not from personal experience of persecution but from second-hand contact with the Holocaust. At least one of them, Sam Rothberg—and there were others—decided to devote himself to Israel after seeing the concentration camps with his own eyes. The sight of the gas chambers, crematoria and the human skeletons who survived moved him to change the course of his life. Then in his late thirties, a man who might have easily contented himself with giving large donations, he reversed his basic priorities, relegated a successful distilling business to second place and pushed his work on behalf of Israel up to first.

Sam came to this initial meeting with his friend and lawyer Julian Venezky. Both Sam and Julian were already leaders within their communities, as was Bill Rosenwald, then the rich aristocratic president of Sears Roebuck ("a prince of a man" mother called him). Then there were Henry Morgenthau, Jr., secretary of the treasury in F.D.R's administration, Rudolph Sonnenborn, the scion of a wealthy German-Jewish family that had made its money in the chemical business, the indefatigable Lou Boyar (construction and development) who was the United Jewish Appeal man in California, Harold Goldenberg, midwestern, jovial,

115

who later came to live in Israel for a while, Henry Montor, vice-president of the U.J.A. and his assistant Meyer Steinglass, paid professionals who organized and administered the great fund-raising drives. Montor was tough, practical, utterly committed and a slave driver when it came to Israel.

By the time that winter campaign was over these people had turned into a clan whose members were passionately devoted to Israel's development and security. For all these men who felt that they must do something to restore dignity and meaning to Jewish life, my mother became a living embodiment of Israel's renascence.

But when she arrived in New York on that bleak Friday afternoon at the end of January 1948, she was relatively obscure outside of labor Zionist circles. Even Eliezer Kaplan, the treasurer of the Jewish Agency, wasn't at all sure she could do what was required. Prior to this tour Kaplan had already been to the States and assessed that five to seven million dollars would be the maximum that could be drawn from U.S. Jews, though it was only about a tenth of the sum needed. Now mother came along and said that the aim should be four to five times that much, twenty-five million dollars! The figure was astronomical. Few people knew better than the men in that room how much American Jews had already given and how many other worthy causes were competing for their money, including Jewish education and community work in America itself and aid to refugees in Europe. So how would mother ever succeed in collecting sums that no other representative had even neared? Till today I remember the raised eyebrows and Henry Montor's heavy jaw fixed in a skeptical hold. Of all of them, perhaps Sam Rothberg was the most optimistic, though I'm not sure of that either; maybe it was just that he and mother took to each other immediately; he drawn to her solidity, pluck and humor, she to his warm, enthusiastic personality.

As foreign minister in 1959 mother was host to members of an Afro-Asian seminar. Here she is shown leading her guests in a spirited <u>horrah.</u>

With David "Dado" Elazar visiting the town of Kiryat Shemonah, prior to the Yom Kippur War. The town, situated on the northern Lebanese border, was frequently the target of attacks.

September 26, 1969 during one of her visits to U.N. headquarters. Here she is shown being escorted by Dr. Ralph J. Bunche, undersecretary general for special political affairs (right). Abba Eban is behind mother (left).

After the lunar landing astronaut Allan Shephard presented mother with a commemorative plaque bearing the flag of Israel, which was taken on his historic journey into space. Here they are in the official office of the prime minister in Tel Aviv. My son Amnon is standing behind mother; my wife is seated at the table.

As prime minister, mother with Defense Minister Moshe Dayan peering at Egyptian lines during a visit to the Suez Canal.

Mother pays her first visit to the Wailing Wall after the war of 1967.

Mother meeting with her old friend, Eleanor Roosevelt. They breakfasted together whenever mother was in New York for meetings at the U.N.

Mother with then Prime Minister David Ben-Gurion He proclaimed her "one of the two most important statesmen of the Jewish people."

Secretary of State Henry Kissinger with mother during the period of "shuttle diplomacy" in the Mideast.

In 1973, mother with Moshe Dayan at the Golan Heights, chatting with Israeli soldiers stationed there.

June, 1970. Mother is pictured here with Walworth Barbour, American ambassador to Israel at the time and a close and trusted friend.

Soldiers of Israel's Women's Army form a guard at Tel Aviv airport in October, 1970 as mother prepares to leave for a three-week visit to the United States.

Mother with Harold Wilson, one of her closest comrades, before the Socialist International meeting in London, 1973.

Mother addressing a meeting of the Israel Bond Organization in New York, 1972.

An historic meeting with Pope Paul VI, January 16, 1973, at the Vatican.

A soldier is overcome with emotion during a visit to the Wailing Wall after the war of 1967.

Mother with President Nixon and his wife, Pat, during a state visit to Washington.

As prime minister, mother shares a joke with David Ben-Gurion and Major Grisha Feigin (center), Red Army World War II hero who had recently arrived from Russia, at the First Convention of Immigrants from the Soviet Union.

During a tour of Asian countries in 1962 mother and I walked barefoot as we visited Shwe Dagon Pagoda in Rangoon, India, guided by Burmese chief of protocol.

Diplomatic talks with President Nixon at the White House.

Israeli Arab leaders met with mother in her Jerusalem office to congratulate her on becoming Israel's new prime minister.

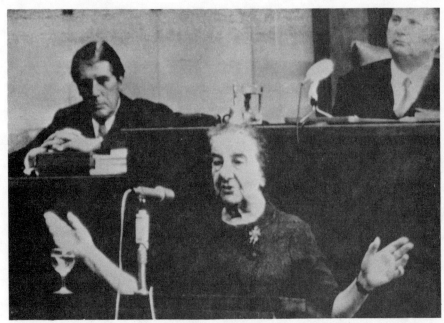

In Strasbourg, France, mother as Israel's prime minister addresses the 25th meeting of the Council of Europe. Behind her (left) is Toncic Sorinj, secretary general and Giuseppe Vedovato, president of the Council.

In 1962 mother made a trip to the U.N. and is pictured here with her good friend Haile Selassie. Behind her is Yosef Tekoah, who was then Israel's ambassador to the U.N.

A reception at the official residence of the prime minister in Jerusalem. To mother's right is Lou Boyar, a businessman and leader of the Jewish community in California, and to her left is Samuel Rothberg, president of the Israel Bond Organization. Across from mother is Sam Rothberg's wife, Jean.

March 22, 1976. Mother chats with Mrs. Margaret Thatcher, then British Conservative Party leader, outside mother's office in Tel Aviv.

Israel's foreign minister speaking at the U.N.

In 1975, mother and Foreign Minister Yigal Allon place a wreath on the wall of the Fasanenstrasse Synagogue in Berlin.

An historic meeting in Jerusalem in 1977 with President Anwar el-Sadat.

On a goodwill visit to South Asian countries in 1962, mother greeted Philippinese President Diosado Macapagal at Malacanang Palace in Manila.

May 1, 1962. Mother holds her hand to her face as she and Sheyna attend the trial of Adolf Eichmann in Jerusalem.

The meeting was very tense. Everyone in the room understood the urgency of our needs, but no one could be sure they would be met, and everyone knew the consequences if they weren't. The word "beleaguered" may be overused in our century, but it describes with frightening accuracy the situation of Israel, surrounded on all sides except the Mediterranean by neighbors who were not only hostile but committed to our destruction.

It is fortunate, to put it mildly, that these were daring and far-sighted men, their pragmatism twinned with imagination and a sense of history. And the Council of Jewish Federations, the powerful fund-raising arm of the American Jewish communities, was holding a convention in Chicago just then, a godsend of an opportunity because it meant that the major Jewish fundraisers could be addressed en masse, thus saving weeks of precious time. Mother was reasonably confident tht if she could only speak to these people, say what she had to say, they would understand and come through. True, the convention had other matters to discuss, Palestine wasn't even on its agenda, and most of the assembled were not the labor Zionists mother was accustomed to addressing, or Zionists at all, for that matter. But these divisions didn't discourage her. The next day she was off, and in the middle of a blizzard so severe that it had shut down all the airports in the East and Midwest, which meant travelling hundreds of miles in a train that seemed destined to get stuck in the snow en route.

In Chicago mother spoke quietly, without histrionics. She told the men and women in the audience why we were fighting:

> Long before we had dared pronounce that word, we knew what was in store for us. Today we have reached a point when the nations of the world have given us their decision—the establishment of a Jewish state in a part of Palestine. Now in Palestine we

117

are fighting to make this resolution of the United Nations a reality, not because we wanted to fight. If we had the choice we would have chosen peace to build in peace.

Friends, we have no alternative in Palestine. The Mufti and his men have declared war upon us. We have to fight for our lives, for our safety and for what we have accomplished in Palestine. Perhaps above all, we must fight for Jewish honor and Jewish independence.

She told them why we needed help:

We must ask the Jews the world over to see us as the front line and do for us what the United States did for England when England was in the front line in World War Two. All we ask of Jews the world over, and mainly of the Jews of the United States, is to give us the possibility of going on with the struggle.

When the trouble started we asked young people from the age of seventeen to twenty-five who were not members of Haganah to volunteer. Up to the day that I left home on Thursday morning, when the registration of this age group was still going on, over twenty thousand young men and women had signed up . . .

We have to maintain these men. No government sends its soldiers to the front and expects them to take along from their homes the most elementary requirements—blankets, bedding, clothing. A people that is fighting for its very life knows how to supply the men they send to the front lines. We too must do the same.

Why we needed it today, not tomorrow:

Our problem is time. The time factor is now the most important. Millions of dollars that we may get in three or four months will mean very little in deciding the present issue. The question is what can we get immediately. And, my friends, when I say immediately, this does not mean next month. It does not mean

118

two months from now. It means now.

Much must be prepared now so that we can hold out. There are unlimited opportunities, but are we going to get the necessary means? Considering myself not as a guest but as one of you I say that the question before each one is simply whether the *Yishuv,* and the youngsters that are in the front line, will have to fail because money that should have reached Palestine today will reach it in a month or two months from now?

Is it possible that time should decide the issue not because Palestinian Jews are cowards, not because they are incapable, but merely because they lack the material means to carry on?

Why in the form of outright donations:

But it would be a crime on my part not to describe the situation to you exactly as it is. Merely with our ten fingers and merely with spirit and sacrifice we cannot carry on this battle, and the only *hinterland* that we have is you. The Mufti has the Arab states—not all so enthusiastic about helping him but states with government budgets.

The Egyptian government can vote a budget to aid our antagonists. The Syrian government can do the same. We have no governments. But we have millions of Jews in the Diaspora, and exactly as we have faith in our youngsters in Palestine I have faith in Jews in the United States; I believe that they will realize the peril of our situation and will do what they have to do.

And she said all this truthfully but without despair, optimistically but without any illusions:

I want you to believe me when I say that I came on this special mission to the United States today not to save 700,000 Jews. During the last few years the Jewish people lost 6,000,000 Jews, and it would be audacity on our part to worry the Jewish people throughout the world because a few hundred thousand more Jews were in danger.

That is not the issue. The issue is that if these 700,000 Jews in Palestine can remain alive, then the Jewish people as such is alive and Jewish independence is assured. If these 700,000 people are killed off, then for many centuries we are through with this dream of a Jewish people and a Jewish homeland.

My friends, we are at war. There is no Jew in Palestine who does not believe that finally we will be victorious. That is the spirit of the country. We have known Arab riots since 1921 and '29 and '36. We know what happened to the Jews of Europe during this last war. And every Jew in the country also knows that within a few months a Jewish state in Palestine will be established. We knew that the price we would have to pay would be the best of our people. There are over three hundred killed by now. There will be more. There is no doubt that there will be more. But there is also no doubt that the spirit of our young people is such that no matter how many Arabs invade the country, their spirit will not falter.

However, this valiant spirit alone cannot face rifles and machine guns. Rifles and machine guns without spirit are not worth very much, but spirit without arms can in time be broken with the body.

She spoke to a galvanized audience. Not a throat was cleared, not a chair squeaked. When she was through, people stood up and cheered, gave—in unprecedented amounts and in unprecedented ways—with community leaders taking out bank loans to finance the immediate purchase of arms even before the pledges came in.

Chicago was only the beginning of two and a half gruelling months. She didn't know days or nights. Breakfast, lunch, dinner were translated into so many speaking engagements. In one month she spoke in over twenty different communities; three, even four speeches a day weren't unusual. She slept and ate in strange houses, strange hotels and in transit, physical fatigue matched only by wear and tear on her nerves. In each house and each auditorium the same basic points had to be made over and over again; the same questions, often coming out of a blur of faces, and sometimes aggressive, had to be answered patiently and politely; indignities had to be endured. Her only respite was on rare occasions an evening at the theater that Steinglass considerately arranged to take her mind off things, and visits with me and Zipke, who came in from her home in Bridgeport, Connecticut, at mother's New York "headquarters."

In the end there were pledges and checks and the satisfaction of having done the job better than anyone imagined possible, and the vastly greater satisfaction of knowing that the word had gone out to our agents in Europe—"buy." And something else as well. Mother had always felt that during the Holocaust American Jews had done less than they might have. She understood the constraints—the U.S. was deeply involved in the war. But surely more immigrants could have been admitted, at least more children, before their annihilation. Now she witnessed a resurgence of American Jewish activism, a renewed unstoppable unfaltering dedication, especially in the men with whom she was working.

After the State of Israel was proclaimed, Ben Gurion sent her back to America. "We now need much larger sums to finance the armaments," he wrote in his diary, "so it is necessary to send Golda Meir to America at once to raise the funds we need. Our activities in this sphere before the establishment of the state were very successful. With the money Golda collected, we were able to purchase rifles, light machine guns, heavy machine guns and artillery pieces . . . Now we need planes and tanks."

On the second trip mother's heart was heavy. Egyptian columns were advancing towards Beersheba. Revivim, with only thirty poorly armed young men and women there to defend themselves, was under constant threat. By a stroke of luck Egyptian intelligence had communicated the misinformation that the kibbutz was well fortified, protected by several hundred men, and Egyptian troops weren't sent in to attack; but there was no way of knowing this in advance. What mother knew was that the road was blocked, food and weapons were being airlifted and her own daughter was in danger. But Montor cabled saying that if she came back, they would be able to raise another fifty million dollars more, and Golda knew what and how much that would buy. "At moments like this," she said, "I'm only a soldier called upon to do my duty." And she was off again—obedient, exhausted and inspiring. Ben Gurion has been quoted as saying: "Some day, when history will be written, it will be said that there was a Jewish woman who got the money which made the state possible."

The mission that left the deepest impression on Golda was her by now famous mission to Moscow, though it was also the one about which at the onset she was least enthusiastic. Her meeting with Abdullah held the promise of possibly procuring peace at least on one of Israel's borders—a bait to which we were to rise many many times in the future. Her fund-raising tours to the U.S. had helped to win the War of Independence—when mother told American Jewry that we could not win it without their money she was telling the gruesome truth. But becoming Israel's first minister to the Soviet Union was something else. She received the appointment in the form of a cable from Moshe Sharett, Israel's new foreign minister, while she was still touring America, and through a curious set of coincidences I was close at hand.

To backtrack a bit, she was actually at the end of her tour of duty, about to leave at last for Tel Aviv. We went to pay a farewell call to the Goodmans, with whom we had stayed in 1932 during my first visit to New York. On the way back from Brooklyn a car crashed into our cab. Mother, sitting wearily in the back with her aching legs stretched out, was thrown forward and a ligament in her right leg was torn (the leg incidentally that she had already injured once at Merhavia when a cart banged into it, a leg that would be injured again in the 50s by the blast of a lunatic's bomb thrown in the Knesset). Well, instead of the ride to the hotel, there was a ride to the New York Hospital for Joint Diseases. Within minutes the woman who had practically been run off her feet in cross-country fund raising was immobilized in a hospital room, the hapless object of much curiosity on the part of television and newspaper reporters who flocked to interview the new state's lady minister to Moscow. A few days later I too was hospitalized for some surgery planned long before. After my operation I could wheel myself into the orthopedic ward, where mother was staying, and when the reporters left and the crowds thinned we were able to talk.

The topic of Moscow was uppermost in her mind. She was being flooded by get-well-soon cables from Tel Aviv, their purport less to inquire about her health than to hurry her on to the post she was to fill. She had endless questions of her own. Am I the right person for this position? What do I know or remember of Russia other than poverty and pogroms, beggars and Cossacks? Certainly not the language, not even French (the *lingua franca* of international affairs then). And what do *I* know of diplomacy? The *Nachshon* was one thing, and fund raising not so different, but aren't I too blunt, too unpolished for the diplomatic game? Besides, what good can I do as minister plenipotentiary? And she laughed wryly at the pompous title. There was also an ideological consideration, a wariness mother felt about the Russian regime. After all, she was a committed socialist, a member of the Socialist International, an outspoken anti-communist. Even in the 30s, when many of her socialist colleagues

123

so blindly admired the Soviet Union, to the point of justifying Stalin's purges within his leadership, mother retained enough clarity of vision to see the Soviets for what they were: a totalitarian regime mouthing the most exalted of principles but wickedly oppressing its own and other peoples.

Nonetheless, there were weighty counterclaims, not the least being the clarion call of duty. She had never said *no* before; was she going to say it now, in the middle of a war? If she was the candidate Sharett thought best and Ben Gurion supported, what justification did she have for pitting her will against theirs?

Her hesitations about the regime were offset, in part, by the fact that the U.S.S.R. had been one of the staunchest supporters of our statehood in the U.N. and indeed followed the U.S. in granting us much-valued diplomatic recognition. If the Russians were motivated mainly by the desire to rid the region of the British, later cooly turning against us, it was also true that mother deeply responded to the suffering of the Russian people who had endured such enormous losses during World War II. But what she really wanted to do, and about this she talked endlessly, sitting up in bed, forgetting her aches and pains in her enthusiasm, was to establish contact with "the Jews of silence," the Russian Jews who had been permitted virtually no contact with the Jews of Israel or elsewhere ever since the 1917 Bolshevik revolution and whose very Jewishness—in the cultural, religious and national senses of the word—was being so ruthlessly and systematically undermined. Not only had the regime pursued a campaign of secularization, but Judaism in particular was singled out for repression—the teaching of Hebrew forbidden, Yiddish barely tolerated and after World War II no longer taught. There were a few synagogues, but only the old dared attend. The official line was that there existed no such entity as a Jewish "people," and that if Jews in the West needed a state because of persistent anti-Semitism in their respective countries, Russian Jews had no such need.

True, temporarily the Soviets abandoned their insistence that Zionism was an arm of Western imperialism, but even in this period of relatively good relations a Russian citizen holding Zionist convictions was treated as no less than a criminal, to be punished by exile or forced labor.

Speeding up her recovery as much as possible in order to accommodate the increasingly frantic appeals from Israel, mother flew back to Tel Aviv more or less resigned to her new assignment and, for all of her doubts, proud, I might add, to be the honored and official representative of the state she had helped bring into being and seen through the trauma of its birth. If the pill was still a bit bitter, Moshe Sharett had added a sugar coating. How would you like to have Sarah and Zecharia (Sarah's fiancé) join the legation as wireless operators, he cabled mother, a suggestion at which she, of course, jumped.

A few weeks later I followed mother to Tel Aviv, packing music and personal possessions in the hope of joining up in the newly formed Israel Defense Force. It was no easy matter to return home, since, with the war, ships simply bypassed Israel's ports and only a few planes flew the Atlantic in those days. Finally, I flew to Paris and from there, in a two-propeller, to the small Haifa airport, where father met me. Lod Airport (to be renamed Ben Gurion), located between Tel Aviv and Jerusalem, was cut off by the Jordanians. I learned from father that having come to Jerusalem to undergo eye surgery, he had been caught in the Jerusalem siege for weeks with little food and water, no cigarettes, and the maddening din of exploding shells and mortar fire.

The ride to Tel Aviv in a *sherut* (the share-a-cab service that is still so widely used in Israel today) was eye-opening, since I had been away from the country for just about the most monumental year in all its recent history. The potholes on the road testified to air strikes; but the soldiers who passed in ill-fitting crumpled uniforms and heavy knapsacks sent a thrill through my heart. Tired-looking, dust-caked—no matter; their rifles were slung freely over their shoulders, Jewish weapons that, only a short while ago, had been termed illegal by the British and had been assiduously hidden lest they be confiscated.

I arrived in time for Sarah's and Zecharia's wedding. The middle of a war is not the time for extravagant festivities, so it was a small, intimate affair, only for family and closest friends. Grandpa had died in 1944, and grandma, who was now in a home for the aged and no longer the woman she had once been, was brought to the wedding. Father stood next to mother, and even so many years after their separation I wondered how and why it all happened.

I had already met Zecharia, a dark, wiry, handsome young man of Yemenite descent who had been active in the youth movement and one of the founders of Revivim, where Sarah met him. He and I liked one another immediately. Mother, who had met him earlier, had already adopted him into her "family" as a second son just as later she adopted Aya as a second daughter. In those days marriages between Western and so-called Oriental Jews were not frequent. Indeed, the first generations of immigrants from Europe and those hailing from Moslem countries were worlds apart, and bringing their children together in a shared Israeli identity was one of the cardinal though not yet perfectly achieved aims of Israeli society. But for mother, who moved as easily between cultures as most people walk from room to room, it was entirely natural for her Jerusalem-born daughter to marry the Jerusalem-born son of a traditional Yemenite family. She took warmly not only to Zecharia, who was, in fact, in terms of ideals and outlook, totally Western, but also to his devout Yemenite parents.

A week later we were at the airport again; mother, Sarah and

Zecharia, the rest of the legation. The charming worldly Eiga Shapira, a close friend of mother's now assigned to serve as her assistant, was there looking after last-minute details; and Lou Kaddar, the clever young ex-Parisian secretary who was to become one of mother's most intimate associates, was also on hand. The foreign minister, Moshe Sharett, said a few parting words and then the delegation mounted a waiting DC-3 army plane and flew off. I remember watching it get smaller and smaller and feeling sad. My induction was to take place very soon and who knew what would happen then? Would I survive the war that had killed and wounded schoolmates and other friends and was finally to take the enormous toll of one percent of the population, though I didn't know that then. And I couldn't help wondering whether mother and I would ever see each other again. Within minutes, the plane had disappeared, and I was on my anxious way to the war.

Moscow. Before setting out, mother had given a good deal of thought to the question of how our legation should be run. As a new state we had no tried and tested procedures to fall back on; and the examples of the legations and embassies of older, wealthier and better established countries—even had mother been familiar with them—seemed inapplicable to a pioneer country still at war and absorbing homeless immigrants. Not for us were the formalities or luxuries for which, in any case, we had no budget. Eiga Shapira advised mother on such matters of furniture, clothes and protocol. But it remained for my mother to set the tone and to determine the image of ourselves to be conveyed to the Soviet Union.

The image she chose was of a kibbutz, a collective settlement, one that accurately reflected both the spirit of the country and suited the sociable personality and modest tastes of a woman who had longed to live in Merhavia. Even in Tel Aviv her lifestyle approximated, as much as was possible under the circumstances, the sociability of communal life.

In Moscow mother would be able to live out her dream of collectivism at the same time as she demonstrated for the benefit of the Russians what *she* considered to be the best and most representative form of Israeli life. The staff of the legation, she decided, would eat together, share preparation and chores (later there was a cook and some household help), and everyone would get the same amount of spending money. As the state had no budget yet, and only a provisional government (the first Knesset elections were to be held in January 1949), at first no one received a salary, an arrangement that suited mother fine and which she would have been prepared to continue, I believe, for a long time.

All told, mother was in Moscow for about eight months, with two trips back home. I remember her sitting on our balcony in the early evening as the sun sank into the sea in bursts of purple and orange, serving tea to guests—friends, colleagues, reporters and foreign visitors—and telling them excitedly about Russia, story after story about Russian Jews.

It was by now clear that the strong emotions expressed by Russian Jews towards mother and the other members of the Israeli legation were in essence the Jews' identification with the young state of Israel. The Russian authorities were quick to understand this: the Jews of Russia had awakened and their long silence was about to be broken.

I suppose that the clearest, the strongest expressions of this feeling occurred when mother, in the company of the full staff of the legation, visited the Moscow synagogue. She did this twice, in September and in October. Though few in the delegation were religiously observant, preparations for the visits had already been made in Tel Aviv; it had been decided that members of the legation would go to each and every place where they might possibly meet Jews. The men were told to bring along prayer shawls and other ritual objects, and married women outfitted themselves with hats or kerchiefs to cover their hair, as Jewish law requires.

Since mother has written in her *Life* about the events that took place in the synagogue, I will only retell them very briefly. The first visit was on the Saturday following mother's presentation of her letters of credence to the Russian authorities (without which the legation would not have been *bona fide* and could perform no official functions). She had arrived at the synagogue unannounced, flanked by the legation staff, and as unobtrusively as possible (how unobtrusive can a Hebrew-speaking group of people be in the middle of Moscow?), they took their seats, the men in the center aisles and the women in the gallery that Orthodox synagogues reserve for them. Looking down from it mother saw some one hundred old men who had come to pray. Just a handful; a token attendance of those whose presence there didn't matter to the government in any way. Toward the end of the service, after the obligatory blessing for Stalin, the rabbi—to mother's amazement—added a blessing for her; and when her name was mentioned the entire congregation turned to stare at her, their gazes fixed on her as though, as she later wrote, to imprint her face in their memories.

All things considered, she decided it was wisest to space her synagogue visits so as not excessively to rile the Russian authorities. The next visit was made on *Rosh Hashana,* the Jewish New Year, the first of the High Holidays, when even those Jews who ordinarily don't go to synagogue make their appearance to pray, to express solidarity with other Jews. Mother had learned that in Moscow a *Rosh Hashana* crowd of about 2,000 could be expected. So imagine her wonder when not 2,000 but 50,000 Jews stood pressed together, people of all ages, infants in arms, children and parents; so tightly jammed together that a way had to be cleared for her for blocks around the synagogue, all come not so much to see her personally—this she realized—as to celebrate the birth of the State of Israel and to affirm their kinship. This time she sat in the gallery, too moved to speak, to smile or wave, just taking in the fact that after thirty years of isolation and suppression these brave people had come to say, yes, we too are Jews. At the end of the service, when she rose up to leave, she could barely pass through the crowd. People gathered around her, grabbed her hands, kissed her clothing, called out, "Golda, our Golda," . . . "A long life to you" . . . "Shalom" . . . "Happy New Year . . ." It was impossible for her to walk back to the hotel, so although it is forbidden to ride on the Sabbath, someone pushed her into a cab. But the cab couldn't move either. She wanted to talk, she wanted to say something to these people who had shown so much love and courage, but for once in her life she was unable to find the words. In the end she stuck her head out the window of the cab and called out in Yiddish, "Thank you for remaining Jews," a sentence which packed into itself all the gratitude of an overflowing heart, but one that *she* always felt was miserably inadequate.

Back in the hotel, mother told us afterward, everyone stayed together, just sitting with each other, too shaken by their feelings to talk. "Eiga, Lou and Sarah were sobbing; I was too drained even to do that," she said. Ten days later, on *Yom Kippur,* the Day of Atonement, the drama was replayed, with variations. This time the police were forewarned and patrolled the area. The authorities told Golda that they did not want a repetition of the *Rosh Hashana* welcome and asked that she not leave the synagogue until everyone else had cleared out. The end of the service came; the rabbi's last words, "Next Year in Jerusalem," echoed through the packed synagogue like a wave billowing—maybe, at last, these words repeated by Jews, year in and year out, would come true; if not the following year then the one after. Mother rose to go; so did the legation staff, including the men whom the rabbi had honored by seating on the dais up front. But no one else moved. Then the men in the congregation surged to the dais; the women surrounded mother. In the end the police cleared a space and whisked mother off through a side door, but the people outside had moved also, and the same kissing, touching, reaching-out, well-wishing and crying was repeated.

These were then the "major" scenes, the unforgettable, intense dramatic occasions when Russian Jews demonstrated their solidarity, their ability to endure and their undiminished sense of peoplehood—despite the decades of silence. The government was not pleased. An article appeared in a Yiddish-language newspaper piously proclaiming that "the State of Israel had nothing to do with the Jews of the Soviet Union, where there is no Jewish problem and therefore no need for Israel." It had been written by Ilya Ehrenburg, the noted Soviet Jewish journalist, and it was a warning: keep away from the synagogue, and keep away from the Israelis! Still, during the first part of mother's stay there was some hope that the prompt Soviet recognition of Israel might be followed by a change of attitude towards the Jews. Not only had the Soviet foreign minister himself stood up in the U.N. and, in an unprecedented speech, declared that the Jews were entitled to a state of their own, but the Russians were making good that assertion by closing an eye to the sale to us of the guns and tanks that enabled us to get through the first terrible weeks of the War of Independence. While mother was still campaigning for funds in the U.S., Israeli agents were buying arms in Czechoslovakia and shipping them through Yugoslavia with Soviet support, at a time when the U.S. government had placed an embargo on all arms to Israel; and while mother was in Moscow, one of the major bits of official business that our legation conducted was to negotiate continuation of these arms sales. Though the dealings between the legation and the Russian government were stiff, the overall atmosphere in some ways was so positive that once when mother went to the Moscow circus she was treated to a little skit showing Abdullah on a donkey being goaded by a clown who mocked him with the taunt, "Ah ha, the Jews have won the war!"

But for individual Jews matters were more difficult. In a campaign against "cosmopolitanism" the Russian authorities forbade U.S.S.R. citizens to converse with foreigners and foreigners to approach Russians, except of course through government agencies. Before she grasped the pervasiveness of this ban, mother had tried to hold an open house at the legation on Friday evenings; but the only Jews who ever showed up were foreign tourists, journalists and people connected with other embassies. She had tried also to print an information bulletin about Israel and had sent it to Jewish communities throughout the U.S.S.R., only to be called into the foreign ministry late one night and ordered to put a halt to the illegal "propaganda."

So the stories that left their strongest impression on me were not of mass gatherings, but of the few souls who approached Golda personally, each such act being one of desperate heroism. One story I remember had to do with an ex-communist, ex-Palestinian Jew who arrived at the legation late one night and somehow was passed by hotel security (read the KGB)—maybe because he still held a Mandate passport that the State of Israel recognized. He asked to speak to my mother and begged her to help him get back to Israel. He had left in the late 30s to fight in the Spanish Civil War, was wounded and taken to Russia for treatment. When he wanted to leave, he was refused permission. Now middle-aged, sick and disheveled, he approached my mother as a last hope. But there was nothing she could do for him, or for others like him, including a second cousin of hers who turned up from Pinsk, having travelled to Moscow without a permit to implore her to intervene on his behalf for an exit permit to Israel. But as mother described the situation, "Not one Russian official would discuss Jewish emigration with me, not for individual Jews nor for the multitudes; not one official would even answer our questions on the subject."

Nor could mother make contact with Russians. Before she left for Moscow she had received names and addresses—this person's sister, that person's aged mother or young daughter. One story I remember is indeed about a woman who asked mother to help bring her daughter to Israel; the two were separated during the Holocaust, the mother caught in Poland until she was able to get to Israel at war's end, the daughter hidden by nuns in Russia. Mother brought the matter to the authorities, but to no avail. But once in Russia she was in an agonizing dilemma. Not that she was afraid for herself, but any letter, package or even regards originating in Israel could cause severe damage to the recipient. Sarah told me, for example, about a call she and Zecharia made to the mother of a friend who received them politely, heard what they had to say, asked no questions and never invited them back. So aside from the synagogue, where the appearance of the police did a great deal to diminish attendance after *Yom Kippur,* pretty much the only place that remained for the legation to make any contact with the Jews of Russia was the Yiddish theater.

There, during intermissions, the audience progressed to the outer hall and, just as they did at the opera and ballet, "corso-ed," walking round and round in a circle, chatting with everyone more or less in line and everyone moving in the one direction. The formal progress, so different from anything that goes on in western theater lobbies, was interesting in itself, but there was also an added feature: the crowds began to circle around mother and her escorts. No one came up close; no one said anything. Only the eyes spoke their yearning and their faith in the inde-structable ties that linked us.

In 1948 the authorities shut down the Yiddish theater in Moscow, the Yiddish newspaper, the one remaining Yiddish publishing house and practically every other U.S.S.R. Jewish organization in Russia. No explanation was given. But the conclusion—that Russian Jews were being made to pay for showing too much enthusiasm about Israel—was inescapable.

CHAPTER 8

"MY SEVEN GOOD years," mother called her time as Israel's labor minister, the one post in her long career for which she felt herself perfectly suited and which she had actually requested. In the winter of 1949, soon after the country's first parliamentary elections, Ben Gurion, now prime minister, invited her to become his deputy prime minister and coordinator of development, whatever that meant. The offer was relayed by Moshe Sharett when she stepped off the plane returning from Moscow, but the next day when she met with Ben Gurion, she said, "If you insist on my being in the government, I have no desire to be deputy prime minister, nor do I want to be coordinator of development, of which I know very little. However," she added, "there is one field in which I have some understanding, it is labor relations." To me she later remarked: "I wanted to tell him that I am also an expert in unemployment, since I had dealt with this problem in my Histadrut days." To her surprise and joy, Ben Gurion at once agreed. So my mother became Israel's first elected minister of labor, public works, housing and social security, a post today divided among three cabinet ministers and whose sweeping title only hints at the formidable range of the responsibilities involved. Only hints, I say, because in 1949 everything had to be created practically from scratch: houses built, public works projects initiated, social legislation passed, and the government machinery to implement and enforce policy established. Mother's experience as a labor negotiator, her standing and relationships in the Histadrut, and the Histadrut's own extensive involvement in construction work and social insurance were all to stand her in great good stead—as I imagine she knew when, departing from her usual pattern, she herself volunteered for the job.

The barrage of problems awaiting solution had to be set against the background or, maybe more accurately, the foreground of a massive and revolutionary change in the very composition of Israel's population. When the British Mandate ended in the spring of 1948, there were fewer than 700,000 Jews in the country. By the end of 1951, the figure had doubled, with about 1,000 new arrivals a day; and by 1956, when mother left the labor ministry for the foreign ministry, a total of 900,000 immigrants had been absorbed. The numbers, though, tell only part of the story. Most of the immigrants arrived with little more than the clothes on their backs and whatever powers of endurance and adaptation each one possessed individually. They came from the DP camps of Germany, Austria and Italy, from the broken remnants of Jewish communities in the Balkans, from the detention camps of Cyprus—and, mostly, they were traumatized in spirit and body. They poured out of ghettos and casbahs of North Africa and the Arabic-speaking countries of the Middle East, in the main bewildered, uneducated and poverty-stricken, a human melange that had to be housed, given jobs, taught Hebrew and somehow turned into useful motivated citizens of a brand new state.

Unlike the early pioneers of the 20s, the majority of these newcomers were unprepared for the shift to manual labor and, unlike the German immigrants of the 30s, totally lacked the capital or know-how with which they might have set up shop, if there had been a market for their products. In short, the adjustment demanded of them was nothing less than monumental.

For us, the established population, this huge flood of immigration meant belt-tightening and a return to rationing: 200 grams of hard cheese per person per month, two eggs a week . . . Just about the only foods that we could get without coupons were eggplant and frozen fish, and even these were in short order. Whatever had been just about adequate for one family now had to be shared by two or three. Nor was this all. Immigrants from seventy different countries, speaking nearly as many languages, each group with its own customs and unique way of looking at the world, somehow had to be welded into one people. Of course we were all Jews, which was saying a lot, but not everything; we were Jews from the East and from the West, hundreds of years of differing cultures and traditions dividing us. Many of the so-called Oriental Jews from the Arabic-speaking countries of North Africa and the Middle East came to the "Holy Land" innocent of even the slightest familiarity with modern technology; the European Jews came with the latter but perhaps without an adequate understanding of or tolerance for people whose lives were so alien to them.

So when mother stepped into the labor ministry in April 1949, she was, in fact—as she herself defined it—stepping into "the most important job in the government," and she was very excited about it. After a decade dedicated to survival, the time had finally come for construction; and mother faced the welcome opportunity to combine the two things that mattered most to her: the rebuilding of the Jewish nation and the promulgation of the ideals of social justice. If any office in her career epitomized who she was and what she stood for it was unquestionably the labor ministry.

It is difficult for me to convey what mother felt about the immigrants who arrived in the late 40s and early 50s and how much it meant to her that they become part of Israeli society. As I've already mentioned, there *were* people who believed that this huge influx of newcomers should be slowed down to match Israel's ability to absorb them. But mother disagreed; she was one of the strongest, most outspoken advocates of a non-selective immigration policy. "Let us," she said, "take in the old and the infirm along with the healthy, the weak and the illiterate along with the strong and the educated. Israel without immigrants isn't worth having," she said often. "The State of Israel has no purpose unless this immigration continues for as long as it is necessary and as long as possible."

She also was probably one of the first Israelis alert to the dangers of ethnic divisiveness. As early as 1950 she told a worker's delegation:

> The reality being created in Israel . . . indicates the lamentable emergence of two separate and distinct groups within our population . . . one group of so-called old-timers and another of new immigrants.

In that same talk she paid special attention to the "Oriental" Jews:

> . . . I am not worried about how long an old-timer has to wait before he can buy a refrigerator. What I want to know is how long will it take for a Yemenite immigrant family to get a roof over his head . . . and when the Yemenite family will come anywhere near to owning a home and the barest minimum for its existence.

138

We are in Nes Ziona ("The Banner of Zion"), an inconspicuous town established at the beginning of the century, that straddles the dusty and busy road connecting Rishon Le Zion ("The First of Zion") and Rehovot. All are close together on the coastal plane these days and by car less than an hour away from Tel Aviv. All three, as is hinted by their somewhat self-important names, date back about one hundred years to the beginnings, in fact, of Jewish settlement in this country. Of the three, Nes Ziona is the smallest and the least flourishing. It is a very hot summer morning. Mother and members of the labor ministry are here to inaugurate a new housing project. From her expression I can see that her mind is not on the wooden podium from which she will soon say a few words, but rather is riveted on the spanking new houses that line the street. "How wonderful they are!" she whispers, with an intensity justified more by what they represent than by what they actually are or how they look: rows of absolutely identical red-roofed two-story houses, a hundred or so apartments in all, each one approximately fifty square meters divided into three rooms plus kitchen, with not an inch of wasted space. Though for large families these apartments are barely adequate, they are a great improvement after the absorption camps.

For Golda every house represents a major undertaking, a significant accomplishment of the state, and a source of great personal gratification. Once the houses are up, a new town or suburb has been created at one go; not only houses but everything else, all the essential if rudimentary services: a clinic, a school, a grocery store, a synagogue. The Nes Ziona project, crude, tatty and incomplete though it is, represents a great advance in the kind of accommodations the state can offer the newcomers. When mother first took office 250,000 immigrants lived in tents. These were replaced by corrugated tin and/or heavy canvas shacks (the first, ovenlike in Israel's summer heat, the second leaking and cold in the heavy winter rains) that gave

139

way to more permanent dwellings starting in 1950, when mother convinced the government it had to build 30,000 apartments. So she has good reason to beam.

The obligatory speeches over, we tour the little community, mother walking methodically from one house to another, from room to room. Whenever she inspects new homes, she looks them over like this, with the eagle eye of a practiced housewife and such total involvement that you'd think she was planning to move in herself. Nothing escapes her. Is the kitchen sink placed conveniently? Is the counter really easy to clean and at a sensible working height? How is the interior space divided? Won't the wall between the kitchen and the dinette make the apartment look and feel much smaller? What about that entrance?

In Kiryat Shmonah, a large development town up in the north close to the Lebanese border, she insists that an additional step be added after she sees for herself that the first step is too high for small children and old people to cope with. She even concerns herself with scenic views, though there isn't much she can do about that, but I remember that when she inspected a project overlooking the Sea of Galilee she wanted to know just why the architects hadn't designed the property so the kitchen window looked out on the water. Whenever we went on one of these tours I could see her brow crease; there is always the same inner conflict; none of the houses is comfortable enough or pretty enough and she knows it; inevitably, almost everything could have been built better. Still it's a miracle that they have been built at all, and the crease vanishes for a while.

For every dollar (building materials must be imported and paid for in hard currency) that goes into housing, there are a hundred other pressing claims. Schools, hospitals and transportation must be brought into existence and maintained; rocky, neglected land must be cleared for cultivation; industry must be encouraged and helped. Nor do our neighbors permit us to

140

forego our astronomical defense expenditures. Even though most of these Arab states signed armistice agreements (not peace treaties) with Israel in the first months of 1949, they had in no way renounced their stated intention of eventually destroying us. Egypt has closed the Suez Canal to Israeli shipping; there is a pan-Arab boycott of companies that dare trade with us, and armed infiltrators regularly cross Israel's borders, wantonly killing and robbing Jews.

Though some people criticized public housing on economic grounds, mother brought to the ministry not only the acumen of an executive trained to respect the economic facts of life but also the instincts of a woman who knew that people without decent homes cannot be good workers, good providers or good citizens. "What I contended during those years," she once recalled, "was that good citizenship and civic behavior don't and can't develop when people for years are forced to live in tents."

So if the housing estate she was officially opening that day in Nes Ziona was far from luxurious, it was—at least to her certain knowledge—the best available under the circumstances. And when she reacted to one woman's bouquet of flowers and stammered thanks by hugging her, it was in a spirit of shared relief and genuine joy.

In 1950 mother was off to the United States again, fund raising but with a difference. This time more money was needed—$1.5 billion over a three year period, $600 million to go to housing and public works, the rest mainly into agricultural and industrial development. This much money couldn't be raised through philanthropy alone. The most generous donations mustered by the U.J.A. could not meet more than the basic needs of resettlement and relief. If Israel was to move ahead, to stand on its own feet, a new way of obtaining money had to be found.

The master plan—in retrospect it was a daring and brilliant

stroke—was to try to raise one-third of the total need through close-to-intolerable taxation on Israel itself, the rest by floating a bond issue. It was a startling idea; who in the world could vouch for the solvency of an infant state so financially drained by the expenses of its War of Independence and the uncontrolled influx of thousands upon thousands of penniless immigrants. But Henry Montor and the other men who had done so much on previous fund-raising drives were very enthusiastic about prospects of the Israel Bonds. And one man in particular at once undertook to lay the groundwork. This was Henry Morganthau, Jr., former United States secretary of the treasury, whom mother greatly respected and with whom she had, amicably and effectively, traveled to so many United States communities in the watershed year of 1948.

Predictably my mother's job was to convince United States Jews, who had already donated so magnanimously to Israel, now to *invest* in it. This was a radically new approach, it called for optimism and faith, and was based on the assumption that such investment could carry financial reward. As for herself, it was far more satisfying, if not less exhausting, to barnstorm for bonds than to ask for gifts, and she did it unsparingly and brilliantly.

I had returned to the United States by then to continue my music studies and was in Washington, D.C., when she talked about Israel Bonds there before a deeply impressed audience. I can still hear the pride with which she explained Israel's need, not for charity but for funds that could be invested and that would be paid back.

> . . . It is our firm resolve to free ourselves at the earliest moment of any dependence on philanthropy. We have to continue receiving large-scale help for the relief and rehabilitation of the newcomers. But if we want to build houses, if we need lumber, we are ready to pay. If we need steel, we also must be ready to pay for

it. If we want to build schools for our children, we shall pay for them. We have now reached that point in our development where we have the potential to borrow funds and, by our own labor and resourcefulness, repay each penny.

After the meeting in Washington we went together to visit old friends and relatives, as mother usually tried to do on her trips abroad—and another kind of bond was floated. This one between myself and the daughter of one of mother's oldest friends. Channah Lutsky was a pretty, bright and unusually self-assured young lady, and after a six month courtship we married. Everything boded well. Channah, who was to become an economist, loved music as much as I did and I was hugely attracted to her composure and independence. Both our families were happy; our mothers were virtually childhood friends; Channah's father, who had joined the Jewish Legion during World War I, had known my father, and Channah herself had met him on a previous visit to Israel. Also, she had already made detailed plans to settle there, something that meant a great deal both to me and to my parents. We were married in Passaic, New Jersey, June 1950. My mother was present at the wedding but my father unfortunately was ill and couldn't come. I didn't realize at the time how grave his condition was. He died in May 1951.

Jerusalem 1954. Channah and I are staying with mother during our summer vacation. At Ben Gurion's instigation the government has moved most of its offices to the nation's capital. Golda now lives in a rooftop apartment—attractive, romantic though too modest to be labeled as a penthouse—that the government has remodeled for her in the Talbieh quarter of the city. From the bay window of her living room where we sit with her in rare moments of relaxation, one can see the Judean hills. From the window that faces south, when the weather is good,

143

Bethlehem is visible. My memories of my mother in that apartment are distinct. She loved it and felt it to be her home, something I think she felt for no other place except perhaps the twin houses in Ramat Aviv.

One recollection that has just surfaced for reasons that will be obvious is of a Saturday afternoon when Marc Chagall came to visit her there. Mother was not a lady of many hobbies; she didn't play bridge or golf or even watch TV much once it made its debut in Israel. In fact, she was singularly not *au courant*—she didn't know who the Beatles were when every child knew about them or even what in the world *The Hite Report* was. But one form of pleasure that she *did* make time for was going to plays and concerts, and among her favorite official duties was the hosting of artists of every sort.

In 1954 Chagall had his first major exhibit in Israel, a retrospective in Jerusalem. Mother invited him to Sabbath lunch. Though he was reputedly very shy they spent the entire afternoon swapping Yiddish stories of their poverty in Russia. But the highlight, an event mother pretended to boast about for years to come, was when Chagall and Moshe Mokady, a leading Israeli artist who also came to lunch with us, made the rounds of the paintings and drawings on the living room walls, works from the Israel Museum that the government lent out to its ministers. Slowly they strolled from picture to picture, discussing the style, technique and inspiration of each, with Mokady delivering little lectures on the personality and background of the respective Israeli artists, until they came to one unsigned seascape. Whose could it be? Mother stood to the side and smiled when Chagall exclaimed, "Now *this* picture has music!" The painting was mine, painted years earlier from our balcony in Tel Aviv.

But for me the recurrent picture from those days is of Golda hunched over the kitchen table, forever stacked with heaps of papers: files, budgets and construction plans, reports, drafts of the National Insurance Law she saw through the Knesset and successions of documents of all sorts and shapes, all neatly arranged. Reading glasses perched on her nose, ashtray overflowing and a fresh pack of cigarettes at the ready, a cup of coffee forgotten and cooling at arm's reach, she pores for hours over what she calls her homework, peppering her papers with instructions and suggestions, stopping every so often to make and take phone calls or talk with the callers who are also an essential part of her work schedule. When she is alone, or just with us, she wears a housecoat (always ironed) and slippers, and whenever she washes her hair it is often wrapped up in a towel turban to dry as she works. She doesn't, I suppose, look much like most people's notion of a tough, hard-driving, no-nonsense minister of labor. What is most surprising to me, in retrospect, is her ability to move from total absorption in one thing to ordinary family chit-chat with Channah and me when we come in. There is always time for her to put up the coffee, to tell Channah that her skirt looks nice, to exchange political comments with us. Left to her own devices she would chat like this all night and then, once we are gone, work to close to dawn, raising her eyes from her papers only long enough to see the colors of the Jerusalem landscape change as the sun comes up.

Mother's regular visitors during that period were the people she worked with in the labor ministry, in particular Ytzhak Eylam and Zvi Berenson, who were her senior colleagues at the ministry. Employment, like housing, was a very personal issue for Golda and not something she took lightly. Not likely to be forgotten was her childhood in Russia when her father, though a good carpenter, was denied employment because he was Jewish, or her years in Jerusalem when Morris wasn't working steadily or paid enough for what he did and she had had to wrangle with the milkman and grocer over credit so she could feed Sarah and myself. The situation of the immigrants was pressing, though foreign relief money made it possible to provide them with food. But charity was no more a long-term solution for an individual immigrant than for the state as a whole. Work had to be created for these disadvantaged men and women since the existing economy couldn't possibly absorb the half a million or so new job seekers.

In pre-state days, the Histadrut had initiated cooperative enterprises that built the nation and employed the people. Now the time had come for the government to do the same with a massive program of public works, not unlike the public works programs with which Franklin Delano Roosevelt had pulled the United States out of the economic doldrums of the 30s. My mother was convinced that this was the only alternative to a perpetual and demoralizing dole, though, just as with her insistence that a roof over one's head is a prerequisite for proper citizenship, so here too there were opposing arguments expressed by some economists.

Most of the immigrants had never planted or harvested, never held bricks in their hands or even seen a drill, never mind use one. So not only did jobs have to be created but people had to be trained to do them. To complicate matters still further, though most newcomers were happy to earn a day's wage, there were many who just plain didn't want to do (or were maybe scared to do) what they had never done before. So why, some argued, the immense bother and gigantic expense of creating jobs for people who were so unprepared for them?

The struggle mother faced was double-edged: against those in government who screamed that public works were a wild extravagance, and against those immigrants who were suffering so acutely from the shock of having to adjust to new demands and expectations.

146

But she was adamant. When experts quoted figures intended to prove that unemployment wasn't so high after all, her answer was instant and tart: "Any unemployed person is one hundred percent unemployed." At a Labor Party meeting in 1953 she spelled it out:

> . . . We have always said, and rightly, that as socialists we see no justification for unemployment anywhere, even less so in our own country. There is no room here for people out of work—there was none before the state was established and there is none now. There is so much to be done here connected both with our security and our political position that it is inconceivable that thousands and tens of thousands of people be without jobs in a country crying out for more production.
>
> Must we repeat the ABCs we know so well: that frontiers are not frontiers when they run through wasteland; that one can only rely on frontiers when people live along them; that the soil is ours only when we work it; and that we can rely on the people to stand up to the harshest tests only when they feel themselves to be citizens of this state—not by virtue of certificates of citizenship but because they work here, build the country and till its soil.

So once or twice a week, Shalom Cohen, in charge of employment, puffs his way up the sixty-odd stairs leading to mother's apartment after a long day out of town to report on the number of unemployed in this region and that, or this or that number of jobs that opened up here or there, or to hash out yet another scheme for creating yet another few jobs in critical areas. Every day, 30,000 to 50,000 laborers leave their homes at pre-dawn hours to clear land and work in forestation, housing and road construction programs launched by the ministry of labor. There may be grounds for complaint regarding the waste and error that seem always to accompany public works to the dissatisfaction of those for whom either employment hasn't been found or

147

who don't like what they got, but the sight of men working with picks and shovels or on the new machines they have just been taught to use, gaining skills, feeding families and becoming like the rest of us fills my mother with a sense of deep satisfaction. She clumps along a new, only partially paved road, chatting happily with the sturdy looking Bulgarian workers or Jews recently arrived from Morocco, perfectly at ease with them, genuinely interested in their problems, their new lives . . .

Usually my mother created an atmosphere of cordiality around herself; the top labor ministry teams drove themselves at the tempo she dictated, fired by the urgency that she brought to whatever she was doing, but each member of a team was given room for individual initiatives that were always acknowledged. One of them, Itzhak Eylam, wrote in his autobiography that Golda was blessed with the knack of choosing the right people for the right jobs and with a personal style of work that stimulated maximum cooperation. I know on the other hand she considered herself "most fortunate to be surrounded by such able and dedicated people." Her connection with, and respect for, the people of the labor ministry lasted to the end of her life.

Years later when she resigned as prime minister, the men who had worked directly with her in those distant days got together to present her with a gift that I knew meant more to her than almost anything else she had ever received. It was a scholarship fund established in her name for higher education in development and border towns as well as in Arab and Druse villages. Her genuine interest in Israel's development towns never faded. Above all, she remained vitally concerned with the education of young people there, the people for whom mileage and lack of money made the acquisition of higher education out-of-reach, but who, she knew, were as anxious to go on with their studies as she had been when she was a young woman. The idea was to award stipends to young people who would then bring new knowledge and skills back to their hometowns. Here again was the dual themes of simultaneous personal achievement and national development that she emphasized throughout her tenure as labor minister. I was sitting with her when the first stipends were awarded. I remember she literally glowed watching the proud winners and their even prouder families. And how happy she was too that at least a partial answer was being found to the question "How on earth will they manage?" that she had asked herself over the years whenever she visited one of these new towns or thought about the people living in them whose well-being so profoundly concerned her.

We are on the new Beersheba Road, one of the major public works that mother has promoted and organized. The opening ceremony has just ended, the ribbon cut, the flowers already wilting in the sun, the obligatory child affectionately kissed, the speeches over. Mother, her personal staff, Batsheva Arianne and Zalman Chen and other members of the labor ministry, some of the people who had worked on the road and a delegation of old-timers whose previously remote settlements this road now linked to the rest of the nation, and myself—all of us set off in a procession of dust-stained vehicles from the junction south of Rehovot, where the old road dating back to Turkish days meandered along the outskirts of Egyptian-held Gaza, making the maiden journey to Beersheba.

Unimpressive by any international standards, this two-lane highway (it has widened considerably since) is one of the events of the year. Peering out of the windows of her car, mother can see tangible vindication of her emphasis on employment and public works. The entire road has been built by Jewish workers, from the design and enginering down to the last detail of laying the asphalt and painting a white line through the middle. Men from tens of countries, speaking in tens of different languages, have worked,

149

sweated and quarreled together, gradually learning to know each other, to identify with a common aim, acquiring the skills with which to earn a livelihood long after this particular road is finished. (In the years when Ben Gurion would popularize the slogan "Go South," it would be this road that would make that population dispersal possible.) Broader and more direct than its ancestor, this road will bring Beersheba, the tiny kibbutzim and settlements on the way—in fact, the entire Negev—within reasonable reach of the center of Israel. It will quicken the transport of goods, open up the way to agricultural and industrial development, make the country safer and bring communities nearer to each other. Last but not least, it cuts an hour and a half off our travel time to Revivim! Just a road, not even Little League elsewhere, but it symbolized my mother's vision of how the country should grow. As we ride, Itzhak Eylam, who has an eye for art and a taste for history, points out the mounds that once marked the Philistine city of Gath, known from the story of Samson, and within minutes we see the raw beginnings of new construction, the first houses in what is to become the town of Kiryat Gat. Within a few years Kiryat Gat will turn into a compact modern city, the home of Israel's finest textile industry. And Polgat will be established by Israel Pollack, a Holocaust survivor who has made his fortune in Chile and invested much of it in Israel . . . after he has been whizzed down "Golda's" road at the traffic-free hour of 5:00 A.M. by Pinkas Sapir, minister of trade and industry, to prove that the trip from Tel Aviv could indeed be made in superhighway-speed!

Moving south, passing the remains of the Arab village of Falujah, where the Egyptian army (including one Colonel Nasser) was trapped in a so-called pocket during the War of Independence, we come upon Beersheba itself, rising dramatically and unexpectedly from the desert that frames it. Spreading out from the old section at the center of town, brash new neighborhoods are already elbowing their way crudely past the sand, much as they are doing everywhere else. At the reception tendered her, Golda listens with unconcealed glee as Beersheba's Mayor David Tuviahu sets out before the minister of labor a draftsman's plans for what he calls "greater Beer Sheva!" Abraham once herded his flocks somewhere very near where we are sitting now, in the improvised town hall of what was a Biblical watering place and is now well on its way to turning into a bona fide metropolis in Israel's south . . .

That is but one ride with mother. There are many others, mostly in the big black shiny American DeSoto that mother's adoring American friends have given her and that is a kind of mobile home for her. She holds meetings there; when she is tired she stretches out on its back seat, props a pillow under her head, if it is cold she covers herself with a blanket and falls into the deep brief sleep of one who has earned the right to rest. But if the day is not too tiring, she often stops to give a lift to hitchhikers! A student, a soldier, a farmer or one of her cherished road builders only has to stand on the road, thumb up, and mother motions the driver to pull up.

Until she became prime minister and the security services absolutely and sternly forbade the indulgence, she thought that this was a wonderful way both to help people directly and to get to know the so-called ordinary citizens with whom high government officials are bound to lose touch. Her car, license number 600, soon became famous on the Jerusalem-Tel Aviv road that she regularly traveled, but there were still enough people who didn't know who she was for many of these encounters to be natural and candid, and sometimes amusing.

One such meeting that I witnessed was with a Yemenite farmer whom mother picked up outside his *moshav* (the type of settlement in which members own their houses and land but share agricultural equipment, marketing services and the like, and where many of the new immigrants of the period have been settled). Slight like most Yemenite Jews, dark-skinned, wearing traditional earlocks but having exchanged the traditional ankle-length robe for sturdy blue work clothes, he has not been in the country very long. He left Yemen, he tells Golda, in the late 40s. He took his young wife and seven children, his Bible, a handful of possessions and like thousands of other Yemenite Jews started out on foot for the Holy Land, fleeing forever the Moslem country in which his people had lived for hundreds of years, much of the time under highly repressive conditions. Walking in weary groups of thirty or forty, eating only the flat Arab bread (*pitta*) and dates they could carry, paying huge ransoms either to Arab brigands or to Arab sultans, they arrived in Aden, to be airlifted from there—these people who had never even been inside a car—to Israel in the huge converted transport planes that made up what came to be known as Operation Magic Carpet and, as such, entered Israeli history. Mother is delighted to have him along. They sit in silence for a while, then she starts up a conversation.

"How are you doing?" she asks. "How are things going for you?"

"Baruch Hashem," (The Lord be praised) he answers.

"Is your wife happy?"

"The Lord be praised."

"And your children, are they doing well?"

"The Lord be praised."

"How do you like the *moshav* you're on?"

"The Lord be praised."

Mother is not one to give up. Besides, she understands that at least for this one man, life may be hard but it's good.

"How are the houses?" she continues, meaning the ones the labor ministry had just built.

"The Lord be praised."

Her hitchhiker has only one complaint. "In Yemen," he says, "the women were so small"—he makes appropriate lowering gestures with his hands and lithe body—"but here they have become so big and free!"

When he gets out of the car mother says, "I wonder whether he credits the State of Israel or the good Lord with the voting rights, the freedom of speech and the dignity his wife has just obtained. . . ."

Perhaps a word is now in order about the labor laws and the National Insurance Law that mother introduced then. Both sets of regulations were based, again, on Histadrut accomplishments. Now the original aspirations for a just and egalitarian society were given legal sanctions, although the regulations were passed in stages so as not to put too heavy a strain on the economy. As early as 1950 mother had spoken on behalf of a maximum forty-five-hour work week "to safeguard workers' health and provide the possibility of rest, and for the sake of efficiency and increased production." And in 1952 she introduced the first national insurance bill so that in the new state "no one would be neglected, no widows and orphans will hunger for bread, no people will be cast out in their old age." Today paid annual vacations, restrictions on night work, factory safety regulations, protection of youth laws, old age pensions, unemployment, workers' compensation and disability insurance plus numerous other social benefits are taken-for-granted features of Israeli life, but all have their origins in the bills that came out of my mother's office in the 1950s.

She was especially interested in getting laws on behalf of women, safeguarding health and making it easier than it had been for her to do the double job of mothering and housekeeping as well as participating usefully and profitably in economic activity outside the home. She saw to it that night work for women was restricted to crucial areas such as nursing, and that mothers in government service worked reduced hours at the same pay. A three-month paid maternity leave was put into law, and maternity grants given to women who had their babies in-hospital—this to encourage both Arab and Jewish women from Moslem countries (accustomed to home deliveries) to give birth in supervised, hygienic surroundings.

Needless to say, all of this was a gigantic financial strain. Up to the last minute before the National Insurance Law was passed, its opponents issued dire warnings: "Golda, we beg of you. Rethink the catastrophe that you're about to bring down upon the nation. Israel cannot possibly survive the kind of fine costly ideals you're making into law . . ." And so forth. But she dug in, and she was right. Instead of catastrophe she was herself to witness a vast improvement in the quality of life of hundreds of thousands of people, the development of a sense of civic belonging in people who paid dues and received benefits, and what was, to her mind, a revelation of Jewish solidarity.

To personal matters: the bond between Channah and myself did not, sad to say, last. We came back to Israel in 1954 and lived for about a year in mother's Tel Aviv apartment. There was some not unusual friction between Channah and myself, but on the whole things seemed, at least to me, to be all right.

Mother came to Tel Aviv for weekends, and the three of us developed a pleasant and effortless routine. She arrived from Jerusalem on Thursday evenings in time to attend the weekly Labor Party meetings. Friday mornings she worked in the ministry's Tel Aviv office and joined us for the midday meal. Toward evening she left for Sheyna's, outside Tel Aviv, where she slept over and spent all day Saturday—an arrangement by means of which she tactfully gave Channah and me weekend privacy and was able to keep her now-widowed ailing sister company.

The following summer, four years into our marriage and in the middle of a difficult pregnancy, Channah suddenly informed, without introductory comment, that she wanted a separation. We were in Yugoslavia then; I was studying the cello with Antonio Janigro, apparently too absorbed to realize how unhappy Channah was or, for that matter, even to sense the incompatability that so troubled her. A month later, we went back to Israel and Channah moved in with her mother.

In January of 1956, four months after Channah left, our daughter Meira, named after my late father, was born. Unfortunately the child was afflicted with Down's Syndrome.

Shortly afterward Channah remarried and the baby had a warm family. For me, visiting Channah's new home was unpleasant. I felt out of place and unwanted, which I suppose I was. Eventually my contact with Meira was only on occasions when Channah and I met to discuss the economic or medical problems that we had to handle together.

Looking back, I think of this as being one of those rare turn of events when mother, who sympathized both with Channah and myself and who generally speaking was of a positive and optimistic nature, was simply unable to help either of us.

Since Channah severed all relations with me and my family, no bonds could be developed between my mother as grandmother, and Meira. Out separation on the one hand and the tragedy of a mongoloid child on the other deeply saddened mother.

CHAPTER 9

IN 1956 MOTHER WAS appointed minister of foreign affairs. For almost a year prior to that appointment—a year during which the idea of the appointment had surfaced with increasing frequency behind various closed doors—she summarily dismissed the very thought. At first she said almost casually, "I haven't finished my work as minister of labor." Then, as Ben Gurion went on pressing her and party colleagues stepped up their urging, we began to hear: "*I* as foreign minister? What do *I* know about diplomacy? Or protocol?" And "anyhow, the whole idea is absurd." On the face of it, she had a point —but not a good one.

Ever since the ministry's inception it had been run by a different sort of personality: the thoughtful, erudite, dapper Moshe Sharett, a master of languages—Hebrew, English, French, German, Arabic, Russian, a connoisseur of propriety and a stickler for form, a man who fervently believed in the well-worded diplomatic protest as a suitable response to the on-going fedayeen terror waged from across the Egyptian and Syrian borders. The fact was that Ben Gurion was sending feelers in mother's direction just *because* she was so different from Sharett, and because he wanted a foreign minister who saw eye-to-eye with him on security matters and who would share, as mother did and to the hilt, his own deepest conviction that the safest and surest answer to the swords of the terrorists were swords of our own—deterrent retaliatory actions. Nonetheless, when mother did finally and inevitably succumb to the call of duty she took with her to the foreign ministry a rucksack full of doubts and a sense of unease that lasted for years. "I'm not among my own," she said more in discomfort than disparagement of the ministry staff that Sharett had selected, trained and worked with for so long. "They're not at home with the kind of person I am and I'm not at home with them. I don't think it's going to work."

Her forebodings not withstanding, for the next ten years, from 1956 to 1966, mother served as foreign minister of Israel and gradually put her own personality into the job and derived satisfaction from it.

Within these years, except for my niece Naomi, who was born in 1952, my sister's son Shaul and my own three sons Amnon, Daniel and Gideon, were born. These were the years of their early childhood, and we used to spend long weeks of our vacations in the lovely, spacious house that served as the foreign minister's residence. And so the ties between mother and the children grew close from the very beginning. She loved to baby-sit for them. I remember quite vividly one evening when Aya and I came home late, only to find the kids dressed up in mother's various hats, which they picked out of her hatbox, and play-acting out before an audience of one, my mother.

When mother was abroad, and she travelled quite frequently, the children missed her and would urge us to take them to the airport to meet her. To an outsider it must have seemed amusing to see the little ones marching at her sides on the runway, or seated beside her during the briefing to the press at the V.I.P.

room of the Ben-Gurion airport.

At home she loved to unpack her suitcases with the presents she fished out for the children. Most exciting were the exotic presents she brought throughout the years when she came back from her journeys to South America, Africa and the Far East. I too shared the enjoyment when mother surprised me with folk music instruments to add to my collection.

In 1959 she went on an official visit to nine Latin American countries—Argentina, Bolivia, Brazil, Chile, Mexico, Uruguay, Venezuela, Guatemala and Peru. I remember how deeply impressed she was by the friendship of these countries. She was overwhelmed by the encounter with the ancient Indian cultures, and her heart warmed when she saw the flourishing Jewish life. She met with leaders of the Jewish communities and was welcomed by teachers and students of the elaborate educational network of Hebrew and Yiddish schools.

I joined mother in 1962 on a tour through Japan, the Philippines, Hong Kong, Cambodia, Thailand and Burma. In the Far East she did not experience the same kind of informal open communication which she was used to in the west. In Hong Kong she made an attempt to reach out to Communist China through a British intermediary, with no luck. But throughout that continent too we were received with generosity and friendship. The old Emperor Hirohito of Japan and the pretty Queen Mother of Cambodia's socialist Prince Sianouk invited her.

And then there was Africa. Between 1958 (when she attended the first anniversary of Ghana's independence and visited Liberia, Senegal, the Ivory Coast and Nigeria) and before the end of her term of office she returned to Africa, visiting some of the same countries again, as well as the Cameroons, Toga, Sierra Leone, Gambia, Guinea, Kenya and Ethiopa, practically every nation in that vast continent except South Africa—the one invitation she turned down. She was touched by the enthusiasm and affection which she encountered everywhere.

"I am so very glad you were able to see something of the problems we face . . . I am sure that when independence comes to Kenya we will be able to draw heavily on your experience in meeting the tasks that confront us," Jomo Kenyata wrote to mother in 1963.

"I can assure you that the government of Tanganyika and I myself were extremely happy to receive you during your visit. In particular Maria and I were very pleased to have you as our guest at State House," wrote President Julius Nyerere.

African newspapers carried such headlines as "Israel Understands Us" and "Israel is like Us" whenever mother visited. And with one African leader, the Ivory Coast's scholar and medical doctor President Houphouet-Boigney, mother formed such close personal ties that, even after the pressures of Arab oil forced all of Israel's African friends to break relations with us, he met with her secretly in Europe.

What was responsible for this extraordinary popularity? I ask myself the question now as I have done on other occasions, not so much because the matter puzzles me—I never thought for a moment that Golda wouldn't be all that a foreign minister should be—but because the phenomenon is so amazing in itself. I think the answer may be simple: She lent to the job an active, humane, personal dimension. She saw it as a bridging of gaps, a cementing of relationships and an opportunity to continue doing the things she had done before—making friends for Israel and sharing the Israeli experience with them.

Her consciousness of the significance of her basic mission never left her when she journeyed abroad. In Asia I saw for myself how well she acquitted herself (if not always comfortably) whenever formal demands were made—for example, obediently approaching Cambodia's queen bent over backward from the shoulders when taking leave, as a sign of respect. She took pleasure in the natural and man-made beauties of ancient and intricate cultures: Japan's gardens and shrines; the magnificent excavations (since destroyed by the Viet Cong) at Ankor Wat; the mysterious, thousand-year-old dances of the Cambodia's Royal Ballet; the rain forests along the Mekong River—the green envy of all desert dwellers.

But what was closest to her heart and made her very happy was the developmental work that Israel was doing in the emerging states. In those days our program of international cooperation and technical assistance embraced over eighty countries throughout Africa, Asia, Latin America and the Mediterranean Basin. So in many of the places that mother visited there were Israeli advisers working in fields, schools, fisheries, hospitals with the native laborers they had trained. In the Philippines I remember she met with our agricultural advisers; in Burma, particularly exciting was her visit to an adaptation of an Israeli-style *moshav* (cooperative farming village) in the Namsang region of North Burma. For years Burma had been practically defenseless against constant harassment along its Chinese border; the similarity to our own situation was striking, and in cooperation with Israel's ministry of agriculture and defense mother had helped introduce in Burma an Oriental version of what had been a viable solution in Israel. Many of our borders were and still are protected by a well-trained, permanently resident civilian population made up of people who, when of army age, had received their military training in conjunction with what is called kibbutz *hakshara,* or preparation, and afterward, having become skillful soldier-farmers, went to live and work on the cooperative border settlements they also helped to defend.

Mother suggested to the Burmese that they too adopt this approach and invited the Burmese Government to send a group of demobilized soldiers and their families to spend a year or so on an Israeli *moshav* or *kibbutz* in order that they experience at first hand the unique cooperative lifestyle. At the same time Israelis were sent to Burma to help to set up the *moshavim* there. Those were the villages that she and I went to see, the fruits of her labor so to speak. Predictably she was especially moved by the sight of the Burmese families that had been in Israel and now met her at the airport singing Hebrew songs and waving Israeli flags. "Look at them, just look," she said, literally overwhelmed by their sense of connection with Israel.

It was this that mattered: the ability to help people to live better, more dignified, more independent lives. When she said in Nairobi once, "The world cannot be a place of peace and happiness while there are haves and have-nots," she spoke out of profound conviction. When she globe-trotted she brought her Israeli values with her—and people understood and responded to that vision—best put into words by her when she spoke in 1960 before the General Assembly of the United Nations on the needs of the emerging nations:

> ... Much has been said and done about what I would call "first aid" about the sharing of food and the transfer of surplus to the hungry. But I wish to say now that we will never be really free as long as our children have to be fed by others. Our freedom will be complete only when we have learned to bring forth what we need from our own soil. The cry that goes out from the African and Asian continents today is: Share with us not only food, but also your knowledge of how to produce it. The most frightening inequality in the world lies now in the gap between those who literally reach for the moon and those who do not know how to reach efficiently into their own soil to produce their daily requirements.

Nor was it only to the disparity between east and west, developed and underdeveloped countries that mother was sensitive; she was also concerned with local inequities. Throughout Asia, with the exception of Japan, mother and I moved to and from the elegant surroundings of thickly carpeted, richly upholstered, beautifully tiled hotel suites to scenes of abject and wide-scale poverty. In the Philippines I remember circling around rows upon rows of tightly packed shanties with their hordes of shoeless children and patently undernourished adults, a sight that horrified Golda more than it would have been polite or possible for her to acknowledge publicly, and left her white-faced and trembling.

One particular incident in Hong Kong stands out in my mind. One evening we had been invited to a dinner given by leaders of the Jewish community that was held in a famous ferry restaurant that could be reached only by walking to the very end of a pier and taking a boat to it. All along the pier we were besieged by children; toddlers; ragged, skinny, barefoot children, the bigger ones carrying younger sisters and brothers on their backs. They pressed as close to us as they could, hands outstretched for money. Mother looked at them, looked away, again at them, again away and down at her pocketbook, wondering what to do. Clearly, however many children actually managed to receive an offering, there would be others who failed and in the inevitable fight more children would be hurt than helped.

But the real reason for the stopover in Hong Kong was to meet a certain colorful General Morris Cohen, "Two-Gun" Cohen as he was known, who was one of those mysterious characters roving the Far East. A British subject, he had lived many years in China and had served as Sun Yat-sen's bodyguard and personal assistant. He was a man of some influence who had high contacts in the Chinese government. Through him, Mother was trying to come to some sort of dialogue with the Chinese authorities. When he arrived at the Repulse Bay Hotel, where we were staying, we met a man in his early seventies, who was solidly built and spoke softly, retaining some of his original

Lancashire accent. After a long conversation, General Cohen promised that he would try to convey to the Chinese authorities Israel's wish to open diplomatic relations. Unfortunately nothing came of this meeting.

As she traveled through Asia and Africa she brought, in addition to aid and instruction, her own universally and instantly identifiable self, thereby disproving by her own behavior all the false and disparaging things that even then were said of Israel. "An extension of western imperialism" . . . "capitalist" . . . "aggressors"—well, the people Golda met with on those trips knew that this couldn't be so: there was nothing racist, condescending or manipulative in her manner. She saw in the people of the Third World friends we could help, equals among equals. "We who are struggling to cement our political independence by rapid economic, social and scientific development feel close to the nations of the great awakening continent of Africa," she said, and it came from the heart.

And whenever she came home from these trips she spoke with love of Africa. One incident that I can still see her telling, a small incident, not so important in itself, is characteristic of the spirit of her ties with these people. On the eve of her departure from Ghana in 1958 she was invited to a gala farewell party attended by government delegates who had previously visited Israel. The room was crowded with Africans (resplendent and colorful in traditional dress and jewelry), Europeans and, of course, Israelis. At the far end, Ghana's best orchestra played away softly. After a while one of the Israelis went over to the orchestra for a whispered conversation, and in five minutes the chords of the *hora* filled the room—and there was mother, leading the Israeli delegates and some of the Africans, who had spent time on *kibbutzim,* in the traditional folk dance. The waiters stopped in their tracks, the Europeans looked shocked and reporters reached for their pads. But soon some of the African cabinet

163

ministers and tribal chiefs began to move to the rhythm, and then others until finally they got tired, one by one dropping out of the circle, leaving mother, perspiring and panting, whirling to the very last with one of her hosts. The crowd applauded, the band changed over to African Highlife—that rhythmic, jazz-like music—and there again was Golda, almost sixty years old, continuing to twirl as if there were no tomorrow.

Good public relations? Maybe. But more than that. Mother was just being herself, the same woman who had once danced through the night into the early morning at Kibbutz Merhavia and who now travelled devoid of airs or pretensions to befriend and make friends for herself and Israel.

Self-interest? Yes, also that. But honest self-interest. Keeping the world informed of the perils threatening Israel was the single most important task facing Israel's foreign ministry, and everywhere the foreign minister went she talked about our need for secure borders, for defense against continuing infiltration from Egypt, Jordan and Syria, for free passage through the Suez Canal that Egypt had closed to Israel's ships, about our readiness to negotiate face-to-face with any and all of our Arab neighbors, and about our legitimate demand that they do the same.

The ten years when mother was foreign minister were framed by two wars: the Sinai Campaign in the fall of 1956, just after she took office, and the Six Day War in 1967, not long after she resigned. The interval was far from peaceful. At least once or twice a year she flew to speak before the United Nations, a closed club, she felt, and one that in no way guaranteed its smaller members against aggression. She went to New York toward the end of 1956 to explain our Sinai action, then back again at the beginning of 1957 to hand over the Sinai and Gaza Strip; and repeatedly thereafter: to refute demands that we return to the 1947 partition borders, to recommend reasonable solutions to the problems of Arab refugees; to answer Argentinian charges that Israel *illegally* kidnapped Adolf Eichmann.

Those appearances at the U.N. constituted, I think, the most difficult, discouraging and draining part of her job; in Africa and Asia she spoke to the hearts of people feeling that she was understood. But at the U.N. she felt "like an unloved orphan at someone else's party." Even when a grudgingly kind word was said, it failed to make her happy. "When people compliment us on being the only democratic state in the Middle East," she once said, "it doesn't really please me much. Who wants to be the only clean family in the apartment house?" . . .

It so happened that I was on the way to Puerto Rico in December 1956 to study with Pablo Casals and thus was able to attend the session at which Golda stood up before the General Assembly to explain the reasons for the Sinai action. As usual she spoke clearly and simply. Of the many strands in that speech, perhaps the central thread was that ours had been a preemptive action designed to defend Israel against certain and imminent attack. Egypt's President Nasser had stockpiled huge quantities of Russian-supplied arms and suddenly massed military forces on our Sinai border; in October he signed agreements with Jordan and Syria whereby their armies would be placed under Egyptian command for the sole purpose of entrapping Israel; contrary to United Nations resolutions he had nationalized the Suez Canal and, in addition, blockaded the Straits of Aqaba to ships going to and from Israel, thereby cutting off our lifeline to oil and other essential goods. All this against a background of continuous fedayeen murders, hailed on Cairo radio and the Egyptian press with statements such as: "Weep, O Israel, because Egypt's Arabs have already found their way to Tel Aviv. The day of extermination draws near. There shall be no more complaints or protests to the United Nations or the Armistice Commission. There will be no peace on the borders because we demand the death of Israel." Statements that left no doubt whatsoever as to Egypt's intentions. The facts clear, our motives expounded, mother made a point that she had made before and unfortunately would have to make again. There had been no choice:

> We are a small people in a small barren land that we have revived with our labor and love. The odds against us are heavy; the disparity of forces is great; we have no alternative but to defend our lives and freedom and the right to security. We desire nothing more than peace, but we cannot equate peace merely with an apathetic readiness to be destroyed. If hostile forces gather for our proposed destruction, they must not demand that we provide them with ideal conditions for the realizations of their plans . . .

And, the war over for the time being, she continued to hold out the hand of peace and to hold up before that august body a vision of growth and development in the Middle East such as she had inspired in Asia and Africa:

> The countries of the Middle East are rightly listed in the category of the "underdeveloped." The standard of living, disease, the illiteracy of the masses of people, the undeveloped lands, desert and swamp—all these cry out for minds, hands, financial means, in technical ability. Can we envisage what a state of peace between Israel and its neighbors during the past eight years would have meant for all of us? Can we try to translate fighter planes into irrigation pipes and tractors for the people in these lands? Can we, in our imagination replace gun emplacements by schools and hospitals?

She might as well have been speaking to the deaf. I watched her walk back to her seat, slowly; aside from a few perfunctory hand-claps and indifferent coughs and shuffles—punctuated by applause from only one nation, Holland—the Assembly was silent. The next month, in January, it was mother's duty to return to that forum to announce Israel's withdrawal from the Sinai, Gaza and the Gulf of Aqaba. There were similar explanations, similar appeals for peace, and, though I wasn't there to witness it, similar indifference: which accounts, I suspect, for much of the impetus into her subsequent reaching out to Asia and Africa. It is perhaps ironic that the enthusiasm she, and Israel, evoked there, when we were judged on our merits only, was so conspicuous by its absence in a world body already dominated by hostile Arab interests.

The only thing that relieved the dreariness and gloom of those sessions were the few personal moments snatched from a hectic schedule. One was breakfast with Eleanor Roosevelt at her tranquil home just off of Washington Square in New York's Greenwich Village. In Eleanor Roosevelt mother found a kindred spirit; a woman like herself—active, creative, involved and dedicated to progress. And Mrs. Roosevelt apparently felt similarly towards Golda. In 1960 in her foreword to a selection of mother's speeches, she praised a "mind constantly probing into the future and how her own service and that of her state can be increased in the world," and she termed mother "a woman one cannot help but deeply respect and deeply love."

Other moments came in her visits with Marie Syrkin, who would come to New York from Brandeis University, where she taught comparative literature. Marie was actually mother's closest female friend, their relationship dating back to the 1930s when Marie, born into one of labor Zionism's founding families, was active in the Pioneer Women, and it was maintained to the end of mother's days. I first remember Marie when she spent some time with us, serving as the English announcer in the still clandestine radio broadcasts of the "Voice of Israel" at the end of the 40s. A small attractive woman, whose wit and vivacity matched her good looks, she spent hours with mother on our Tel Aviv balcony, exchanging opinions, sharing life's ironies. Mother relied implicitly on Marie's ability to cut through to the center of any issue and relaxed in the company of a friend whose grasp of Jewish issues matched her own. "I always come away from conversations with Marie refreshed," she used to say. I too enjoyed the company of a woman ready at the drop of a hat to discuss with me, a green twenty-year-old, such lofty abstract topics as the goals of egalitarian societies and the destiny of man. Marie, fine writer and polemicist, was mother's first biographer (she wrote *Golda Meir: Woman of Valor* in 1955, when mother was still minister of labor). Golda looked forward to Marie's visits, both in the U.S. and in this country, and regretted only that Marie had never made Israel her home.

Writing about Marie, it occurs to me that I have said almost nothing about mother's other women friends, though they played an important role in her life. In addition to Leah Biskin (who lived with us for almost twenty years and was practically like an aunt to Sarah and myself) and Marie, of course, three other women stand out.

One is Regina Hamburger-Medzini, the childhood friend who had helped mother to run away from Milwaukee to Denver and came to Israel on the *Pocahontas* with her and father. In Israel, inevitably and naturally their paths crossed: Regina worked first as an English secretary to Ben Gurion and Sharett in the Jewish Agency and then in the foreign ministry in Jerusalem and Washington. What bound them to each other over so many years were the long-standing ties of memory and affection; and though mother was seldom inclined to reminisce, with Regina she could and did occasionally indulge. Her friendship with Beba Idelson was of another kind, less sentimental. Russian-born, a pioneer of the Women's Labor Council for which Golda had worked,

Beba, like Golda, was a very political person, active in the Labor Party and a member of the Knesset. She was one of those women mother admired and liked, an early exemplar of the natural, unassuming feminism that righted ancient wrongs without bravado or bra-burning. Beba, her hair, like mother's, combed back in a bun, and gold-rimmed glasses forever perched on the tip of her nose, was, of all of Mother's friends, the one who seemed to know best how to relate to children and who paid most attention to Sarah and to me.

And there was Henia Sherf, warm, pleasant, understanding, soft eyes matching her soft voice. She had spent her life raising three children, working hard as a volunteer for the Women's Labor Council, always ready to help everybody and endlessly assisting her husband Zeev, who served first as government secretary and then as minister of housing and minister of finance when mother was prime minister. Motherly and low-keyed, Henia was the only individual with whom Mother ever discussed personal matters and feelings, the only woman with whom she had what might be considered a purely woman-to-woman friendship.

As foreign minister, mother's role, I should emphasize, involved more than the making of friends and augmenting of understanding—vital as those were. Two of mother's concrete achievements stand out:

One, having among other things to do with foresight, was the shifting of Israel's singular orientation towards France to include also the United States. During the 1950s it was to France that Israel had looked for arms and support. France was our major supplier of weapons, the only one of three foreign powers (the other being Britain and the United States that, having signed the tripartite agreement to oppose any aggression on the Suez Canal, kept its word when Nasser closed the international waterway to Israeli shipping. On the other hand it was President

Eisenhower's threat of sanctions that forced Israel's premature withdrawal in 1957 from the Sinai and Gaza Strip.

So the ministry of defense had good reason to be satisfied with the orientation that existed and feared that if overtures were made towards the United States we would forfeit French friendship. But Mother was convinced of the folly of putting all one's eggs in a single basket, and sure that France was no less guided by self-interest than other nations and would reverse her pro-Israel policy whenever this no longer seemed opportune. So when John F. Kennedy became United States President in 1961 mother tackled the nay-sayers in the defense ministry, brought Ben Gurion around to her point of view and went calling. The rest is, as they say, history. Kennedy and Johnson understood Israel's vulnerability as Eisenhower never had. We began purchasing and receiving weapons from the United States, and when the Six Day War came around in 1967 and de Gaulle, angered that we defended ourselves without his permission, imposed an arms embargo, the wisdom of mother's insistence was clear: it was the United States that provided life-saving support.

The other achievement was one of skillful diplomacy in the field of economics, helping to obtain for Israel associate status and preferential treatment in the European Common Market. In the spring of 1964, I accompanied mother to Europe, on what came to be known as the "Common Market Tour," that Moshe Allon, head of the Economic Desk at the foreign ministry, had asked her to make with him.

"Shouldn't Eshkol be the one to go along?" mother queried. "After all, he's the finance minister and knows more about these things than I do."

"I don't think so," Allon answered. "He'll work out the economics, but it's you, Golda, that we need to talk to the people."

So we were off. On the plane, Allon asked me to switch seats with him so he could brief mother on some of the financial intricacies involved; only enough, he said, for her to present Israel's needs with respectable familiarity and conviction. For most of the ride they sat, heads together, bent over papers, graphs, and charts. And mother grasped more than he ever expected.

In Europe she met with the foreign minister of France Maurice Couve de Murville, with Italy's President Guiseppe Saragat, whom she knew from the Socialist International, with Italian Prime Minister Aldo Moro, with Britain's Prime Minister Harold Wilson (an old crony of hers) and Belgium's Foreign Minister Paul Henry Spaak. Though she spoke neither French nor Italian, she found a common language with each and presented our needs with authority. Seragat was also an old friend and invited us for the only informal dinner we had on that entire trip. But Couve de Murville, reserved and chilly, was a more difficult nut to crack; I was therefore amused to see my mother smoke between the courses of the magnificent formal dinner he gave on her behalf. Nonetheless, and despite even this, she managed to warm him up.

She left Europe with pledges and promises that culminated in important tariff concessions of up to fifty percent on our agricultural and industrial produce, as well as economic cooperation in the form of development loans—both advances of great importance to the State's economy. "Without Golda's hard work and skill," Allon told me, "we would never have gotten such an agreement."

One of her personal pleasures on that tour was meeting with the legendary Angelica Balabanova, that extraordinary exile from Russia who had been a socialist leader of the 1920s and Mussolini's mentor before he turned fascist. Mother was not, as one may imagine, particularly agog to meet more celebrities, but Balabanova was one of two women socialists (the other being Rosa Luxemburg) whom she tremendously admired and she

171

wanted to pay her respects. On our first free afternoon we went to Balabanova's flat in an old part of Rome. We met a tiny woman in her eighties, dressed all in black, still in possession of all her dignity and fire. I have rarely seen my mother so moved by any encounter. We didn't stay long; they didn't talk much but, for Golda, it was, I felt, like going to see some legendary and mysterious figure.

Another interesting encounter was with the Italian socialist leader and philospher Pietro Nenni, who was not known to be pro-Zionist. However, after several hours of conversation, Nenni perceived Israel and its problems in a different light and became a true friend. He visited Israel to the delight of Israel's Labor movement.

In the summer of 1956, just before mother moved into the foreign ministry, she hosted a wedding in the large airy living room of her labor ministry apartment in Jerusalem: my wedding to Aya Pinkerfeld, an old schoolmate with whom I had renewed my friendship following the break with Channah, a wedding, with only family and close friends, far more to my liking than the gala affair in New Jersey had been. Of course Sarah and Zecharia, Sheyna and my cousins were there, but of all of mother's friends, only Zeev and Henia Sherf and the Zuckerman family attended, who were also within our extended family.

Mother and Aya's family were connected through a series of coincidences of the sort that are understandably not uncommon among Israel's old timers. Both of Aya's parents, Gila and Jacob, came from assimilated Jewish-Polish families and had joined the *Shomer Ha'tzair* ("Young Guards"), a Socialist-Zionist youth movement as teen-agers. Her father had emigrated to Palestine first in 1921 (just about the time mother did) and worked clearing swamps in Emek Hefer, the valley that lies between Tel Aviv and Haifa; he was part of a group, by the way, that was to go on

172

to refound Kibbutz Merhavia, to which my parents had come before. But like so many others, he contracted malaria and tuberculosis and returned disconsolate to Europe, having been told that he would certainly never be able to live on a kibbutz. Resigned, he turned to the study of architecture in Vienna, then married and came back to Palestine in 1925. In the following decades he took up archaeology too, becoming one of the country's leading experts in ancient synagogues, a subject on which he wrote and lectured. Whenever he met my mother, he invited her to tour "my excavations," to which she always said, "Yes, I'd love to, when I have time." To her lasting regret, she never found that time. About four months after our marriage and shortly before the Sinai Campaign, Aya's father was one of four Jews killed by Jordanian sniper fire during an archaeological convention at Ramat Rachel, just south of Jerusalem, in which he had delivered a lecture about old synagogues in Jerusalem.

In Israel, life creates unexpected ties: mother had already known Aya's aunt and uncle, Helena and Karl Reich, eight years before our marriage when their son was one of thirty-five Hebrew University students killed by Arab ambush on their way to rescue beseiged settlers at Gush Etzion, and she had been involved in transferring their bodies. With Aya's other aunt, Anda Pinkerfeld-Amir, a well-known children's poet, the connection was made many years before. We had all met Anda when the family was still young and mother read her verses to Sarah and me. In 1963, in Kenya while attending a Freedom Day reunion for one hundred Kenyan students who had completed courses in Israel, mother was delighted to watch the performance—in Swahili—of a play that Anda had written. Anda spent a year in Kenya with her husband, Arie Amir, the agronomist, who was assisting Kenya in planning its agricultural reorganization, and she helped establish ties with African writers.

I imagine that the most important thing for mother about my

173

second marriage was seeing me out of the doldrums and on the way to a happier life. Until the end of the summer of 1959, we lived with our son Amnon in mother's apartment on Hayarkon, facing the sea. Then we all moved to Ramat-Aviv where we lived next door to each other for almost twenty years. Actually, from this point on our lives intermeshed. The major advantage was unquestionably that we were all together, three generations enjoying each other—generation gap notwithstanding. Our three sons, Amnon, Daniel, and Gideon, gradually became Saturday morning regulars at Golda's hospitable breakfast table; they wandered freely in and out of her living room, at ease with all her important guests; and, when the mood took them, they explored her refrigerator with similar ease, or dressed up in her various caps and gowns. Most remarkable was that my mother even tolerated the boys' dog—though I remember, with just the smallest twinge of envy, that whenever I, as a boy, brought a stray animal home, no sooner was it bathed and fed than mother got home from work and firmly demanded that it be removed. On the other hand, Aya and I became mother's most reliable aides and escorts—Aya in particular because, as a doctor, she could keep a watchful eye on Mother's health and when the need arose, as it often did, had the authority to evict visitors, gently, if they lingered too long. On Friday nights we always ate together. Mother made it a rule not to accept other engagements, political or social; and, after dinner, if she hadn't invited her own guests, she happily joined Aya's and my friends, chatting with them as easily as if they were her own age.

During the week, of course, she lived in her official residence in Jerusalem. This was now the foreign minister's residence, a two-story stone house on a quiet street whose spacious charms befitted mother's new role, though not her temperament. The ground floor, the public part of the house, had a large, well-equipped kitchen where Yehudit, the housekeeper and cook, prepared food for the endless luncheons, dinners and cocktail parties mother was now required to give; a formal dining room for dinner parties; and a damask-curtained drawing room with doors that opened onto the garden. Here the distinguished guests were received and entertained: one day the Ambassador of Ghana, the next day the Ambassador of the United States; one day a delegation from Burma, the next, representatives of the Common Market. And also a steady procession of non-diplomats; many being musicians whom she liked to invite for after-concert gatherings: including Pablo Casals, Arthur Rubenstein, Leonard Bernstein, Rudolph Serkin, Isaac Stern, Gregor Piatigorsky and Mstislav Rostropovich.

Upstairs were the private rooms, bedrooms, a living room and a library stuffed with mementoes of mother's travels, a dining room in which she rarely ate and a kitchen in which on the rare evenings when she was alone she fixed her own snacks, brewed tea for the guards on night duty outside, and, as always, worked on her stacks of papers, signing this, crossing out that, putting something aside for further reference. It was here, too, in the kitchen, that mother's closest friends (and, in this sense, most honored guests) made themselves really comfortable.

She often claimed that she didn't feel at home in that house whose elegance and functioning had to be maintained by a professional staff. But it was difficult for me to detect signs of her discontent. She seemed quite happy to me whenever I saw her at the kitchen table chatting with Yehudit, with Esther who did the daily cleaning, with the woman who came several times a week to bake, and with Itzhak, her driver. Also, almost always there were overnight or live-in guests. Sheyna's granddaughter Ruthie lived there while she studied at Hebrew University and other members of the family bunked there when in Jerusalem. Two sons of dear friends of hers stayed with her in Jerusalem during their school years at the University. "They lower the

average age," mother, now in her sixties, commented. On weekends, if mother couldn't get to Tel Aviv, Sheyna often went to
Jerusalem; Sarah and Zecharia used to drive up from Revivim
with Naomi and Shaul, and Aya, me and our entourage would
meet them there. During summer vacations it was not at all
unusual for us to come to Jerusalem to enjoy the cool mountain
air or even to deposit our children with their grandmother and
go off by ourselves.

"Why don't you take a vacation in Safad and leave the children
with me," Mother would say, encouraging our truancy. One
summer, I remember, Aya and I went to Europe. Aya's mother,
who had once been a high school teacher and was now a social
worker, moved into the foreign minister's residence to take care
of our children in the mornings, playing with them and taking
them out for nature walks. Then in the afternoons it was, if only
her schedule allowed, Golda's turn to take them walking or to
a children's movie or the circus, where a good time, so it was
duly reported, was had by all.

> Mother's term as foreign minister began with a change of
> name. For years Ben Gurion demanded that all public servants
> Hebraize their family names. Now that mother was to represent
> the State, he was insistent. So one morning, Meyerson metamor-
> phosed into Meir, an easy abridgement that retained something
> of the old identity and had other resonances as well: "Meir" is
> the Hebrew word for "illuminate" and the Hebrew version of
> my father's first name.

By the time her term of office ended, she had become a famous
woman. "A major symbol of Israel," the Jerusalem *J Post* called
her, putting into print the spoken and unspoken admiration of
the foreign leaders she had come into contact with, her name
equated with Israel's renascence, survival and continual struggle
for existence. For millions of others she came to stand for liber-

Greeting Mstislav Rostropovich in Tel Aviv. He first stopped to perform in Israel after defecting from the Soviet Union.

From left, Aya, my wife, mother, Pablo Casals. Next to me is Alexander Schneider, a conductor, violinist and close friend of ours and Pablo's wife, Martha. Standing behind us is Mr. and Mrs. Aaron Z. Propes. Mr. Propes was head of Israel's Summer Music Festival.

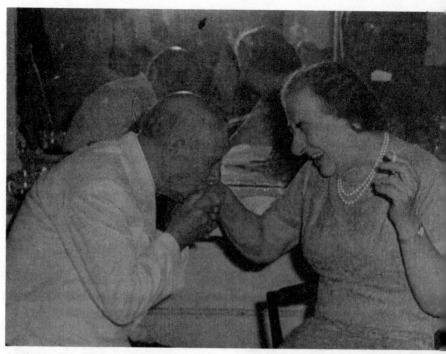

Mother is obviously charmed by Pablo Casals following a concert.

Mother dining with Arthur Rubinstein (far left) and former
Israeli ambassador to the United States Eliahu Eilat.

Mother with one of Israel's leading dramatic actresses of the time, Chana Rovinah of the Habimah Theatre in 1957. There was a mutual admiration between the women, and Miss Rovinah was a great friend of mother's.

ated womanhood, liberated but not deprived, the personification of motherhood and grandmotherhood. She was, for the public—friend and foe alike—a unique, impressive and hard-to-forget personality; the archetypal Jewish grandmother who was also a gallant, infinitely canny and tireless spokesman for an embattled people. Her face, her voice, her clothes, her dry *bon mots* and, above all, the straightforwardness and clarity with which she expressed herself were known and recognized everywhere.

But by 1965, having served in every cabinet since the first, mother wanted to go home and be just herself again. At the beginning of 1966 she resigned as foreign minister and moved back to Ramat Aviv full time. Now she was free for pushing swings, supervising seesaws and even an occasional idle afternoon for sewing bathrobes for three boys, who, to this very day, keep them as remembrances. Never going to sleep before the midnight news, she rose at eight instead of seven; read books that Marie Syrkin brought or sent; indulged in an orgy of concerts, plays, and movies and called up long-neglected friends. She spent weekends at Revivim (it now boasted a profitable plastics industry and thanks to water piped in from the Sea of Galilee, had tea that was fit to drink as well as acres of flourishing peach trees). Also there were day trips to the development towns—Dimona, Kiryat Gat, Kiryat Shemonah—none of which she had been able to visit properly as foreign minister but in all of which she saw the true future of Israel and the continuation of her own pioneering.

Enthusiastically, almost girlishly, she cooked, dusted, did her own washing and ironing (she never allowed anyone to wash her underthings for her, even when she travelled: "It's the sort of thing I do for myself," she said). All told, I think she much enjoyed being Golda Meir, private citizen.

"Do you know what happened to me at the bus stop this morning?" she asked me one day.

"No."

"A woman came up and said, 'Are you Golda Meir's sister?' "

"What did you answer?"

"I said, 'No.' "

In truth, though, mother's life still wasn't all that private. She had kept her seat in the Knesset, continued her activity in the Labor Party, and began each day with a thorough reading of the morning papers. Then, after about a year without homework in the evenings and an air-tight engagement schedule, she was asked to become Secretary-General of the Labor Party, for the express purpose of uniting factions whose divisions had deepened since Ben Gurion formed the so-called dissident *Rafi* splinter party.

"You're the only person who can clear the air and bring about Party unity, Golda," her colleagues told her.

How well they knew her; the outcome was a foregone conclusion. "They're right, you know," she told us. "If we don't get together, the Party may very well lose the next elections." And she was off again, in orbit, meeting with leaders of the various factions, lecturing at *kibbutzim,* talking peace to the ranks of the warring Laborites. Now the evenings were again filled with people from the Party and the government. I would open the door and usher in the visitors; Aya, without having to be asked, would come over with cake and pour coffee while those who preferred alcoholic beverages poured their own, since mother's knowledge of juices and soft drinks was matched by an equally deep ignorance of fermented grape and grain. On Saturday mornings, after the children had had their pancakes, Golda's kitchen once more became the scene of political analysis and debate, and when the phone rang promptly at eleven, the kids knew that it was from Yisrael Galili again, "the Party brains," as mother called him, not knowing that soon he would serve in her cabinet as an indispensable minister without portfolio.

Eventually the mission was accomplished. But if I try to pin-point mother's contribution to the State of Israel during her time out of the cabinet. I'm not sure that I'd say it was her unification of the Labor Party, important though that was. Nor was it in her ongoing endeavors in the field of fundraising—she went on several U.J.A. and Bonds trips. Nor even in the cement-ing of new ties with Jews of the Diaspora, her lifelong though not especially publicized preoccupation.

I think what mother really gave the country then was moral support. One incident may illustrate what I mean. It was just before the outbreak of the Six Day War in 1967 Omens identical to those that had preceded the Sinai Campaign had been ac-cumulating for about a year. Terrorist action, again supported by Nasser but now including Yassir Arafat's PLO, had been stepped up; a united Egyptian-Syrian command (to be joined by Jordan later) had been formed and Syrian forces receiving heavy infusions of aid from the USSR were mercilessly shelling the *kibbutzim* of the Hula Valley and eastern Galilee from safe per-ches on the Golan Heights. In the Gaza Strip and Sinai, Nasser was massing troops and armor and then made two moves whose meaning even the most optimistic and self-deceiving of observ-ers could not mistake: he demanded that the U.N. Emergency Forces stationed for the past ten years in Sharm el-Sheikh (at the tip of the Sinai Peninsula) and Gaza be removed at once; and he closed the Straits of Tiran to Israeli shipping. Mother, anxiously noting these developments, said over and over again, "Look how history repeats itself."

There was no question in anyone's mind that war was in the making; it was only a question of time before the tightening noose was actually pulled. The month before the outbreak of the Six Day War was, I think, something that no one who ex-perienced it in Israel will ever forget. There was incredible ten-sion and growing fear. On the international front, Aubrey Eban, now Israel's foreign minister, paid frantic calls on the powers in Washington, in Paris, in London, appealing for diplomatic intervention from those who had publicly guaranteed Israel's safety. It was to no avail. Wherever he went he was met at best by ambivalence and tentativeness; at worst by blank faces and averted gazes. At home, Prime Minister Levi Eshkol (until the end of May when he appointed Moshe Dayan for the job he was also minister of defense) quietly and efficiently readied the army for the looming onslaught but failed to proffer much-needed reassurances to a jittery public.

Not that anyone gave way to panic, but as the days passed and as the news from Israel's southern borders worsened, we went about daily life with heavy hearts, making makeshift arrangements for self-defense in the event of air raids or even invasion. Slowly people began to clear out basements and cellars, restocking them for use as emergency shelters; we dug pathetic trenches in our gardens and in the public parks and then helped dig similarly pathetic trenches in the children's school yards as well. Women all over the country, everyone actually, dutifully packed overnight bags with the bare essentials we were told to prepare against the moment when sirens might start wailing. Mother blacked out the window of her kitchen so there would be at least one room in which we could read at night, and took to nagging Aya and myself about the blackouts next door.

Although she was no longer a cabinet member, she was turned to frequently for advice and support, and often, in those weeks of what was known in Hebrew as the "The Waiting," drove to Jerusalem for urgent meetings, and a number of ministers became frequent visitors to the house. Whenever they came, I made myself scarce but, of course, I knew that the subject matter of those hours of intense talk concerned nothing less than how to avert the grim threat to Israel's existence.

180

On the first or second day of June, mother was in bed with a debilitating and infuriating bout with the flu when Eshkol, the prime minister, his face ashen and drawn, came himself to speak to her. They were together for a long time. Occasionally either Aya or I went into the room with a cold drink or a cup of coffee. The evening wore on, but Eshkol showed no signs of leaving until finally, at about midnight, Aya reminded him gently that mother was not well and that she particularly needed to rest. When he left, despite the hour, it seemed to both of us that he looked calmer than when he had arrived. I had taken for granted his visit and those of his colleagues, but now it is clear to me that they had come to this woman, who was no longer in the cabinet, not only to hear her views but to derive strength and optimism from her.

A couple of days later, she said with more than usual sharpness, "Tape up your windows tonight." It was the nearest she would come to indicating her certain knowledge regarding Israel's extraordinary preemptive strike, today known as the Six Day War.

The spectacular outcome of the Six Day War is too well-known to bear or need retelling here. What mother could never quite fathom was how was it that those people who were so sympathetic to a weak and vulnerable Israel found it so hard to forgive us for surviving once again against such unexpected and large odds. Nations, whose leaders had barely raised their voices against Nasser's provocations, again, as after the Sinai Campaign, clamored for Israel to withdraw from the territories she had captured. But this time Israel's answer was different. And mother, who had felt so impotent at the United Nations ten years before, now stood up before a giant audience in New York's Madison Square Garden to explain why we wouldn't repeat the error of handing back the same territory without a negotiated peace and firm guarantees for the future:

181

All fair men in the world . . . should in this hour ask themselves this question: Should Israel be urged to withdraw, and if urged, should Israel comply with the request? Consider our situation. Here we are. We're a wonderful people, they tell us. We win wars, though few against many. Boys fall. Many of those that fought in the War of Independence fell. Their younger brothers went to war ten years ago. The younger brothers of those that fought ten years ago went to war only last week.

There are some families who lost sons in all the three wars, but they are wonderful people, these Israelis. Look what they can achieve against such odds. Now that they have won this battle, let them go back where they came from so that the hills of Syria will again be open for Syrian guns, so that Jordanian Legionaires, who shoot and shell at will, can again stand on the towers of the Old City of Jerusalem; so that the Gaza Strip will again become a place from which infiltrators can be sent to kill and ambush.

Is there anybody bold enough to say to the Israelis, "Go home! Begin to prepare your nine and ten-year-olds for the next war, perhaps in ten years." You say "No." And I am sure that every fair person in the world in power and out-of-power, will say, "No" and, forgive me for my impudence, more important than all—the Israelis say, "NO!"

Chapter 10

I N JUNE 1968 MOTHER, aged seventy, resigned as secretary general of the now united Labor Party; the job she had undertaken was done; an amalgamated Labor Party had been formed, and now she felt entitled to live her own life. "I have only a few years left," she said, "and each one of them counts."

Six months later, in February 1969, Levi Eshkol died. Inevitably, factionalism flared up again within the Party, with Moshe Dayan, who was minister of defense, and Yigal Allon, who was deputy prime minister, openly competing for Eshkol's place. Again the cry went out: only Golda can keep the Party together; it is Golda who has the stamina, the skill, the brains to head up a cabinet suddenly deprived of Eshkol's experience, tact and control.

Aya and I were living in New Haven then. Aya was doing research at the famous Yale University Child Study Center and I was performing and teaching cello and doing graduate work at the University of Connecticut. One evening early in March the phone rang. It was mother, from Israel. How were we? she wanted to know. Was all well? Yes, and you? we asked. Well, she was all right too. There was just one thing she wanted to discuss, and then she told us about the prime ministership. "What do you think? What shall I say? Should I say yes? Sarah and Zecharia think I ought to. What do *you* think?"

I don't for a moment want to suggest that Aya and I played a very weighty role in mother's final decision, but we provided her an additional forum for airing her various and grave doubts and I am quite sure that it mattered to her how we felt about it. There were several things that worried her. One was the matter of her health; the formidable list of maladies, beginning with arthritis, migraine, recurrent thrombo-phlebitis of both legs and going on to mild congestive heart condition and cancer of the lymph glands.

"What do the doctors say?" Aya asked her.

"They say to go ahead." mother answered. "They've been telling me to rest for years, but no one seems to think that I can't cope well enough if needs be."

Which was how we saw it too. Whatever her ills, she wasn't some sick old lady. The cancer was in remission, her heart, lung and vascular problems intermittent. The medication she took didn't stop her from rising early in the morning, going to bed late at night and concentrating hard in the hours in between. Her walk was rapid, her voice, though husky, strong, and heaven only knew, her mind was as keen as ever. Now and then she drove herself to exhaustion and went to bed for twenty-four hours, but the next day she'd be up and about as though nothing untoward had happened.

A more serious concern was whether she really *wanted* the job or not. Every time she'd managed to wrench free of the tyranny of public office, she'd been called back again. And the prime ministership, of course, was no ordinary assignment. In all countries, the head of state bears enormous responsibility. In Israel, where

184

war unfortunately has so often been the order of the day, the responsibility is awesome. For mother, to say yes meant, as she saw it, no less than taking upon herself personal responsibility for each and every casualty—whether of terrorist bullets or one of our neighbor's warplanes—and, more than that, responsibility for Israel's continued if much challenged existence. Later, she used to say self-mockingly, "Anyone who wants this job deserves it." But that night, on the phone, she was very tense.

We talked for a long time. Aya and I took turns, sometimes interrupting each other in mid-sentence and taking the phone out of each other's hand. More than we felt competent to advise, we wanted to be sure how mother herself felt. "Well, you know," she said, "I never dreamed of becoming prime minister or planned anything remotely resembling this." As though she couldn't believe that it was she, Goldie Mabowitz, who had been called upon. But in the end, I think it was the very responsibility —and urgency—that helped her to make up her mind. "Someone had to lead this nation," to use her phrase. It wouldn't do to have Dayan and Allon battle each other to the death for the honor; Allon himself had come to her and said as much. Pinchas Sapir, Yisrael Galili, they and others were pressing heavily. "How can I say no?" she asked herself as much as us. And finally, of course, she said yes.

Mother served as prime minister for five years, from 1969 to 1974; five years in the life of a country like Israel is a very long time indeed. Everything happens here with incredible density, so many events, so many crises are crammed into a single year, a month, sometimes a day that they can barely be absorbed and certainly not judged with any perspective or objectivity. But for my mother, they were years of doing what she had always done, and in more or less the same way. The hurdles and pitfalls that faced her, the authority that was needed, the diplomacy and self-discipline called for must have been there, part of her nature, from the start—just as essentially Israel, in those five years, faced the same kind of problems it had faced from the beginning; the absence of peace and security, difficulties attending the absorption and integration of its population made up largely of relative newcomers, and the intricacies inherent in the State's relationship with the Diaspora.

Now that mother was prime minister, those problems—especially the country's peace and security—became the absolute focus of her attention, her perpetual and cardinal concern. It seems ludicrous now—after all those years when the facts should speak for themselves—to feel it necessary, as alas I do, to repeat once again that she was *not* the intransigent narrow-minded militaristic woman that certain circles chose to depict. Her main crime in the eyes of those circles being, I suspect, that while she desperately wanted peace, she did *not* want it at any price and certainly *not* at the price of Israel's annihilation. Moreover, the record shows that as prime minister she voiced this eagerness for peace incessantly, everywhere and to everyone who would listen from the day she assumed office until the day she could no longer voice anything.

Her very first statement as prime minister contained an unequivocal and obviously sincere invitation, addressed to the leaders of the entire Arab world. I have it before me as I write. "We are prepared" she declared, "to discuss peace with our neighbors any day and on all levels."

Nasser's response was published three days later: "There is no voice transcending the sounds of war, and there must not be such a voice—nor is there any call holier than the call to war."

Nonetheless mother reiterated her readiness "to enter immediately into negotiations, without any prior conditions, with everyone of our neighbors in order to reach a peace settlement."

186

The Arab states at once heaped scorn on the proposal. An editorial in a Jordanian newspaper published at that time is indicative of the spirit with which her overtures were received:

> Mrs. Meir is prepared to go to Cairo to hold discussions with President Abdel Nasser but, to her sorrow, has not been invited. She believes that one day a world without guns will emerge in the Middle East. Golda Meir behaves like a grandmother telling bedtime stories to her grandchildren!

Nonetheless mother went on trying; she sent messages to which no one reacted; she authorized a series of third-party envoys—from Britain, from Rumania and from other places still not to be mentioned—all of whom were promptly rebuffed. Undaunted, she continued to indicate her readiness to engage in direct or indirect negotiations, any time, any place, with anyone empowered to talk to her.

In March 1968, just as mother took office, Nasser opened up what was called the War of Attrition, its declared purpose being to enable the Egyptian army to resume control of the Sinai Peninsula from which it could once again launch an attack on Israel proper. Within less than two years of the Six Day War, the Soviet Union had replaced, virtually free of charge, all of the planes, tanks, missiles and munitions that Egypt had lost in that war. Egyptian soldiers bombarded our defensive fortifications on the east bank of the Suez, their commando units regularly crossed the Canal to attack Israeli positions, and Russian experts poured in *en masse* to install, man, and operate the batteries of the SAM2, and later SAM3 interballistic missiles they also supplied.

For Israelis, accustomed to short, swift, instantly victorious wars with the Arabs, the long, drawn out War of Attrition with its daily casualties was a nightmare, and for my mother it was, quite literally, an agony, the source of dreadful if unjustified soul-searching and a constant gnawing anxiety. It lasted for months, from the spring of 1968 until the summer of 1970, and ended with a cease-fire, rather than the sought-after peace. But imperfect or not, it was the best that could be done and that too was something mother had to accept, however grimly. The immediate aftermath brought little cheer. At home, opposition leader Menachem Begin, objecting strongly to the whole idea of the cease-fire, removed his right wing *Gahal* faction from the coalition government that mother had inherited. And, far far worse, in Egypt Abdel Nasser used the cessation of hostilities in order to install, on the west bank of the Canal, the SAM2s and SAM3s that in the Yom Kippur War were to cover the Egyptian forces crossing into Israeli territory. Still, for the time being, the bloodletting had ended, and my mother took a break from the torment of attending weekly, when not daily, funerals and paying the condolence calls, each of which was so shattering.

Then, on a Friday night toward the end of September, when mother was sitting around with Aya and me and some of our friends after an ordinary pleasant Friday evening dinner, we turned on the radio for the eleven P.M. news to hear the history-altering announcement that Gamal Abdel Nasser had died of a heart attack. What now? Who would take over in Egypt? What would happen? "Well, one thing," mother said, "whoever the new president will be, he can't be worse for us, and maybe he'll be better. And maybe, just maybe, he'll want peace."

At first, it looked as though she might be right. Anwar el-Sadat seemed to be a great deal more reasonable than Nasser, more attuned to the genuine and dire economic and social needs of his people, more aware that Egypt's national resources had to be transferred as soon as possible from war into the other spheres if the unspeakable and pervasive poverty was to be at all alleviated. Also his relations with Russia were less felicitous, and

188

he was less prepared to trade his country's independence for military aid. There was another reason for some optimism; Jordan's Hussein awoke to the extreme danger posed to his own authority by the Palestinian terrorist organizations he had happily allowed to operate against Israel from Jordanian territory, and in a bloody civil war he put them down. Adding two and two together, hoping against hope, mother at once put out feelers to the new Egyptian President. Efforts were made through an undisclosed European envoy; the U. S. Secretary of State William Rogers was asked to arrange talks; attempts were made to establish contacts through West Bank emissaries with Hussein —all in addition to ongoing efforts undertaken through the good offices of the U.N., mainly, by Gunnar Jarring. All to no avail.

But in the spring of 1972 mother flew to Rumania for a marathon meeting (it totalled fourteen hours) with Rumania's vigorous President Nicolae Ceausescu. What he had to say seemed too good to be true: Sadat had expressed his willingness to embark on a dialogue with Israel. Not in the highest level perhaps (which meant, mother assumed, not to meet with her) but with someone, with some Israeli, some representative of the Jewish state.

"It is the best news I have heard in years," she told the Rumanian president and, of course, it was. I don't know whether any non-Israeli can fully grasp what it meant to us to bear within ourselves this utter hopelessness (mostly not to be publicly admitted) about ever reaching some reasonable solution to what is variously called the Palestine Problem, the Middle Eastern Problem, the Arab-Jewish Problem, and to have to try to resign ourselves—though my mother never did—to the idea that lasting peace, secure borders, normalcy, in fact, are out of the question—barring a miracle, that is. So naturally Golda came back from Rumania elated:

189

"It looks as if the ice may really finally thaw," she said. Then she waited, and waited, and waited for the other shoe to drop. A week went by, then another, then a month. Nothing. Not a word from Sadat; not a word from Ceausescu, who had undoubtedly conveyed what he had been assured was a bona fide offer. So what was wrong? Had Sadat changed his mind? And if so, why? There was no way of knowing—and there was no one to ask. The disappointment was as bitter as gall, and it was not appreciably less bitter to be the continuing target of charges from various voluble quarters (in Israel, but mostly from abroad) that she wasn't *really* making an adequate effort on behalf of peace or sufficiently committed to the idea to risk anything for it.

Luckily, over the years, she had grown fairly philosophical about such grossly unfair criticism. When reporters asked the same questions *ad nauseum,* she answered calmly, with a smile, tirelessly repeating the same points over and over again, as though to first graders. Once an official in the British foreign office accused Israel in mother's presence of having started the Six Day War because we opened preemptive fire. "I wanted to tell him," she said later, "that it was like saying that they had started the war with Hitler, which might have brought the point home. But I thought it wiser to hold my tongue and smoke another cigarette instead."

Gradually she accustomed herself to the world's cynicism, ceasing to expect fair play—from the United Nations or from her friends of the Socialist International. And I think she also consoled herself with historical and psychological explanations. "A *strong* people does not have to demonstrate the justice of its demands," she observed. "Nobody ever asked Nasser, 'Why did you mass your army in the Sinai Desert in 1967? Why did you fill it with tanks and bombers and guns and 100,000 men?' Nobody ever asked Sadat or Syria's Assad, 'Why did you attack Israel in 1973?' Only a weak people has to prove the justice of its cause. And then, however it tires to do so, it's never enough."

But since I myself never attained mother's eventual relative equanimity in the face of such accusations, I feel that I must, in duty to her and to the Israel that she led, say something about exactly where it was that she stood, and what the principles were that she held fast to.

The first was that there *had* to be a negotiated peace, culminating with Arab recognition of Israel's right to exist; there had to be free intercourse, open borders, the kind of mutual relations common to all friendly states. Why was recognition so important? Why has no Israeli premier, of any political persuasion, ever been willing to forego it? Well, as mother used to put it, she wanted "the real thing," not merely another unstable, fragile armistice agreement that would crumble as soon as Arab leaders felt strong enough to have another go at us under one pretext or another. Peace, she felt, had to be solid. In her first foreign press conference as prime minister, she defined what it was that she was after:

> Nobody has ever proved to us why it is so outlandish for us to expect—after three wars—a peace settlement, a signed peace settlement, something that usually takes place between the parties of any war. The only peculiar aspect of our situation is that the party that is asking for this contractual agreement is *not* the party that lost the war but rather the one that won it . . .
>
> Secondly, nobody has yet been able to prove to us that anything else will create that hope, the basis for that hope, that the war fought in 1967 will be the last war, which is what we want. We don't want to win wars any more. We just don't want wars, that's all.

She was convinced that there could be no real peace so long as the illusion was nurtured in the hearts of Arab leaders that there *might* be a solution without negotiations.

The second principle from which she was not prepared to budge was that peace had to be based on secure and recognized borders. There has been some misunderstanding as to just what this meant to her, so let me try to clarify: It did not mean territory *per se*. When she proclaimed, at the end of 1967, that Israel said no to withdrawal, what she meant was that Israel refused to withdraw for the second time without a signed peace. In fact, she repeatedly offered to withdraw from most of the Sinai in exchange for just peace, either with Nasser or Sadat. In 1971, in talks with Henry Kissinger, she indicated that Israel would be willing to make the first withdrawal from Sinai, and in March 1973, she informed President Nixon that Israel was ready to recognize Egyptian sovereignty over the whole Sinai Peninsula on condition that Egypt agree to a limited Israeli military presence at a number of strategic locations there. But all that she ever got in return was the insistence on withdrawal without the making of peace or any agreement regarding permanent borders, this usually accompanied by an addendum calling for Israel's consent to the return of all the Arab refugees who had fled the country back in 1948.

True, she was not ready to give back every inch of the territory we had taken, but territory *qua* territory was not the issue. "We never set out to conquer anything but the desert," she said. And as for the Arabs, if the 1967 borders were what they wanted, why had Egypt, Syria, and Jordan attacked us in 1967 when those were exactly the borders on which we sat? The Egyptians already had Sinai; the West Bank was in Hussein's hands; and there weren't any Israeli settlements on the Golan Heights then. No, it was "occupied" Tel Aviv, Jerusalem and Haifa that they wanted; and this no one in Israel, least of all Golda, was about to hand over.

So what did mother actually want Israel to keep? And what

192

was she willing to return? Well, as long as there was no one to talk to, there was no point, in her view, to drawing maps. But it is quite clear that she never wanted the whole of Judea and Samaria, as does the Likud Government which is in power as I write. As long as those territories were administered by Israel, Golda felt that it devolved on Israel to see to the health, education and welfare of their inhabitants. But she wanted Israel to be a Jewish State, with a Jewish majority, and if King Hussein had ever agreed to a signed peace, she would gladly have handed him back most of the West Bank.

The Golan Heights, however, are something else. Anyone who has ever visited the Golan immediately understands why it is inconceivable to permit the Syrians to return there or to allow a situation in which the Israel Defense Forces gives up control.

After the Six Day War General David Elazar (known as "Dado"), then commander of the northern front (he was to become chief of staff during mother's prime ministership), took all of us and our children on a tour to the Golan Heights. I know a great deal has been written about the Russian-built Syrian bunkers on the Heights, but nothing can ever lessen the shock of seeing with one's own eyes the concrete enclaves carved into the depths of the mountain at the end of barely perceptible footpaths from which for nineteen years Syrian gunners had shot at Israeli farmers working fields and tending fish ponds in the *kibbutzim* below. Many of the bunkers were connected by labyrinthine passages, and there were complicated underground networks of dormitories, officers' quarters and supply rooms packed with weapons, ammunition and sensitive communications equipment—much like, though less sophisticated than, the Egyptian underground facilities discovered in Sinai. How easy it was for the Syrians, with their targets so exposed and almost stationary in the pastoral valleys beneath them. Even mother, with access to so much information, was horrified, and

I saw on her face an inner iron resolve that these hills would never again be used as shooting ranges.

Other territories not for relinquishing were the Gaza strip, pointing like a knife toward our central cities and from which over the past nineteen years Egyptian fedayeen had infiltrated and killed, and Sharm-el-Sheikh, used twice to block Israeli shipping through the Straits of Tiran and the Gulf of Aqaba; and, of course, Jerusalem.

About Jerusalem, what is there to say that has not already been said. Except, perhaps, that for mother—as for many others —the City of Peace held deep significance, not only for national reasons (though these were always uppermost in her mind), but also because for years she had worked in a city cut in two by barbed wire and unbreachable walls and not a day had passed that she had not resented and abhorred the division.

Although according to the U.N. resolution that brought Israel into being, Jerusalem was to be internationalized and its holy places protected and made available to all, during the War of Independence King Abdullah—without compunctions—had sent his Arab Legion into the Jewish Quarter shelling and desecrating ancient synagogues and cemeteries and turning Jews into the only people in the world forbidden on pain of death to set foot in David's City. And so the situation would have remained had King Abdullah's grandson refrained from joining forces with Egypt and Syria in 1967. "If you don't enter into the war, *nothing* will happen to you," Levi Eshkol had signalled to Hussein. But the Arab monarch made his calculations and decided otherwise. This time the Old City fell to us. "What does Hussein expect now?" mother said. "That we give Jerusalem to him as a consolation prize for not having managed to destroy us?"

Like thousands of others, on her first visit to the Western Wall after the Six Day War, even before the dust of battle had blown away, following tradition mother wrote the word *shalom* on a scrap of paper and pushed it into a cranny between the stones. But her craving for peace was more than merely sentimental; it went hand in hand with her certainty that the one overriding imperative was to insure Israel's survival and protect its people. What she rejected, utterly and persistently, was the idea that one could trade the reality of secure borders for the ephemeral promise of international guarantees that in the past had been rescinded at will. And by the same token, as prime minister, she refused as adamantly to bargain or deal with terrorists. "Give in to their demands," she said, "and we shall all be hostages." So when terrorists fired Katyusha rockets at civilians in Kiryat Shemonah, attacked school-children in Ma'alot, or crossed over from Jordan to plant a bomb on a Jerusalem street, the IDF hit back hard, retaliation was the order of the day, and the terrorism ended.

Hard line? Yes, in matters pertaining to Israel's security and defense, though it didn't always enhance her, or Israel's, image. Paradoxically enough, it was Israel's enemies who often understood her stand better than did her friends. One example was Sadat. In the message of sympathy sent to Israel's government upon mother's death, he wrote: "I credit her for her undeniable role in the process of peace . . . She proved herself always a political leader of the first category." And I think it probable that other Arab leaders, Hussein included, also grasped fully just why it was that Golda drew the lines where and when she did.

Among the many who misread mother, though, of course not deliberately, was her sister Zipke. Four years Golda's junior, perhaps the most relaxed and easy-going of the Mabovitch sisters, Zipke was the one for whom Russia and its pogroms were only a blurred memory, if that, whose relationship with her parents was free of the conflicts that had marred both mother's and Sheyna's growing-up, and who did not join the rest of the family to settle in Palestine. Instead, she married a social worker, Fred Stern, a man who regarded Zionism as a somewhat reactionary movement and, furthermore, made no secret of his "liberal" opinions. Though mother appreciated his keen mind and awesome fund of general knowledge, his attitude towards Israel inevitably cramped their relationship and it was only in her widowhood that we really spent substantial time with Zipke.

The Sterns had lived through years of poverty almost as bad as what my parents had suffered in Jerusalem, but eventually they established themselves in the middle-class Bridgeport, Connecticut, Jewish community, and Zipke in particular became very active in communal life, winning both recognition and respect as the lively executive director of the town's United Jewish Council. And Fred, until his health deteriorated, was highly respected during the years he spent working with delinquent youth of all faiths.

After Fred died of diabetes and Bergers disease, through which Zipke nursed him with characteristic Mabovitch devotion and stoicism, she began to visit my mother, and Israel, regularly. By then she was all alone; tragically, her only son David Raphael died at the age of eighteen from encephalitis contracted while in the United States Army. When Mother became prime minister, Zipke began—at mother's insistence—to spend months at a time with us, and the sisters took great comfort in each other's company. Unfailingly mother saw to it that Zipke was invited to all official functions, while Zipke did her level best to protect mother from her proclivity for overwork.

But in politics they remained worlds apart, and my aunt's common sense and consideration tended to fail her when conversation turned to the Middle East. I remember how it irritated my mother when Zipke used to say—as she did all too often—"Golda, why don't you try to put yourself in Nasser's shoes?

196

Why don't you ever try to understand *his* problems?" And one day in the very middle of the War of Attrition, Zipke painstakingly and infuriatingly explained to mother that the prime minister of the State of Israel—"of all people"—should understand how unbearably humiliated Nasser was by defeat in the Six Day War and how he had no alternative other than to start the fight up again to save face! Mother, anguishing over the Israeli casualties, had a hard time controlling herself. And once, when Sadat came to power, Zipke decided that the sort of interpersonal dynamics and role playing she practiced as a social worker with her clients in Bridgeport might be just the thing to solve the convoluted problems of the Middle East.

"Why don't you sit down and make a list, Golda?" she said one day. "You write down all the things that are most important for Israel, and Sadat will write down everything that matters most to Egypt. And then go through the list together. If Sinai really means all that much to him, give it back, exchange it for something that's high on *your* list. In the end you'll discover that you *can* come to an agreement all right!" It was mother again who showed what I can only call remarkable patience, just pursing her lips and rapidly changing the subject.

One person who did comprehend mother's brand of firmness was Richard Nixon; there was much mutual rapport between mother and Nixon, and it was to stand Israel in great good stead during the Yom Kippur War. Whatever other people said about him, mother always publicly credited Nixon with being a true friend of the Jewish State and one of the few world leaders who had understood and accurately assessed the invidious Soviet role in the Middle East throughout the late 60s and early 70s. Zipke, for whom Nixon, naturally, was anathema, used to ask Golda in amazement, "How on earth can you like that man?" But mother did appreciate him. Had she been a United States citizen, she wouldn't have voted for him—and she certainly

197

didn't condone the follies (and worse) of Watergate. But it was not her practice to pass judgment on the internal affairs of other countries, and she could and did always answer Zipke with the statement that "Nixon has never broken a single promise he made to Israel."

Mother visited Nixon's White House several times. Thanks to his courtesy, my family, I, and Zipke were invited when mother called there the first time, about six months after she took office as prime minister. The War of Attrition was taking a close to unbearably heavy toll by then, and mother's trip to Washington was with a "shopping list": Israel badly needed Phantoms, Skyhawks, and millions of dollars worth of low-interest loans to help pay for them. Of course, she came equipped with all the explanations. Why were we conducting such relentless in-depth bombing on the Egyptian side of the Canal? Because *that* was the only way we could keep Egyptian troops from undermining the defensive fortifications on our side of it. Why were we opposed to the Four Power talks that United States Secretary of State William Rogers suggested? Because Russia had no genuine interest in peace, only in gaining a foothold in the Middle East, because France had adopted a clearly pro-Arab policy, because Britain's self-interest also lay in placating the Arabs, and because the U.S. was the only country out of the four with any reliable commitment to Israel's security. It was of critical importance, mother felt, that Nixon, friendly toward Israel, should be kept fully in the picture and actively back her.

Traditionally, state visits to the United States start in Philadelphia. We met mother at the airport and drove with her to Independence Square, where she was to be formally received by the Philadelphia officials. At the airport she had been greeted by hundreds of people, including a group of school children bearing a placard, "We dig you Golda"; and at the park no less than

30,000 American Jews awaited her, enthusiastically waving Israeli flags. In Washington, she was greeted on the White House lawn by a nineteen gun military salute, a U.S. Marine band playing "The Star Spangled Banner" and "Hatikva," and by President and Mrs. Nixon.

Aya and I attended the formal dinner that was held in her honor at the White House on the evening of her arrival. I must say that, of the many state dinners I attended with mother, this was the most impressive. Not simply that everything was so beautifully arranged, but that we were made to feel so welcome. And when the president rose to speak after dinner, he began by praising Golda as a woman of "unusual capabilities." She reminded him, he said, of "the old Jewish proverb to the effect that man was made out of the soft earth and woman out of the hard rib." Then he recalled that ". . . strong women have played a remarkable and important part in Israel's history," citing the story of the prophetess Deborah, who 3,000 years before had served her people so well by "bringing peace in the land for forty years."

"Madame Prime Minister," he went on to say, "as we welcome you here at this dinner, and as we meet with you today and tomorrow . . . what is really deepest in our hearts is the hope that history will record that after your service as prime minister there was peace in the land for forty years and longer . . .

"We can say to you that while it is fashionable in the great councils of the world to talk rather casually about peace, and while it is, of course, expected that at events like this we use that term almost in an off-hand way, we feel it very deeply. We feel it because the people of Israel deserve peace. They have earned peace, not the fragile peace that comes with the kind of document that neither party has any interest in keeping, but the kind of peace that will last . . ."

In her turn mother emphasized the need for a "real partnership between large powers and small, rich and poor," and concluded by expressing her personal gratitude to Nixon: "You made it possible for me, Mr. President, to bring before you all of our problems, all of our worries, all of our hopes and aspirations, and, if you will forgive me, I have never had the feeling, for one single moment, that I, representing little Israel, was speaking to the president of the great United States . . . I have always felt that I was speaking to a friend who not only listens . . . but shares what I have to say . . ."

The dinner was climaxed by a concert that featured Leonard Bernstein and Isaac Stern.

The next day, while mother was in conferences, Aya and I and the children were given a deluxe tour by the secretary of the White House, and the boys were permitted to sit in the president's high-backed swivel chair.

From Washington mother travelled to New York, Los Angeles and Milwaukee, then back to Atlantic City and New Haven. She met with U Thant and with George Meany, addressed several meetings and conventions and attended a diplomatic reception given by Foreign Minister Abba Eban and a banquet sponsored by the United Jewish Appeal. But in the welter of functions the one that was least routine was the talk Golda gave in front of Amnon's sixth grade class in New Haven's Roger Sherman public school. Just as she made little distinction between the generations and social classes at home, so here she felt that every audience, no matter how young or humble, was worth reaching, and she spoke to the children seriously and without hurrying about Israel's problems.

Though she didn't announce it, mother returned home from the States with a pledge for the Phantoms, the Skyhawks and the low-interest loans.

Mother had thrown herself into her work as prime minister

with such vigor and so fruitfully that there could be no question of her being only an interim premier, and in October 1969 she was reelected to another four years in office.

Matters of security, though they dogged and to some extent defined the years of her highest office, were not the sole claimant of her energies nor were they Israel's only problem. Her first term was marked and marred also by the upsurge of long-existing social tensions and unrest within the country. One episode was a case of much pain and misunderstandings: a somewhat violent rally of Israel's so-called Panthers (named, of course, after the Black American organization they sought to emulate). The local Panthers consisted of Middle Eastern and North African Jews, largely and ironically the offspring of the immigrants whom mother had done so much to help settle. Though a relatively small if loud group and not representative of the political views of the majority of the community, the Panthers did accurately and bitterly reflect the frustrations of a generation that had been reared in poverty despite all the attempts to eliminate it; young people who felt more uprooted than the rest of Israel's immigrant population and were hostile to and alienated from the overall ideology and aims of the country's leadership. Their grievances, usually submerged in a welter of long-simmering discontent, were expressed at this particular demonstration not only via the standard speeches and noisy threats, but also by hurling stones and even a Molotov cocktail at the police.

A few days later, speaking at a meeting of North African Jews, mother condemned this violence, motivated by the same abhorrence of indiscriminate physical force that, among other things, had led her into conflict with the IZL and the Stern Group back in the 40s. One of the movement's leaders responded to what she said with: "Ah, but they're very nice people," to which mother snapped, "Surely people who throw stones and Molotov cocktails aren't so nice, are they?" Looking for sensationalism, the press promptly picked up the second part of the sentence, "... not so nice," and mother was instantly branded a racist, the three words becoming the rather lame battle cry of anyone opposing the Labor Party, the Histadrut—or her. As far as I'm concerned, the only possible significance in the absurd accusation is that in itself it reflects social and cultural tensions that, to an increasing extent, divide the country.

I won't attempt to analyze the origins and manifestations of an extremely complex and also highly charged situation, but I'd like to try to give at least a very superficial summary of the background of that social problem that mother was about to tackle. To begin with, as she herself observed and repeatedly admitted, Israel had not yet achieved longed-for social equality. Most of the "Oriental" Jews came to Israel from Moslem countries that had not yet developed industrially at all and in which, generally speaking, they had been discriminated against and persecuted. Mostly of a higher cultural level than the surrounding population, they had been deprived of the opportunity to express intellectual capacity and acquire the education and skills given to Jews who came from the highly developed countries of the west. In the slightly over two decades that had passed since the immigrants' arrival, over 400,000 units of public housing were built; schools sprouted in each single community—from nursery through to public high school and vocational training centers—and a vast network of clinics and hospitals was spread throughout the country. But undeniably a big disparity still existed between the "Oriental" and "western" Jews. Quite bluntly, on the whole, relatively few "Oriental" Jews graduated from high school and university, and so few were able, on account of lack of qualification—to earn what was considered a good living, and almost none could make their way into influential positions in the government, in the business world and in the army. Many still lived in poverty. Starvation is not part of the Israeli landscape, but families of ten were crowded into two tiny rooms, and crime, juvenile delinquency, and the alienation and disengagement characteristic of desperately poor people anywhere were prevalent and alarming.

Moreover, at the same time as the Oriental Jews were becoming aware of their own deprivation, they could look with understandable and growing resentment at the greener pastures next door. Israel was no longer as austere as it had been in the early 50s, and an increasing number of people spent more money more lavishly and more conspicuously than before. Also, this was the time of an influx of new immigrants—from Russia, but also, following the Six Day War, from the west, and many of the Oriental Jews felt threatened by them; since the country was in a better economic situation than it had been in 1948, these immigrants received significantly greater assistance in housing and absorption than had the families from which the Panthers sprang. Also, like other western Jews before them, many now came with the vocational and technological skills that eased their integration into Israel's economic and cultural life. Mother was well aware of all these factors. And in the early 70s, when frustration found expression in anger, in shrill accusations of intentional discrimination, and in the demonstrations that, at last, drew public attention to long-smoldering problems, mother decided to go into action, to clear up some of the misunderstanding on both sides and to find out for herself what exactly she could do to improve matters. In a speech delivered before the Knesset in July 1971 she clarified what she saw as the core of the problem:

> Beyond doubt, the two issues that call for a special effort are housing and education. Our education laws apply in equal measure to all children in Israel, but it cannot be said·that this equal-

ity is implemented in practice. We cannot claim that there is equality between two children studying in the same class and with the same teacher if one comes from a home in which four persons live in three rooms with a houseful of books and parents able to assit in the preparation of homework, while a classmate comes from a two-room house with ten inhabitants with no one able to help the child to make progress at school. Let us face it: there is no genuine equality between these children . . .

Better housing, more help at school, better jobs, and increased participation in the daily life of the country, these, in mother's view, were items linked in a chain, the last dependent on the first two or three.

But what did the Panthers want first? For once in her long career there seemed to be a real failure in communication, and she couldn't quite fathom their grievances. Housing? she suggested. After school tutoring? More vocational training? Loans and grants could be extended to people who couldn't afford it. No, these didn't seem to fit the bill either. As mother relayed it to us, what the Panthers seemed to want was power, government jobs, seats in the Knesset, here and now. That most people want to regulate their own lives and to determine their own destinies, mother understood better than most. She also knew all about the eroding effects of poverty, but when she thought of implementation, she thought in terms of concrete, practical, tangible and maybe gradual measures; of establishing what had, in fact, been done and what was left to do. But these didn't seem to be quite the things that were on the minds of her angry young opponents. Her meetings with the Panthers became less and less constructive as mother offered one specific suggestion after another and they spoke, with increasing rage, about more things beyond her control, such as the way they were addressed or their sense of being perpetually excluded from the mainstream. She offered remedies—they responded with rhetoric. No one was getting anywhere.

At home mother talked about these frustrating confrontations very often, for however unaffected by it she may have appeared in the public eye, she was a woman quite sensitive to criticism and she always felt that there was *something* more that she should be doing. One Shabbat over breakfast, mother brought up the subject of intercommunal tension again. This time Aya had a suggestion. Why not set up a committee? Not —she anticipated Golda's objections—a committee that would sweep the problems under the carpet or that would issue a report doomed to gather dust on some shelf. What Aya had in mind was a large, prestigious commission, with all the status and weight that the head of state could give it, something, she said, like President Kennedy's Committee on Mental Retardation that in the United States had revolutionized the public's attitude and approach toward mental retardation. We too, she went on, needed a new approach here. Everything that the government had done so far was not enough. Something was going on in Israel that neither mother nor other people in the government seemed to fully to understand. What's more, there was need for sound and full information; the people who suffered from poverty knew where the ache was, but how many such people were there? How many kids actually dropped out of school and at what ages? And why? These and other basic things were not common knowledge, and without more specific information one couldn't really even begin to tackle the problem.

Mother sipped her coffee and said nothing, but, as always, she listened. The result: the Prime Minister's Committee on the Problems of Disadvantaged Children and Youth, which, in fact, encompassed most areas of social welfare. It was the largest single committee ever established in Israel, with 126 experts, each working on a volunteer basis: distinguished educators, public health experts, social workers and psychologists, city planners, economists, representatives of the disadvantaged groups themselves and representatives of the finance, housing, labor, education, and health ministries that dealt with these problems on a day-to-day basis. The specialists explored matters pertaining to housing, to social insurance, to education, to health, to community work and so forth, as well as to such elusive issues as psychological attitudes, their cause and possible cure. Divided into subcommittees, they interviewed witnesses, gathered data and ordered surveys; they met in plenary sessions that mother chaired, pooling and coordinating information. At the end of two years—much longer than mother expected or wanted—the committee issued a three-volume set of recommendations, some of which had already been implemented. Child allowances for large families were increased; low income housing was boosted, including the subsidized rental housing which is rare in Israel; when prices on staple foods were raised, low-income families were given compensatory tax benefits, etc.

The report on which she placed such hopes was published only a few months before the Yom Kippur War broke out, and mother never got the chance to see it fully implemented. But one project did make her happy and gave her the feeling that things were changing. At the time this committee of her's was established, the army set up a parallel committee of its own. I went with mother to visit an army training center in which classes had opened for soldiers who hadn't completed their schooling. Previously the army had simply not accepted recruits with inadequate educations, a policy that not only contained the seeds of a manpower problem but that, in a country in which all job applicants are asked about their army service, stigmatizes and may handicap army rejects for life. The visit was an eye-opener both for mother and for me, neither of us having had much contact with this aspect of Israel before. Each class, in Hebrew, math, geography, history, consisted of some twenty young men, and a teacher, who was often a pretty young woman soldier. Mother would ask the soldiers a few questions. Where do you come from? How many brothers and sisters do you have? How long have you been in the army? From their answers she knew that doors which had once seemed locked and barred now seemed to be opening to them, and she was tremendously encouraged and pleased that she had not turned to her separate ministers and said, "Do something about health; do something about education," and so forth, but that she had taken the responsibility on herself.

In recent years, community centers offering courses, lectures and social activities for children and adults alike have sprung up like mushrooms all over the country; and an extensive program of urban renewal has been undertaken with joint funding by U.S. Jewish communities. Both these developments—taken for granted today—had their roots in that prime minister's committee and its recommendations.

Another of mother's most satisfying, if least known, activities as prime minister was encouraging immigration from the Soviet Union. Just about the time that she took office the gates that Moscow had barred to Jewish emigrants in order to "punish" Israel for the Six Day War were opened again and exit permits began to be issued. Applicants wishing to leave were still run through a gruelling, often prohibitively expensive, obstacle course. Virtually no applications were processed in under a year; most took a lot longer and there was enough arbitrariness in the procedure so that no Jew could ever know in advance whether a request would be granted or not. At best, potential emigres were fired from their jobs and prevented from getting other work or demoted, or, if they were students expelled from the university or technical school in which they were enrolled. At worst, they were arrested on trumped-up charges of subversion or, if unemployed, jailed as "parasites." In between, there was no end to the subtle tortures devised by the regime. But, since the USSR was interested in détente then and thus vulnerable to pressure from the United States and western Europe, Jews were let out as bargaining chips.

For the most part, mother worked on behalf of the immigrants without benefit of the media. Getting Jews out of the Soviet Union was the responsibility of a special government Department for the Rescue and Immigration of East European Jews; and getting them settled in Israel was the job of the Ministry of Absorption. But emotionally, intellectually and practically mother was deeply involved with both procedures and, most particularly, with the immigrants themselves. The busiest of days would often enough be capped by a visit from new Russian immigrants to her home in Jerusalem or Tel Aviv. Over tea that she sometimes served herself she would shower them with questions about their troubles in getting out of Russia, how their absorption in Israel was progressing and what more could be done to help them. On her own initiative, and quite often in the middle of the night, she would receive groups of immigrants arriving at the airport from the transit post in Vienna. She took a personal interest in the individual situation of dozens of these newcomers, getting them in touch with the proper authorities and securing speedy action. For their part, they thought of her as "Golda *shelanu*"—"our Golda," as she had been called by them in Russia. I myself saw many former Russians approach her at various times with: "I saw you in Moscow," or "I was in the synagogue that Yom Kippur," or "I passed your car then," and questions such as, "Do you remember me? I gave you a letter for my cousin." Just as she had been before, so now for these immigrants mother was a symbol of Zion itself.

Actually, her involvement with Russian Jewry had begun even before she was appointed minister to Moscow, as early as 1942, when Shaul Avigur, the modest, dedicated man who had taken upon himself practically the entire responsibility for organizing and conducting "illegal" immigration from Eastern Europe to Palestine, introduced Mother to a twenty-two-year-old, Zvi Netzer, the first Jew to come out of Russia during World War II. Polish-born, Zvi had been active in helping Jews escape from Nazi Europe when he was arrested by the Russian secret police during a cross-over from Russian-occupied to German-occupied Poland and imprisoned in a Siberian camp. When he was freed he made his way to Teheran, met Shaul's people and from there to Palestine.

Shaul introduced him also to Ben Gurion and Berl Katznelson, but it was mother who showed the most avid interest as he sat with her in the Histadrut's executive offices. "I started to tell her about the Russian Jews," he told me, "but I hadn't gotten five sentences out of my mouth when she stopped me and said, 'This has to be recorded!' She called in a stenographer, and for three or four days we spent three to four hours together as my testimony was taken down. I told her about how Jews fleeing into Russia were arrested and, like me, sent to camps; I described the brutal conditions of the camps, which were not then the public knowledge they are today and the way Russian citizens collaborated with Nazi executions of Jews. She listened so intensely that I felt as though she was absorbed in each and every word. From that point on we became fast friends, allies in a common cause. 'Call me when you get to Tel Aviv,' she made me promise when I left for the kibbutz where I was to start my new life as a farmer.

"Over the years we met frequently. In 1945 she asked to see me just before I was sent to Poland once again to bring out the survivors. By this time I had a wife and baby daughter, and Golda thought it wasn't fair that I be separated from them. 'Can't you find someone else?' she asked Shaul. Well, he couldn't, and when I was back in Palestine again in 1948 she summoned me to hear what I had to say. By then everybody was involved in the life and death struggle that had already started with the Arabs, so her calling me in then ment a lot." As time passed, she became more and more passionately concerned about the Jews of Russia, and whenever she could she raised the banner high.

In 1953 mother went to the U.N. to protest the anti-Semitic campaign Stalin conducted so ruthlessly in the last years of his life and to refute the age-old lie of the so-called Jewish conspiracy to undermine the regime. As foreign minister, she kept close tabs on what was being done for East European Jews; and when she became prime minister she felt the need to transfer many operations in this sphere from the supervision of the foreign ministry to her own office.

From there she also contributed to disseminating information about the Soviet attempts to "spread fear and terror among (Jews) so that they should not dare to express their longing to emigrate to Israel," to quote the words she used in the Knesset in 1971 describing the significance of the Leningrad trials of Soviet Jews who were seeking to emigrate to Israel. In the same year the first world conference on Soviet Jewry was held in Brussels, Ben Gurion its chairman. Mother didn't attend in person, since she believed that this would be tantamount to engaging in direct political confrontation with the Kremlin, but her instigation and prompting, as well as her assistance in planning and organizing, was in no small measure what got the conference under way and helped it mobilize world sentiment on behalf of Soviet Jewry. A second Conference was held in 1976, and at this one mother, no longer in office, was a major speaker.

"What is there decent, revolutionary, or socialistic about not letting people live where they want," she asked, addressing delegates from thirty-five countries.

At home in Israel, an important decision she made as prime minister helped turn the tide in Jewish immigration. In August 1969 mother received a petition signed by the heads of eighteen observant Jewish families in Georgia, with a copy enclosed for the U.N. Human Rights Commission in New York. It was an extraordinary document; written in Russian, it explained that for months, and in many cases years, though the necessary papers allowing them to join relatives in Israel had been in their possession, these Jews had still not received the essential exit permits and that the hundreds of imploring letters they had sent to the authorities as, with growing desperation, they waited, had, to use their own phrase, vanished like "tears dropped on desert sand." The reason, they stressed, for their yearning for Israel was not so much their desire to leave the USSR but their intense spiritual hunger for Zion, for the land of their forefathers, for a Jewish State. And for this they would wait, if they had to, forever. Also they made clear that they were writing in the name of many many others, and they asked that the government of Israel transmit their peition to the U.N.

Mother was shaken by their courage and by the intensity of their sense of belonging to the Jewish people. From the Knesset floor, addressing humanity as a whole and the Soviet Union in particular, she responded:

> . . .We shall do whatever we can. We shall spare no effort to see to it that all men of good conscience—be they Jew or not—all those who cherish liberty will raise their voices with us in defense of the liberty of others . . . For those who seek to enslave are themselves never free. They may rule and dominate but their spirit remains that of slaves . . . The State of Israel is firmly

211

resolved that under no circumstances will it compromise the inalienable rights of the Jews of Russia nor surrender its own right to welcome them here, however long and hard the struggle may be . . . This government has never accepted the position (regardless of how well-intended its advocates) that our voices must not be raised lest we further endanger those who are already imperiled . . . I solemnly promise the heroic Jews of Russia, who have risked so much in order to reach out to us in their distress, that we shall not lag behind . . .

It was the reverbation throughout the world of the State of Israel's repeated and uncompromising demand to free the Jews of Russia, a demand articulated and personified by Golda, that was eventually to shame the Soviet government in the eyes of the world and thereby make possible the emigration of thousands of Russian Jews.

CHAPTER 11

A S I WRITE, Israeli soldiers are still in Lebanon in the sequel to the controversial and protracted war; the country, bitterly divided, is in a somber mood; and Prime Minister Begin has handed in his resignation. But for me and for much of the rest of the country the Yom Kippur War that began in October 1973 is still the traumatic event it was ten years ago. It is the war that caught us off guard, and thus constituted a turning point in the nation's history, forcing us to reevaluate our view of Arab military capabilities and issuing in a new era in Israeli politics. It was that war, in a way, that marked the end of my mother's career, finally, and somewhat ironically, obtaining for her the retirement she had so long sought.

For the country as a whole and, of course, for Golda personally, the Yom Kippur War was deeply tragic. Though no one considered her directly responsible for the terrible blunders that had led to our lack of adequate preparedness on that Saturday afternoon of October 6 when Israel was simultaneously attacked on two fronts, she herself never quite recovered from "a nightmare that will always be with me."

The facts of the matter can be simply noted; the people in charge of Israel's military affairs had misjudged the situation and thus inevitably and inadvertently had misled mother. Complacency was caused in large measure by the lightening and total success of the IDF's Six Day victory just six years before, the euphoria that followed the war and the dreadfully mistaken conviction held by almost the entire military establishment that the Egyptians neither could nor would cross the Suez Canal, that even if they tried to do so our forces would trap and crush them within a day.

Along with this extreme confidence in our military power, there was something deeper, a desire for peace so strong that it was difficult to accept that the Arabs didn't share it, especially since it seemed so impossible ("unlikely" was the word most often used) for them to embark once again on a losing battle with us. As mother phrased it afterward, "We had talked ourselves into thinking that because we saw no point in war, the Arabs didn't either."

In retrospect the indications of war were visible earlier, particularly that September when first Syria, then Egypt, bolstered their forces at the northern and southern borders respectively. Hadn't there been buildups often before, notably the previous May? At that time our reserves were mobilized and then the tension subsided, either because of this response or maybe of itself. In any case, if today hindsight makes those September signals glaringly visible, at the time—which is what counts—they misinterpreted them in line with the prevailing notion of Arab capacities and intentions. While the amassing of enemy forces was duly noted, it was explained as a defensive Syrian response to Russian-instigated propoganda that *we* were about to attack plus autumn maneuvers in Egypt.

Not surprising then that at the end of September mother felt efficiently confident to take off for Austria to deal with what was, in her eyes, another emergency. But prior to the meeting with Chancellor Bruno Kriesky she was scheduled to address the Council of Europe meeting in Strasbourg. A few days earlier two Palestinian gunmen had broken into a train carrying Soviet Jews at last bound for Israel just as it crossed the Austrian border at Schonau (where they were to be met and cared for by Israeli representatives), took seven hostages and informed the Austrian government that if the transit station wasn't closed at once they would violently retaliate against Austria itself. Chancellor Kreisky responded to this blackmail at once, and mother, feeling as strongly as she did both about Soviet immigration and about not giving way to terrorism, decided to go to talk to Kreisky and to implore him not to surrender to the threats. She came back empty-handed, dejected and appalled by the chancellor's easy compliance. To this day no one knows whether that attack at Schonau was by way of being a diversionary tactic or not, but it did succeed in distracting government attention from the Sinai and Golan, and after the war mother was criticized in some quarters, I think most unfairly, for having left the country at so crucial a juncture.

In the few days she was away the military situation had appreciably worsened; at once on her return she met with members of the cabinet and representatives of the intelligence community. She asked again if the Arab armies were not capable of launching an attack from their present positions. The answer was yes, they theoretically were; but all of those present (their number included two former chiefs of staff and the present C.O.S.) reiterated their interpretations of Syrian defensive moves and Egyptian maneuvers, and gave as their considered opinion that imminent attack was *most improbable*. It was, however, decided to report on the situation to the full cabinet right after the Yom Kippur weekend.

215

On Friday morning another meeting was held after it had been learned on Thursday night that Soviet families stationed in Syria were being sent home. This had happened before just prior to the outbreak of the Six Day War, and it lit a red light in mother's mind. But again her advisors assured her that there was no immediate threat and that in the unlikely event that war did break out, we would have more than enough warning time for the regular army to cope until the reserves reached the front lines. Minister of Defense Moshe Dayan, then-Commander in Chief David Elazar, and the head of intelligence were all of the same opinion. Meanwhile the army was placed on alert, just in case; and mother decided to convene another meeting of the cabinet members in the vicinity.

I saw mother shortly after noon when we paid a condolence call together on Simcha Dinitz, whose father had just died. Dinitz was currently Israel's ambassador to the U.S. and had worked closely with mother ever since she was foreign minister. She was uncharacteristically tense and nervous. "The Russian families are pulling out of Syria," she told Dinitz glumly, and added that she was alarmed by the troop concentrations on the Suez and the Golan.

Nine cabinet members were present at the emergency meeting called for that afternoon. Others had already left to spend Yom Kippur at their homes in Jerusalem, Haifa and on *kibbutzim*. Yom Kippur is the most solemn fast-day of the Jewish calendar, the one day of the year in which everything in Israel, with the exception of emergency services, closes down. There is no radio, no TV, and public and private transportation alike come to a halt. Technically, Yom Kippur (like all Jewish fasts and feasts) begins at sundown, but by mid-afternoon activity has already stilled and people begin making their preparations at home. Under the circumstances, recalling ministers who had already left seemed unwarranted. Anyway, those in Tel Aviv

216

convened in mother's office with the chief of staff and the chief of intelligence, and they passed a resolution permitting mother and the minister of defense to authorize a call-up, if need be, without the approval of the full cabinet, something usually required.

Mother joined us for the traditional pre-fast meal. She was restless and tired. Aya and I were expecting friends, and normally mother would have spent the evening with us. But this time she excused herself. "I'm not in the mood," she said, and left for her own house.

Inevitably, the question arises: Could she conceivably have done other than she did? In her memoirs, she answers in the affirmative:

> Today I know what I should have done. I should have overcome my hesitations. I knew as well as anyone else what full-scale mobilization means and how much money it would cost, and I also knew that only a few months before, in May, we had had an alert and the reserves had been called up, but that nothing had happened. But I also understood that perhaps there had been no war in May exactly because the reserves had been called up. That Friday morning I should have listened to the warnings of my own heart and ordered a call-up. For me, that fact cannot and never will be erased, and there can be no consolation in anything that anyone else has to say or in all the common sense rationalizations with which my colleagues have tried to comfort me.

And she often said the same to us, though I remain unconvinced. I think she did all she could do, that it was much more her colleagues who let her down.

At any rate, that afternoon Bar Lev had come to the house and on the way out, patting mother on the shoulder, said in his quiet, reassuring way, "Golda, I will sleep well tonight." Bar Lev was then serving as minister of commerce and industry, but had formerly been chief of staff; the fortifications he had designed along the Suez saw us through the War of Attrition; he was surely in a position to know how our forces could best be deployed in case of an attack. Dayan also exuded confidence in Israel's fortifications, planes, military and men; and though mother had never been mesmerized by his famous charisma, she had worked well and closely with him during the previous four years; and certainly his military acumen was not to be disregarded. To these voices were added that of Elazar, the chief of staff who had won the Golan for us during the Six Day War and whom mother had always regarded highly; Yisrael Galili, her invaluable minister without portfolio, whose opinions mother sought on all matters of importance; our intelligence experts, known to be among the best in the world; and the input of U.S. intelligence that concurred with our own. For mother, for any prime minister for that matter, even one more intimately familiar with military affairs, to have pitted intuition and unease against such seasoned judgments would, it seems to me, have been rather arrogant and foolhardy.

Once war was under way, however, mother gave the country the required leadership. In the midst of uncertainty she provided moral authority. Reeling herself from the high casualties and grim forecasts of the first few days of that awful war, she radiated a steadying faith in the IDF's capacity to meet the challenge. And at seventy-five, repeatedly called upon to judge between conflicting opinions of experts, she arrived at decisions, universally hailed as sensible and well-timed, without fuss or panic. . . .

We realized that something had gone terribly wrong early on Saturday morning. Aya and I were awakened by the strange whirr of a plane flying back and forth overhead; and since I was up and worried about mother, I went to see how she felt. I found her in the process of dressing, getting ready to leave for her office to meet with Elazar and Dayan, among others. She had received a four A.M. phone call from her military secretary, telling her that the Egyptians and Syrians were to launch a joint attack late that afternoon.

That morning she made two crucial choices. One concerned the size of the troop mobilization now immediately required. Elazar pressed for a general call-up and to begin an immediate counter-attack; Dayan recommended limited mobilization, arguing that a larger mobilization before any shots were fired would leave us open to charges of aggression. Mother, reasoning that if an enemy attack were, in fact, to be launched, Israel's forces must be in the best possible position to repel it, sided with Elazar. The other question was whether or not to open up with a preemptive attack of our own. Elazar favored repetition of the tactic that had been so effective in the Six Day War and that, he argued, would save hundreds of casualties among the front line troops. As for Dayan, he opposed a preemptive strike on the same grounds that led him to advocate only a limited call-up. This time mother sided with Dayan; a preemptive strike might cause us to forfeit U.S. help if we were indeed to need it later, as it turned out that we did. After the meeting she notified the U.S. ambassador of the pending Arab attack and our own resolve not to strike first, and at noon she assembled the full cabinet, its members called away from homes and synagogues.

By eleven A.M. news of the mobilization had spread, the streets were alive with ominous movement. At home, we waited for mother to phone, but the first we heard from her was at six P.M. with the rest of the nation, when she broadcast to the people of Israel:

Shortly before two P.M. today the armies of Egypt and Syria started an offensive against Israel. They launched a series of air,

219

armored, and artillery attacks in Sinai and the Golan Heights. The IDF has entered the fight and is beating back the offensive. We have no doubt that we shall be victorious.

She spoke gravely and firmly, and it was clear that in her heart she had total faith in the ability and courage of the IDF. But the first days of the war, when Israel was outnumbered in guns, and tanks, and planes, and men, and at the severe psychological disadvantage of having so grievously erred, were literally harrowing for her. She often came home after midnight, showered, changed her clothes, caught a few winks of telephone-interrupted sleep, and was off again. Composed, pale, only her posture hinted at her heavy heart—and her fears.

Moreover, with the reversals of the first bloody few days, something inside Dayan, so confident before, seemed to have snapped, and mother had not only to help maintain the morale of cabinet and country but also to counter his unexpected, potentially contagious pessimism. When Dayan suggested withdrawal of our battered troops in the Golan, Golda asked Bar Lev to assess the damage for himself, authorizing him to give whatever orders he deemed necessary—a move that was to result in the strong counterattack that pushed back the Syrians. When Dayan made the same suggestion regarding our positions in Sinai, she agreed with Elazar that we go on with a counteroffensive and dispatched him there to supervise it. And, at the same time she refused to accept the resignation Dayan offered, knowing how damaging the departure of a national hero would be to the country's already shaken self-confidence.

The tide of the war began to turn only on October 10, with the recapture of the Golan, the IDF penetration into Syria and, in the Sinai, the smashing of the Egyptian armored advance. Mother knew that the tide had finally turned when Elazar phoned her, "Golda, it will be all right. *We* are back to being ourselves and *they* are back to being themselves." That evening she announced on television, with more relief that her viewers probably realized, "The Golan Heights is in Israel's hands and Israeli forces are in pursuit of Syrians and on the offensive on the other fronts." And she added, "We, as Jews, most especially cannot afford the luxury of despair."

But all was not well yet. The IDF had still not crossed the Suez nor fully routed the Egyptians; and its ability to continue the offensive was hampered by a critical shortage of armaments. England and France had crumpled before Arab threats, and indifferent to our life-and-death struggle, had embargoed all weapon shipments to us, including already promised parts and replacements. President Nixon had agreed to send us tanks, ammunition, rockets, and planes, as well as clothing and medical supplies as soon as possible. But the five or so days that their arrival was held up, first by the bureaucratic maze in Washington, then by the refusal of European countries to permit the Skyhawks and Phantoms destined for our use to refuel on their territory, seemed like decades. There were frantic calls back and forth to Dinitz in Washington, including one at 3 A.M. in which mother shouted, "Call Kissinger now. Never mind the time. We need the help today because tomorrow may be too late." Finally the precious cargoes arrived, massive aid, so vital in itself, that also reaffirmed America's commitment to us. To President Nixon, mother remained grateful to her very last day.

Militarily Israel had won the war. The IDF had routed the Egyptian and Syrian armies, obtained air superiority on both fronts and deeply penetrated into both Egyptian and Syrian territory across the Canal and the former Golan lines, even before the Russians came to the rescue of their defeated clients to demand a cease-fire. In the course of the next months, disengagement agreements were reached first with Egypt, then with

Syria; reservists came back from duty and eventually prisoners of war began to return. It looked as though life was returning to normal. Cafes reopened; street lamps lit up night-time streets; men took over the wheels of busses that women had been driving.

But nothing and no one remained the same after that Yom Kippur. The country was stricken by a loss of faith—in itself, its aims, its leadership that still has not altogether been resolved. People went about their day-to-day activities feeling somehow disoriented, their worlds shaken. Heroes were toppled, certainties revealed as deceptive, and, above all, two thousand five hundred men had died in battle, and soldiers and POWs returning from the fronts told and retold the stories of what it had been like to find themselves in unequal combat; in tanks inadequately prepared for battle, waiting for reinforcements that were deadly slow in coming. We had won the war, the enemy had been defeated, but much had gone awry and the public mood was almost as bleak as though we had lost.

Throughout Israel, protest movements sprang up. On the right, ultra-nationalists protested mother's close cooperation with United States Secretary of State Kissinger in reaching the disengagement accords that let the boys come home and what they saw as her willingness to make concessions in order to maintain the friendship and assistance of the United States. On the left there were renewed charges of inflexibility and outspoken, often hysterical demands that the government quit, that it pay the price of its awful mistake, that compromise and withdrawal be the order of the day. In between there was the proverbial silent majority, bewildered if not actually on the barricades. Much of the national rage (and it is not, I think, too strong a word) focused on Dayan, whose pre-war glory made him ripest for a fall, but mother too came in for her share of reproach.

Daily she faced lines of young demonstrators bearing placards that said, "Golda, go home!" read the same words published in huge ads that appeared in the newspapers and heard them again in radio and TV interviews with protesters, among whom were soldiers whose comrades had fallen next to them and women who had lost husbands, brothers and children, plain people whose grief mother had no desire to ignore and whose anger hurt her deeply. Whatever the specific political affiliations of the protest movements, they were alike in the clamor for "new leadership" and "change."

Mother never questioned the legitimacy of the protests, or of protest itself. "We are a democratic state," she said. "Freedom of speech and criticism are innate rights respected in all democratic societies. In the present situation it is only natural that questions be asked which need explanation and reply." And where someone else might understandably enough have become withdrawn or set off on a lengthy campaign of self-justification, mother kept her mind on the job and did her best to provide the country with strong, determined leadership.

When the fighting stopped, mother did some travelling. First she went to "Africa," as the territory we held on the Egyptian side of the Canal was called, and then to the Golan Heights to see for herself and to talk personally and directly with the troops. Finally she went to London and Washington. In London, she opened a meeting of the leadership of the Socialist International that she herself had asked to convene. For years she had attended the meetings of the International and most of the heads of the Socialist parties, both those in power and those who led the opposition in their countries, were old and presumably staunch friends and allies of hers, extensions as it were of her cronies and colleagues in her own Labor Party. Now, tired and tormented as she was, she made it her business to meet with them again. She had a very important question to ask: how did it happen that the socialists who headed various European governments had not permitted planes that were en route to Israel during the war to refuel on their respective territories, en route, she repeated, to one of the few states anywhere that had been led by a socialist party since its birth and of which she—with her impeccable socialist credentials—was the prime minister? She knew that she would get no solid answer, but she needed badly to express some of the sense of outrage at their desertion of us —and of her.

In Washington she spoke personally with President Nixon presenting Israel's position on the disengagement of forces with Egypt. Ever since the ceasefire she and members of her government had been conducting the most complex and delicate negotiations to this end—via Dr. Kissinger. As sympathetic and boundlessly attentive as Kissinger was to Israeli interests, there was at times much pressure placed on Israel to make unacceptable concessions, and mother wanted to make quite sure that we would not be asked to withdraw unilaterally (something that Egypt and Russia were pressing for), and that certain minimum demands of our own were met (as they were), including an Egyptian-Israeli meeting and immediate prisoner exchange.

When she came back, in addition to everything else, mother also tackled the job of keeping the ever-fragmenting labor "alignment" together. To avert a cabinet crisis in the midst of an already restive national mood, she once again prevented Dayan from resigning. Then, following the December elections (due to the war they were moved up from October), in which the Labor Party under her leadership again won the largest number of seats but not enough to form a majority on its own, mother set out to form a coalition government under the most trying of circumstances. The divisiveness that was so badly afflicting the country as a whole was also permeating the Alignment itself, and inordinate and nerve-wracking bargaining and persuasion were required to form a new government—which mother did manage to do by the middle of March.

But a month later, on April 11, she handed the President of Israel her written resignation. Why? What had happened? In her autobiography she wrote only that she "was beginning to feel the physical and psychological effects of the draining past few months." There was, of course, much more she might have said, but in the main that was it; there was no single straw that broke the camel's back, nor any one episode, but rather a growing burden that could not longer either be diminished or be borne —even by her. She had never even wanted a second term in office. As far back as the winter of 1972 she announced publicly that she would not run in the '73 elections. Besides, Golda had done what she set out to do; the War of Attrition was over; the borders were quiet. She had had her fill of saying over and over again—and to much the same people—that Israel would accept nothing less than a negotiated peace and secure borders. She longed for personal liberty, to step into her car without body-guards, to go to a play or concert whenever she wanted without thought of security. Also, her illnesses were beginning to catch up with her. At one point there was a series of exhausting cobalt treatments that only we, her doctors, Lou Kaddar, her devoted secretary and Mordechai Gazit, who now headed the prime minister's office knew about, and which were discreetly administered at Jerusalem's Hadassah Hospital at six before other A.M. clinic patients arrived.

But all this notwithstanding, the Party was not ready or willing to let her go. One day that summer I received an urgent telephone call from Pinchas Sapir and Yigal Allon asking that we help persuade mother to lead the ticket once again. So we met —Aya, I, Sarah, Zecharia, mother and a number of cabinet ministers—around the big table in the dining room of the prime minister's residence. Before the meeting began mother took me aside and whispered, "Menahem, I *am* very tired. Please remember that I have really had enough. All of my life I've worked but now I *must* rest." But, as had happened so often before, the familiar arguments were put forward once again: "There *is* no one else, Golda—and you know it—who can keep the Party together. Please, please don't let us down." She had never let anyone down, and she wasn't about to do it now. So she sighed and said yes.

After the war she made two more tries at getting out. Before the December elections she called for and received a vote of confidence from the Party's Central Committee. The ballot was secret; those who felt that mother should, or could, no longer represent the Party were given the opportunity to say so without anyone being the wiser. But the vote was 291 out of 341, and mother could not claim that the majority didn't want her. In March, while the factional struggles were still much in progress, she again said wearily that she wanted out, only to be called back by the pleas of the frantic Party leadership.

But, somehow, despite the vote of confidence, the importuning and the stated wish of most members of the Party, mother was denied the absolute backing that she needed. The very people who had begged her to run for office in December, her lifelong friends and comrades, proved unwilling to stand up— as she expected them to—and speak out on her behalf against the barrage of public criticism.

In fact Dayan not mother was at the center of the storm. True, he had been cleared of "direct responsibility" for the mishaps that occurred preceding and during the war itself by the Agranat Commission of Inquiry established in November. But the terms of reference of the Commission did not include investigation of "ministerial responsibility"; for many people both within and outside the government the contrast between the Commission's harsh judgment of Elazar (whose resignation it recommended) and of people within the intelligence establishment on the one hand, and its gingerly exoneration of Dayan on the other, was unacceptable. At this point mother would have preferred that Dayan leave the government on his own; but, once cleared by the Commission, he felt it was no longer incumbent upon him to do so; and Golda's asking for his departure, she suspected, would have sparked the coalition crisis she was trying so hard to avoid.

But mother was also criticized not only for her refusal to throw Dayan to the wolves but for something entirely different: her so-called "kitchen cabinet." Since there has been misunderstanding, at least in Israel, on the subject, this might be the time for me to say a few words about it. The "kitchen cabinet" comprised her most trusted ministers, those with whom she felt the need to meet and talk whenever the situation required consultation. Cabinet members got into the habit of dropping in on a Saturday night, before Sunday's formal cabinet meetings. They came to air ideas, to exchange thoughts, to see where winds blew without the constraints of agenda and protocol. None of these meetings resulted in binding decisions; they were not mini-cabinet meetings or substitutes for such meetings. They were just mother sitting around in her kitchen with her friends and advisers. Why in the kitchen? Because kitchens were a place she liked, maybe because she was a woman whose own kitchen was warm and spotlessly clean and always orderly so people could be invited in for a cup of tea. When she had an hour to spare abroad, one of her favorite occupations was window-shopping for kitchen gadgets, and she often brought something in this line home for Sarah or Aya. But the people who talked with such hostility about the "kitchen cabinet" hinted dreadful things that might have been brewing over those cups of tea. And that didn't help either.

The Agranat Report not only cleared mother of all and any misconduct during the war, but warmly commended her:

Golda Meir acted fittingly during the critical days that preceded the outbreak of the war. Immediately upon returning from overseas she met with the deputy prime minister, the defense minister, Minister without Portfolio Galili and the chief of staff mainly concerning the situation in the Golan Heights. At the end of the consultation she decided to bring the situation along the borders to the attention of the cabinet at the coming weekly session scheduled for Sunday, October 7.

On Friday, October 5, she decided on the basis of disturbing reports reaching her that day to convene all ministers who were in Tel Aviv at that time. At that meeting the ministers asked the minister of defense and the prime minister to decide on mobilization of need for this should arise during Yom Kippur . . .

The prime minister used her authority properly and wisely when she ordered mobilization of the reserves on Saturday morning, despite the weighty political factors involved.

But in the still-hurting public mind, the idea that mother, Dayan and Galili made crucial decisions, on their own, that were detrimental to the nation and had even led to the war, became an *idée fixe,* and even those personalities in the Party who knew better failed to rise effectively to her defense. They had wanted and relied on her to lead the party, but now she was older, would not stand for election again in any case, and was, from that point of view, not quite as indispensable as she had been.

On April 12, the day after her resignation, mother stood before the Knesset and announced:

> The public ferment cannot be ignored. After much thought I have come to the conclusion that the public and its representatives must be given another chance to choose a new government.

She stayed on loyally as the head of a caretaker government until June 4, when a cabinet was finally formed and the new prime minister became Yitzhak Rabin, a Jerusalem-born *sabra* and a former chief of staff. This is how it should be, mother felt, her generation making way for the next. She moved back to Ramat Aviv at the beginning of July. Sarah, Zecharia and Zipke helped her pack her personal belongings and a few momentoes— books, paintings she had received as gifts from famous artists, family photographs and an Israeli flag embroidered by eleven prisoners of war in Egypt and presented by them to her on their return home.

She was back full time on our quiet street, back in her half of the house, next to Aya and me. But she was not inactive. Like the rest of her life, her retirement was filled with movement and content; abroad she remained in great demand as a speaker; in Israel she was turned to as mentor and adviser. And most of all, she avidly, knowledgeably followed Sadat's peace overtures with the eagerness, curiosity and enthusiasm of someone whose own most fervent wish was perhaps now finally being fulfilled.

CHAPTER 12

THE REQUESTS THAT Golda write a book, pen her memoirs, dictate her autobiography, were incessant. She turned each publisher down with a resounding "absurd" or "nonsense" or just "tell him no again." She wasn't a writer; she didn't have time to read, let alone to try to write, and anyhow who cared? My mother, whatever her other faults, was totally free of false modesty; in the main she knew her own value, was able with accuracy to assess the impression she made on others and abhorred hypocrisy. Her adamant refusal to do more than let herself be interviewed by would-be biographers was based on her honest belief that nobody could possibly be interested in the story of her life. Anyhow, she had told it repeatedly. Everybody, she said, knew about the pogroms of her childhood, about Milwaukee, about Merhavia. And so forth. She would not, she insisted, make a fool of herself by attempting some self-serving project doomed to failure.

Inevitably when she began to talk about retiring for the second and last time, various publishers made fresh attempts to persuade her to change her mind. One such was Sir George (now Lord) Weidenfeld of London, a frequent visitor to Israel who had already talked a number of prominent Israelis into signing contracts with him for books. Denied earlier, he now faced mother with the one and only argument in favor of an autobiography that could possibly have worked—and did.

"It's not a question, Mrs. Meir," he said, ignoring her stony look, "of who cares about your life. It's a question of being able to tell the world, the thousands upon thousands, maybe millions who will read your book in tens of languages, through your life, about this country, about Zionism, about what Israel really stands for. It is, if I may say so, a rare opportunity to explain to the world what the Jewish state is about. Frankly, I can't think of a time when Israel has stood in greater need of a book like this, in particular the young people all over the world. It is, forgive me for saying this, your duty to write it." He had uttered the magic word "duty," and in the end it was that to which, with great misgivings, mother succumbed—though while she was still prime minister she gave The Book (as it was known at home) and the editor whom Weidenfeld assigned to work on it with her very little time indeed. And when the Yom Kippur War broke out, and, after it the months-long War of Attrition, the project was abandoned.

It was only when mother actually retired, and after the first weeks of her move back to Ramat Aviv, when she was an ordinary citizen again, as it were, that Weidenfeld reminded her of her obligation to him—and reluctantly she got down to work, but not before she had reminded him of the ground rules, which —given her natural reticence and sense of propriety—were predictable:

"I will *not* write about my private life," she informed him. "I will *not* settle political or other scores with anyone. I will *not* take advantage of the high office I have just left, or of anything I learned there."

Some of the co-publishers from abroad rushed to Israel to appeal personally to her that she write candidly about the men who had served in her cabinet, that she reveal the "truth" about the Yom Kippur War and who was "really" to blame for Israel's having been taken unaware, that she go into frank detail regarding her relationship with Morris "and others." That, they all said, was what the public wanted. "In which case," said mother, "there won't be a book at all."

The book was written just as she wanted—and to her enduring astonishment it became a bestseller throughout Europe, the United States and even the Far East. Newspapers and magazines in London, Helsinki, Berlin, Bangkok, Paris, etc., all published long, illustrated installments, and it was translated into close to twenty languages, including Japanese and Burmese, with special editions in Braille and Yiddish on which Golda waived all royalties. Published in 1975, *My Life* is still being brought and read and still evokes remarkable response. In fact yesterday's mail brought a typical letter, this one from Holland. Addressed to me, as Mr. Meyerson (sic), it is written by an enthusiastic teenager:

> . . . one of my subjects is history. We have to make a project about something or someone. And I choose your mother, Golda Meir. I started in March '83 and have to tell you that the more I've got to know about her, the more I admire her.
>
> I've just read her autobiography. I hope you would like to do something for me. Could you write me something about your mother. Just a few notes. Or maybe something about your childhood. Or a copy of a photo of you and your mother . . .

Without telling tales out of school, without turning on those who had injured her, without breaking any of her own private rules and regulations, by being herself, Golda had scored a huge

A portrait of Golda in her late twenties.

Mother looking pensive at age nineteen.

Mother relaxing with a book on the porch of our home in Tel Aviv, looking out over the Mediterranean Sea. We lived in this apartment for over twenty years.

Mother working in the kitchen at the official residence of the foreign minister in Jerusalem.

Mother relaxing in one of her favorite chairs in our apartment

This was taken in the late '60s, during her last days as foreign minister.

This is one of the official portraits of mother as prime minister.

Israelis shown paying their last respects to mother.

success with her book. And I think that as the weeks of working on it passed, she had gradually come to see it—though *she* never used such grandiose words—as a final statement about herself and some of what happened to her in the course of an amazing life, and was glad, ultimately, to have done it.

Golda the play, however, was, one might say mixing metaphors, a chapter unto itself; although, of course, not to be compared with the kind of blows she had faced up to in the last years of her life, it was nonetheless, however minor, a source of embarrassment, anger and disappointment for my mother. And it constituted one more occasion for having to square her shoulders like the good soldier she was and call upon her considerable inner resources in order not to give way to her real feelings or disclose the extent of her emotional fatigue.

It was not the first time that a play or a film about her had been suggested to her. In many ways, after all, she and her life were indeed ideal subjects for dramatization, containing all the necessary ingredients from pogroms to the prime ministership; a woman, a pioneer, a broken marriage, a thrilling suspense-filled career and the final peak of success—all this plus the Jewish State, its many trials and tribulations to serve as background. But whenever the topic was broached mother said no. Not we'll see but a flat, final *no*. She gave interviews selectively, only when she believed it to be for the good of Israel and actually liked the give-and-take, of alert and sensitive journalists. Also, she had participated conscientiously in such good-for-Israel projects as the BBC's excellent Panorama TV program about her. As for the Book, it was doing well. But "a play? They must be mad!" she said, reading a letter that arrived in the summer of 1976. "It's a ridiculous notion. I won't hear of it."

It took a lot of persuasion and skill combined on the part of playwright William Gibson (whose "Miracle Worker" mother had seen and been greatly moved by) and producer Philip Langner of the Theater Guild to get her to reconsider the project of a play ("about Israel, not only about you," Gibson said cannily), particularly one with a plot pegged on the tragic scaffolding of the Yom Kippur War. But Langner persisted, and Gibson travelled back and forth for a while between Israel and the United States, each time listening and talking to Golda and eventually finding a common and comfortable language with her. Arthur Penn said he would be proud to direct a play about mother, especially one written by Gibson, and Anne Bancroft, with trepidation and delight, agreed at once to star in the title role.

It was a play that interwove many themes; mother's life, the Holocaust, Israel's bloody birth and painful growth and the last terrible war—and Gibson had orchestrated these big themes in a way so complicated that, when he first read the play to us in mother's living room, I felt troubled by its very complexity. Still, most everyone thought it sounded fine, that it was exciting and informative and conveyed a sense of Israel's stubborn struggle for existence as well as presenting a touching portrait of the one woman who, more than anyone else alive, had been so strongly identified in the public mind with so many stages of Israel's development.

Since everyone liked it and seemed to understand it, it made no sense for me to do anything more than say what I thought once or twice and subside. As for mother, she accepted what she considered genuinely expert opinion. After all, the combination was formidable: Gibson, Penn, Bancroft, the Theater Guild, the best and most glittering talent that could be assembled on Broadway—and this, at a time when Israel so badly needed a boost and renewed good will. So who was she to cry halt just because to her, too, the play seemed convoluted and confusing. Initial reports from the tryouts weren't good, but the advance sales were "fantastic," and when the Israel Bonds decided to turn the opening night in Manhattan into a gala fundraising event, provided mother was there, she decided to go and, what's more, to give the family a treat and take to New York whoever wanted to go along. All told, we were seventeen, including Sarah and Zecharia, though Aya, as it turned out luckily for her, opted to stay at home with the boys.

The play was a disaster. Mother sat through that first night pale but composed ("like marble," Gibson wrote later) and afterward quietly asked those most concerned to meet with her in her hotel suite and told them that had she "looked and sounded like Bancroft" she would never have been elected prime minister and that Israel deserved better than this rather garbled and unmoving account of its history. As for me, I saw the play three times, disliking it more and more and desperately wishing that we had somehow nipped the project in the bud—if only to have saved mother this additional ordeal.

The book, the play, the press, TV . . . nothing apparently was enough to satisfy peoples' desire to know more about Golda Meir. After her death we turned down one offer after another: to be interviewed ourselves, to endorse another play, to help with other dramatic versions of mother's life and times, including a film. Finally there was something about which no one consulted us until it was already far in the making: the much-publicized, three-part Paramount-TV special starring Ingrid Bergman as mother and Leonard Nimoy as Morris. When we learned that the script was being shown to various people for their comments, we asked to see it too but were ignored; when, following the family's repeated requests, it finally arrived, it was too late for anything we had to say to make a difference. There seemed no purpose in our taking a public stand against what had appalled us in it, so we made no comment at all and I merely sent a note to Ingrid Bergman to explain why I felt it impossible to accept the producer's belated invitation to us to attend a reception in her honor.

She wrote back, charmingly, to say that she fully understood and sympathized and later told Aya and Sarah that she herself would never have permitted a film to be made about *her* mother without reading and approving the script. Both Sarah and Aya liked her, were impressed by her, and were touched by the depth of her feeling for Golda, whose autobiography she knew almost by heart. It was moving, too, that she had chosen to make this film —despite her constant pain and the certainty of her imminent death, and I wished that, circumstances being different, I could have felt free to tell her this myself. But she died in London even before the film (which I have not seen) was shown in Israel.

It was, I believe, entirely typical of my mother that when toward the end of her scheduled stay in the States in connection with the opening of the play it appeared that Sadat's visit to Jerusalem would actually take place, she chose not to catch the first plane back but to wait until she was asked to return. If not by Prime Minister Begin, then at least by her own Labor Party colleagues. "I'm not going to have people say, 'Look who's here,'" she said. "If I'm invited to meet Sadat, fine. If not, not." She didn't have to wait long, though the hours of uncertainty took a toll. Still, when the invitation at last came, she didn't stand on ceremony or jockey for position or make any conditions. She packed and took off, flying through the night to be on time for what she wryly termed as her *next* theatrical appearance, having no inkling of what her meeting with Sadat would be like, not dreaming that she would indeed steal the show.

When they met it was at a special session at which Sadat was formally greeted by the entire leadership of the Labor Party and at which he shook mother's hand, smiling with unconcealed pleasure at the bracelet she presented to him for his brand-new granddaughter. "As grandmother to grandfather," she said warmly. Then, very briefly, she spoke about peace, in her capacity, she said, as the Old Lady. "I know, Mr. President, that you have *always* called me that," she added with a chuckle that further delighted Sadat.

For those like myself who watched the highlights of Sadat's visit on television with baited breath—and who in Israel did not? —it was those two or three minutes of human exchange that contained within them all the promise of real peace and the hope of true communication.

Her health became increasingly precarious. Throughout 1978 mother was in and out of hospital, often in pain, forever battling exhaustion. But between the bouts of illness she was on the go as usual. Her relationships with the doctors who took care of her were always good and marked by mutual respect, and for the most part she did what she was told. Years before she became prime minister she had been admitted (due, it turned out, to some fairly minor cardiac trouble) to the hospital in which Aya was then an intern and therefore able to drop in on Golda at odd times. Once she found mother most uncharacteristically dejected. "I think my doctor has changed his whole attitude toward me," she said, reluctant as always to share feelings but obviously sufficiently upset to have to do so. "Something seems to have gone wrong between us. I think, Aya, that he's not telling me the truth anymore about what's wrong with me. And I *must* be told the truth."

She was right. Aya investigated and learned that a lymph node biopsy had unexpectedly revealed malignancy, a lymphoma in fact, but mother's doctor, not certain it was right to tell patients that they had cancer, had not informed her. She passed on to him mother's exact words and, wisely, he proceeded to tell

237

Golda what was the matter and assure her that—as turned out to be the case—the prognosis was good. But while she insisted on knowing the truth, she was fiercely opposed to discussing it. "My health," she said repeatedly, "is *my* affair. The Jewish people have other problems to worry about!"

In the autumn of 1978 after a summer punctuated by pain, she was hospitalized in Jerusalem, in the Hadassah-Hebrew University Medical Center's Hematology Ward. And it was here that she spent the last fifteen weeks of her life, except for one four-day interval when she came home for what we hoped and prayed might be a longer break but wasn't.

That spring we had celebrated her eightieth birthday. Actually there had been a series of celebrations, including a festive concert given in her honor at Revivim (the Kibbutz' new auditorium bore her name) that was especially meaningful for her, topped by a party we gave at home. Resplendent in a "best black" dress adorned by her "best" pearls, surrounded by dozens of friends, she made her entrance through mounds of flowers, cables, letters and gifts, hugging and being hugged, and spent the evening telling stories and interrupting them herself with peals of laughter and an occasional tear.

The way she looked and sounded that evening, it was as if only one more milestone had been passed and many more were to come. It seemed only yesterday that we had all trooped to her seventy-fifth birthday party at the beautiful campus home of one of her dearest cronies, Meyer Weisgal, the builder, then president and finally the chancellor of Israel's noted Weizmann Institute. Unlike her eightieth birthday party, this had been, in the strictest sense, a family gathering: the Weisgals, Golda's children, the grandchildren, Zipke, Lou Kaddar, one or two other "intimates" and Simcha Dinitz with his wife plus a surprise, Nancy Kissinger, whose husband shuttling for the nth time to Damascus (in those days he virtually commuted from one Middle Eastern capital to another, establishing what was to become the traditional route for United States peacemakers in this part of the world), had asked as a special favor if she could join the party for the lady they so much admired and with whom he had lost so many arguments! Relaxed, happy, the weight of the world off her back for a while, I remember that mother and Meyer kept the rest of us waiting, famished, for dinner while they sat for an hour listening to long-playing records from Meyer's precious collection of Jewish liturgical music.

That had been five years earlier. Now, on her eightieth birthday, despite everything she had experienced in the interim, her vitality seemed to me undiminished, though, of course, it was not so.

Although the hospital room in which mother spent those terminal weeks in Jerusalem was like all such rooms, by her second day there it had undergone a transformation: somehow her presence, and the "trappings" that had always been part of her life, had turned it into a room in which her family—and those of her friends she wanted to see—felt at once comfortable. Coffee, tea, the clatter of cups, the radio, the rustle and smell of newspapers brought in twice a day—and mother directing traffic and issuing low-voiced orders from her bed . . . "Menahem, see if someone needs milk." "Aya, remind Yonah (Sheyna's son) to speak English so Zipke can follow the conversation." "Would someone please ask Lou to have Sarah picked up at the bus stop." . . .

Not that she or her doctor permitted the tens of people who begged to see her to come. On the contrary, for once she was averse to having company and glad to be protected against the invasion of non-family. But, of course, there were exceptions: children who turned up with bunches of flowers; soldiers, often delegated by their units, who just said *shalom* awkwardly and departed; Labor Party leaders, assorted VIPs, cherished friends (Sam Rothberg was one) who came for an hour or so with her and whose eyes brimmed as they left. And others. But most of the time the vigil (which I suppose is what it really was) was kept by those who were nearest. We were there every day.

The mail came from all over the world, from wherever people learned that she was so ill, from Indonesia, Costa Rica, France, Mexico, literally from the five continents. Orchids arrived from Hawaii, roses from Canada. A picture of the Madonna, besprinkled with sequins, sent by cloistered nuns from somewhere in the north of France . . . "We know you are not of our faith," the Mother Superior wrote, "but we pray hard for your recovery." She weakened daily; the list of admitted well-wishers was shortened drastically; the bodyguards outside her room ordered to make fewer and fewer exceptions to the hospital's new "no visitors" decree. Some days she rallied and felt better, but it was clear that she had no illusions and when she stopped smoking and drinking coffee, my heart sank; it was as though some ultimate signal was being sent. Once I heard her say to a nurse, "See, even steel weakens sometimes," and on another day, when she was quiet for a long time and I asked what she was thinking about, she looked at me and said, "About the after-world." And the bulletins on her health sent daily, at their insistence, to Israel's President Yitzhak Navon, to Prime Minister Begin, to the Deputy Prime Minister Yigal Yadin, to Labor Party Chairman Shimon Peres and former Premier Yitzhak Rabin were equally terse, and realistic.

Slowly, under the loving gaze of those whom she so loved, mother began to go. On the morning of December 7, 1978, she lost consciousness and at 4:30 P.M. on December 8th she died. One of the last to be in touch with her was Danny, our middle son, who reported to her on a tough high school final that he had just successfully passed. Golda couldn't talk anymore or move, but her eyes opened and shone for him before they closed again.

> . . . She died biblically, within sight of peace. And if it is attained, no Israeli will deserve a greater share of the credit. Farsighted even about herself, she always predicted that someone, someday, would proclaim the ultimate joy of peace—"and I envy him already."

This was from the New York *Times* editorial of Saturday, December 9, 1978.

The day of my mother's funeral was bitterly cold. It poured rain. Drenched to the skin, tens of thousands of men, women and children walked slowly around her plain wooden coffin, covered by the national flag, as it lay in state in the Knesset forecourt. There were also the dozens of dignitaries and friends who had flown to Israel to take their leave of her: the United States president's mother "Miz" Lillian Carter, United States Secretary of State Cyrus Vance, Henry Kissinger, the former British prime minister, her old friend Harold Wilson, Marie Syrkin, senators, ministers, diplomats.

Golda had laid down the ground rules herself, firmly and for reasons of her own. In an envelope on which she had written "to be opened only after my death" and deposited in 1967 with a trusted Labor Party aide, was a stern note: "A few years ago, on the eve of surgery regarded by my physician as major, I wrote to the family that I forbid any eulogies and want nothing to be named for me. Since I am not sure that this request ever reached the family following the operation which turned out to be successful, I want now to repeat those words, even more emphatically, to the Party. I am sure that my request will be honored."

Mother had left little room for argument but even she couldn't stop or diminish the massive wordless tribute. From a gallery of the Knesset's crowded Chagall Hall—where she had attended, and then presided over, so many official functions and where her coffin was placed at the start of the funeral service— Orna Porat, the Israeli actress she had liked so much, read two short excerpts from mother's writings. They said, I thought, what mother would have wanted to say by way of a summing-up of the decades of involvement and leadership. One was about the need for peace with the Arabs and taken from a speech she had made at the agonizing height of the War of Attrition; the other was from the last paragraphs of her autobiography and for me, listening to Orna's clear restrained reading of it, was almost like listening to Golda herself.

> . . . Finally, I wish to say that from the time I came to Palestine as a young woman, we have been forced to choose between what is more dangerous and what is less dangerous for us. At times we have all been tempted to give in to various pressures and to accept proposals that might guarantee us a little quiet for a few months, or maybe even for a few years, but that could only lead us eventually into even greater peril. We have always been faced by the question, "Which is the greater danger?"
>
> And we are still in that situation or perhaps in an even greater one. The world is harsh, selfish and materialistic. It is insensitive to the sufferings of small nations. Even the most enlightened of governments, democracies that are led by decent leaders who represent fine, decent people, are not much inclined today to concern themselves with problems of justice in international relations. At a time when great nations are capable of knuckling under to blackmail and decisions are being made on the basis of big-power politics, we cannot always be expected to take their advice, and therefore we must have the capacity and the courage to go on seeing things as they really are and to act on our own most fundamental instincts for self-preservation. So to those who ask, "What of the future?" I still have only one answer: I believe

that we will have peace with our neighbors, but I am sure that no one will make peace with a weak Israel. If Israel is not strong, there will be no peace.

My vision of our future? A Jewish state in which masses of Jews from all over the world will continue to settle and to build; an Israel bound in a collaborative effort with its neighbors on behalf of all the people of this region; an Israel that remains a flourishing democracy and a society resting firmly on social justice and equality.

And now I have only one desire left: never to lose the feeling that it is I who am indebted for what has been given to me from the time that I first learned about Zionism in a small room in czarist Russia all the way through to my half century here, where I have seen my five grandchildren grow up as free Jews in a country that is their own. Let no one anywhere have any doubts about this: Our children and our children's children will never settle for anything less.

Then, while her own words still echoed in that huge and hushed hall, as an honor guard of IDF cadets snapped to attention, preceded by fifty young women soldiers solemnly bearing wreaths, she was taken in the driving rain on her last journey, through the wet streets of Jerusalem on which, weather notwithstanding, drenched hundreds stood to pay their respects.

"Golda's gift," cabled the President of the United States, "was extended beyond the bounds of her people. She spoke to all humanity." And in Washington, suspending a rule that paintings must not be hung until ten years after the death of a subject, the National Portrait Gallery put Raphael Soyer's portrait of mother on view "for an appropriate period of time." Without exception Europe's television stations devoted long filmed biographies to her memory and broadcast detailed accounts of the funeral. And from Cairo, Sadat saluted her as an "honest adversary in the circumstances of confrontation between us which we hope has ended forever," honoring her and gladdening Israel by not using the word "enemy."

Although the number of mourners on Mount Herzl was limited, huddling beneath the mass of dripping black umbrellas were many of those whose lives mother had touched and often changed: the president, the prime minister, colleagues from the labor movement and the Histadrut, a delegation from Revivim and we ourselves, the tight knot of the family and a handful of its closest friends, and with us some of the "boys" who had been Golda's adoring bodyguards and whom, only a day before, I couldn't have imagined giving way to tears. An army cantor chanted verses from Proverbs, the Chief Chaplain recited Psalms, I said the *Kaddish* (the prayer of praise to God that is the Jewish burial prayer) and Mother's coffin was lowered into the soaking earth, only steps away from Levi Eshkol's grave, and covered with earth. "We and the House of Israel pray for the uplifting of the soul of Golda, the daughter of Moshe Yitzhak," intoned the cantor. And then, while the former United States Supreme Court Justice Arthur Goldberg and Sam Rothberg stepped forward to recite the *Kaddish* together, there was a moment, perhaps only a split second, when the rain stopped, the sun came out and like a sign, a rainbow fleetingly hung in the sky.

Like her own self, in character with the way she had chosen to live and to bring up Sarah and myself, in tune with the directness, the modesty and the grace that were for me her hallmark, mother's tombstone is inscribed only with her name and the Hebrew date of her death. It is often visited, and flowers are left by people whom we do not know but who, it seems, also miss her profoundly.

The letters still come, the references stay vivid in the contemporary histories now being written in and about Israel; all of last week we watched and heard mother as a local TV documentary series on the period between the Wars of Attrition and Yom Kippur unfolded; at least two books have been written since she died. But her ban on commemoration has almost held. In addition to the little pocket garden around the corner from our house, there is only, in distant Milwaukee, the library dedicated in her name. Its historical marker, unveiled in 1979, reads:

GOLDA MEIR
1898–1978

The UWM Library is named for Golda Meir. Born Goldie Mabo-wehz in the Ukraine, she migrated to Milwaukee in 1906, was educated at Fourth Street School, North Division High School, and in present Mitchell Hall of Milwaukee Normal School (1916–17). She and husband Morris Meyerson settled in Palestine in 1921. There she helped found the Israel Labor Party, held high political and governmental posts, and eventually became prime minister (1969–74).

Despite her severe injunction, I think mother would very much have liked that. And, oddly, it leaves little more to be said. History will fill in the rest.

Index